The Life and Campaigns of
Field - Marshal Prince Blücher

Engraved by Hopwood from an original Painting

Field Marshal

PRINCE BLÜCHER

Wahlstatt

THE

LIFE AND CAMPAIGNS

OF

FIELD-MARSHAL PRINCE

BLÜCHER,

OF

𝔚𝔞𝔥𝔩𝔰𝔱𝔞𝔱𝔱,

FROM

THE PERIOD OF HIS BIRTH AND FIRST APPOINTMENT IN THE
PRUSSIAN SERVICE, DOWN TO HIS
SECOND ENTRY INTO PARIS, IN 1815:

COMPREHENDING

*Not only authentic biographical Incidents of the leading military Characters of
both the French and Confederate Armies,*

BUT ENRICHED LIKEWISE WITH
MUCH NOVEL AND INTERESTING MATTER.

𝔗𝔯𝔞𝔫𝔰𝔩𝔞𝔱𝔢𝔡 𝔦𝔫 𝔓𝔞𝔯𝔱 𝔣𝔯𝔬𝔪 𝔱𝔥𝔢 𝔊𝔢𝔯𝔪𝔞𝔫

OF

GENERAL COUNT GNEISENAU,

Quarter-Master-General to Prince Blücher's Army;

WITH CONSIDERABLE ADDITIONS,

BY J. E. MARSTON, ESQ.
Of the Hamburgh-Bürger-Guard.

Wo ist das Deutsche Vaterland?
So weit die Deutsche Zunge klingt,
Das ist das Deutsche Vaterland!

ON MILITARY MATTERS

Published in the United States by
ON MILITARY MATTERS

Copyright © 1996 On Military Matters

Library of Congress Cataloging-in-Publication Data available

ISBN 0-9653-2840-6

Manufactured in Great Britain

HIS MAJESTY

The King of Prussia.

SIRE,

In presenting the following pages to Your Majesty, I perform a duty at once pleasing to myself and useful to the world. To me it is a feeling of unmixed delight, that I am thus enabled to record the illustrious deeds of your great General; and that delight is augmented by the hope, that this faithful history of them will obtain Your Majesty's approbation; while to the world it must ever afford a useful example, to behold the career of a successful Conqueror, fighting in the cause of liberty, of virtue, and of honour, and nobly rewarded by his Sovereign for the achievement of his renowned deeds.

Your Majesty must have experienced no common sentiment of exultation and felicity, in the brilliant termination of that contest in which you so promptly engaged when the auspicious moment presented itself for a wise and efficient co-operation; nor can Your Majesty recal the series of warlike triumphs by which that success was obtained, without finding the name of Blücher visibly stamped on all. It would be difficult to determine whether it be more glorious to have conquered in such a cause, or with such a General.

But while we thus pay the tribute of our gratitude and admiration to the virtues of Your Majesty, and the transcendent exploits of the venerable Hero, let us not forget the patriotism, the ardour, the intrepidity, and the fortitude of the people: they seconded with a noble zeal, worthy of themselves and their ancestors, the efforts of their Sovereign. The cry of battle rang in their ears; the love of independence was in their hearts. They remembered the deeds of their forefathers, and, as if animated by one soul, they arose in the fulness of their strength, buckled on their shield, and marched to victory or death. The descendants of Hermann were not slow to chase the foul invader from their fields: they sprang to arms—they fought—they conquered. They carried their avenging swords to the doors of their oppressors, and there they sheathed them; thus exhibiting to the world the affecting and sublime spectacle, of an insulted but magnanimous nation, proudly shaking off the fetters that tyranny and fraud had imposed, and generously disdaining to retaliate upon the vanquished the evils they had suffered.

Such, Sire, is the picture which the following volume displays; and in the various groups of which it is composed, Blücher, the idol of his army, the favourite of his Sovereign, and the benefactor of mankind, stands pre-eminently conspicuous.

With feelings of the most profound respect, permit me to subscribe myself,

Sire,

Your Majesty's most faithful,

And most devoted Servant,

JAMES EDWARD MARSTON.

Hamburgh,
August 1815.

CONTENTS.

PREFACE............,..................,.........Page xi.

List of French Marshals, &c. mentioned in the Work ....Page xiv.

Plans of the Battles, with Explanations.

CHAPTER I.

Blücher's Memoirs—Enters into the Swedish Service—And afterwards into the Prussian .. Page 1

CHAPTER II.

Colonel Blücher's Campaigns on the Rhine in 1793 and 1794—The King makes him a Major-general in 1794, and a Lieutenant-general in 1801—Is appointed Governor of Münster in 1802. Page 19

CHAPTER III.

General Blücher's Campaign in 1806—Battle of Jena—Capitulation of Lübeck ....Page 34

CHAPTER IV.

Introductory Reflections—Armaments of Prussia— Opening of the Campaign by General von Blücher, prior to the Armistice . . . . Page 50

CHAPTER V.

Battle of Lützen—Retreat to Bautzen. . . . Page 76

CHAPTER VI.

Battle of Bautzen—Retreat to Schweidnitz—Blücher's Ambuscade at Haynau—The Armistice
Page 110

CHAPTER VII.

Denunciation of the Armistice—Opening of the Campaign—Blücher's Victory on the Katzbach
Page 149

CHAPTER VIII.

Our Veteran's masterly Manœuvres in Silesia— Battle of Dresden—Progress of the allied Armies —Blücher crosses the Elbe—Battle of Wartenberg . . . . Page 175

CHAPTER IX.

Victory near Möckern—Battle of Leipsic—Progress of the Allies .... Page 225

CHAPTER X.

Field-marshal Blücher pursues Napoleon after the Battle of Leipsic—Co-operation of Bavaria—General Count Wrede—Battle of Hanau—Blücher passes the Rhine—Progress of the Crown Prince of Sweden—Hamburgh ...... Page 267

CHAPTER XI.

The March of the Silesian Army into France—Battles of Brienne and La Rothière—Progress of the allied Armies .... Page 306

CHAPTER XII.

Blücher marches his Army on Paris—Retreat to Chalons—The Field-marshal out-manœuvres Napoleon—Forms a Junction with the Corps of Bülow, Woronzow, and Winzingerode .... Page 332

CHAPTER XIII.

Blücher concentrates his Army near Soissons—Victory of Laon—Progress of the allied Armies—Triumphal Entry of the confederate Monarchs into Paris. .... Page 351

CHAPTER XIV.

The allied Monarchs in Paris—The King of Prussia returns to his Dominions—Marshal Prince Blücher arrives at Magdeburgh—The Congress at Vienna. .... Page 383

CHAPTER XV.

Napoleon Buonaparte's Escape from Elba—Renewal of Hostilities—Battles of Ligny, Les Quatre Bras, and Waterloo—Our veteran Prince Blücher enters Paris a second Time ...... Page 394

General Index.

Map of Germany, with Explanation.

PREFACE.

It is the duty of the biographer to detail every trait of character, to portray every feature, whether stamped with the image of virtue or of vice. Each page is to present something to praise or admire, or to display a portrait that may create disgust and contempt. But when he fortunately has for his subject one of the most valiant, skilful, and prosperous commanders of his time, his only aim must then be to render the theme of his memoirs interesting as well as useful. The limits of such an undertaking cannot be strictly defined. Contrast is the soul of narration; and in noticing the illustrious actions, greatness, and military genius of our Hero, we ought surely not only to embrace the mention of those gallant soldiers, who may with justice be ranked in the line of his equals, but also those who have disgraced humanity, though the recollection of their deeds must ever create both horror and detestation. This is the system upon which the present volume has been formed, and our exertions have been principally directed to the procuring and collecting every information, that could be derived from original and authentic sources; we are therefore willing to hope, that no material occurrence has escaped our diligent and extensive search, as every sketch that has appeared in the German language of Blücher's life, and the events of the late war, particularly what has been written by General Count Gneisenau, and General Müffling, has been carefully examined and faithfully translated. It is a grateful task which we have taken upon ourselves, to single out an individual as an example of heroism, and uncommon resources of mind, and to render him more distinguished, who is already so universally and deservedly known and admired. We feel conscious not only of the utility of our attempt, but of the delight arising from it.

In opening the domestic tent of our veteran warrior, we bring forward the private actions of one of the bravest and noblest generals the world ever produced, and we find every personal qualification that can dignify man, supported by a military reputation which valour and discretion, when united, never fail to beget.

The public are well aware that anecdotes and biographical incidents are more apt to be the production of some fertile brain than founded on fact; we can, however, with truth assure our readers, that no one anecdote is introduced into this work, which has not been obtained either from the most undoubted authority, from eyewitnesses themselves, or from our own personal connexions.

Might we be permitted to boast of success in any part of our undertaking, the execution of the Plans of the several Battles would tempt us to become our own panegyrists. They are fac-simile copies of drawings taken on the spot, and owe their particular and uncommon correctness to those Prussian engineers, whose office it has been to lay them down upon paper. We flatter ourselves, therefore, that the military reader will find every wish gratified, on their near and detailed inspection,

A LIST OF NAPOLEON'S

MARSHALS AND CIVIL OFFICERS,

WITH THEIR TITLES,

Whose Names occur in this Volume.

Arrighi, Marshal—Duke of Padua.

Augereau, Marshal—Duke of Castiglione.

Bernadotte, Marshal—Prince of Ponte-Corvo, Crown Prince of Sweden.

Berthier, Marshal—Prince of Neufchatel and Wagram.

Bessières, Marshal—Duke of Istria.

Cambacères—Duke of Parma, Arch-Chancellor of the Empire.

D'Avoust, Marshal—Duke of Auerstädt, Prince of Eckmühl.

Duroc, Marshal—Duke of Frioul, Grand Marshal of the Palace.

Fouché—Duke of Otranto, Governor of Rome.

Kellerman, Marshal—Duke of Valmy.

Lefebvre, Marshal—Duke of Dantzic.

Macdonald, Marshal—Duke of Tarentum.

Marmont, Marshal—Duke of Ragusa.

Mortier, Marshal—Duke of Treviso.

Ney, Marshal—Duke of Elchingen.

Oudinot, Marshal—Duke of Reggio.

Savary—Duke of Rovigo.

Talleyrand de Perigord—Prince of Benevento, Vice-Chancellor of State.

Victor, Marshal—Duke of Belluno.

EXPLANATION

OF THE

PLANS OF THE BATTLES

OF

LÜTZEN AND BAUTZEN.

Explanation of the Plan of the BATTLE *of* LÜTZEN *(see Page* 76), *fought May* 2, 1813.

a a.	The Bivouack of a French Division near Gröss-Gorschen.
b b.	The Attack of Ziethen's Brigade, at Half past eleven o'Clock, A. M.
c c.	Von Klüx's Brigade, in Order of Battle.
d d.	Von Röder's Brigade, in Order of Battle.
e e.	Von Dolf's Brigade of Cavalry.
f f.	General von York's corps.
g g.	General von Berg's Division.
h h.	General von Winzingerode's Corps.
i i.	Prince William of Prussia's Charge of Cavalry on the French Squares of Infantry, two of which were broken up.
k k.	The Position of the allied Army at three o'Clock, P. M.
l l.	Their Position at six o'Clock, P. M.
m m.	Position of Napoleon's Army, at six o'Clock, P. M.
n n.	The Charge of Cavalry at Half past eight o'Clock, P. M.
o o.	The Position of the combined Army at ten o'Clock, P. M.

━━━━━━

Explanation of the Plan of the BATTLE *of* BAUTZEN *(see Page* 110), *fought May the* 20*th and* 21*st,* 1813.

On the 20th of May.

a a.	Position of the Vanguard under General Miloradowitsch.
b b.	Position of General von Kleist's Corps.
c c.	Position of the Artillery, as Napoleon endeavoured to force the Passage of the Spree, at five o'Clock, P. M.

On the 21st of May.

d d.	Position of the Corps of General Miloradowitsch and the Prince of Würtemberg.
e e.	Left Wing of the Army.
f f.	The Russian Foot-guards.
g g.	The Russian Cavalry of the Guards.
h h.	Position of General von York's Corps.
i i.	Position of General von Kleist's Corps.
k k.	Position of General von Blücher's Corps.
l l.	Position of General Barclay de Tolly's Corps.
m m.	Position of Barclay de Tolly's Van-guard, under General Tschapliz.
n n.	Attack of Napoleon on the left Wing of the allied Army, at eight o'Clock, A. M. Completely repulsed at ten o'Clock, A. M.
o o.	Attack of the French on Barclay de Tolly at nine o'Clock, A. M. Retreat through Preititz at ten o'Clock, A. M.
p p.	Preititz carried at the Point of the Bayonet by the Prussian Guards.
q q.	The Attack of Generals von Kleist and von Röder to facilitate the Reoccupation of Preititz.
r r.	General von Blücher attacked in his Position.
s s.	Position of General von Kleist's Corps, to cover the Retreat.

Published by Sherwood Neely & Jones Paternoster Row July 20th 1815.

EXPLANATION OF THE PLANS

OF THE

BATTLE OF CULM,

AND THE

AMBUSCADE OF HAYNAU.

Explanation of the Plan of the BATTLE *of* CULM *(see Page* 187), *fought on the 30th August* 1813.

a a. Division of the Prince of Hesse-Homburg.

b b. Division of General Bianchi.

c c. The Corps of Count Colloredo, and a Russian Brigade.

d d. The Russian Troops under General Ostermann.

e e. The French Corps under General Vandamme.

f f. The Corps of Prussians under General von Kleist.

g g. The Russian Guards in Reserve.

———

Explanation of the Plan of the AMBUSCADE *of* HAYNAU *(see Page* 130), *on the 26th May* 1813.

a a. Twenty-one Squadrons of Prussian Cavalry lying in Ambush.

b b. The first Column of the Prussian Rear-guard, under General von Tschapliz.

c c. The second Column, under Colonel von Mutius.

d d. General von Ziethen's Brigade.

e e. The French Van-guard.

f f. The first Charge of Prussian Cavalry upon the Enemy's Infantry.

g g. The second Charge of Prussian Cavalry.

h h. French Columns in Advance.

i i. The Mill on fire.

BATTLE of CULM,
fought
August 30th
1813.

Geo.l Ins.t at Weimar.

Prussians ▬ Russians ▬ Austrians ▬ French ▬

Ambuscade near
HAYNAU,
26th May 1813.

L.t Wenzell of the Prussian Engineers.

Published by Sherwood Neely & Jones Paternoster Row July 20th 1815.

EXPLANATION

OF THE

PLANS OF THE BATTLES

OF

DRESDEN AND THE KATZBACH.

Explanation of the Plan of the BATTLE *of* DRESDEN *(see Page* 184)*, fought on August* 26, 1813.

a a. Positions of the allied Armies on the 27th in the Morning.

b b. Positions of the French Corps on the Evening of the 26th.

c c. Positions of the French Army on the 27th towards Noon.

d. The Spot where General Moreau fell.

e e. Columns of French Troops marching into Dresden from Silesia on the 26th.

f f. Batteries of the Allies.

Explanation of the Plan of the BATTLE *on the* KATZBACH *(see Page* 162)*, fought on August* 26, 1813.

a a. Positions of the French Army on the 25th of August.

b b. Positions of the allied Forces on the same Day.

c c. The Attack of General Lauriston on the 26th.

d d. Two Batteries of the Allies.

e e. The French Army advance in Line.

f f. General von York's Attack on the right Wing of the French Position.

g g. General von Sacken's Attack on the left Wing of the French Army.

h h. The Charge of the allied Cavalry on the left Wing of the Enemy.

i i. The Retreat of the French.

k k. The Attack of Macdonald's Reserve at the Close of the Battle.

m. The Allies driving the French down the Steeps towards the Katzbach.

Geo^l Ins^t at Weimar

Prussians ▬▬ Russians ▬▬ Austrians ▬▬ French ▬▬

Geo^l Ins^t at Weimar del.

Published by Sherwood Gilby & Jones Paternoster Row July 20th 1815.

EXPLANATION

OF THE

PLANS OF THE BATTLES

OF

DENNEWITZ AND WARTENBERG,

AND

GROSS-BEEREN.

Explanation of the Plan of the BATTLES *of* DENNEWITZ *and* WARTENBERG *(see Page* 199 *and* 210*), fought September* 6*th and* 3*d,* 1813.

a a. Position of the Northern Army, under the **Crown Prince** of Sweden, on the 5th of September.

b b. The Attack of the French upon General Dobschütz, on the 5th of September.

c c. The Attack upon General von Tauenzien, on the same Day.

d d. Position of the French Army, under Marshal Ney, on the 4th of September, before Wittenberg.

e e. General von Tauenzien's Position, on the 6th, in the Morning.

f f. The Attack of General Morand upon the Van-guard of Tauenzien's Corps.

g g. General von Bülow's Corps, on the 6th.

h h. Marshal Oudinot's Attack upon the Corps of General von Tauenzien.

i i. General Reynier's Corps, as Support to Bertrand's Corps.

k k. General Bertrand's Corps.

l l. The Swedish and Russian Corps, on the Advance.

mm. Position of the Prussians, on the 6th in the Evening.

n n. The French flying in all Directions.

A. Blücher's Passage over the Elbe, on the 3d of September.

B. Position of Bertrand's Corps, at Wartenberg.

C. General von York's Attack.

D. Prince Charles of Mecklenburg's Brigade storms Bleddin.

Explanation of the BATTLE *of* GROSS-BEEREN *(see Page* 191*), fought August* 22*d,* 1813.

a a. Position of the Northern Army, on the 22d August.

b b. The Attack on General von Thümen's Corps.

c c. Position of the French Army, on the 21st August in the Evening.

d d. Position of Oudinot's Army on the 22d August.

e e. The Attack on General von Tauenzien's Corps.

f f. The French Attack on Gross-Beeren.

g g. General Bülow's Attack on the 7th French Corps.

h h. The French 12th Corps.

i i. Prussian Brigade under General von Hirschfeldt.

Published by Sherwood Neely & Jones Paternoster Row July 20th 1815.

BATTLE of LEIPSIC,
Fought
October the 18th & 19th
1813.

Prussians ▬ Russians ▭ Austrians ▭ Swedes ▬ French ▬

BATTLE of LEIPSIC,
Fought
October 16th and 17th
1813.

Explanation of Plan No. 1, *of the* BATTLE *of* LEIPSIC
(*see Page* 232), *fought on the* 16th *of October* 1813.

The 16th of October.

1°. The Grand Confederate Army.

a. Austrian Corps under Count Giulay, in the Morning.
a i. His Attack upon General Bertrand's Corps.
a ii. His Position after the Attack at Noon.
b. Austrian Corps under Count Meerveldt, in the Morning.
b i. His Passage over the Pleisse with a Battalion, in the Evening.
c. Prussian Corps under General Kleist, in the Morning.
c i. Its Position at Noon.
d i. Prince of Würtemberg's Attack on Wachau.
e. Russian Corps under Prince Gorczakow, in the Morning.
e i. Its Position at Noon and in the Evening.
f. Prussian Corps under General Klenau, in the Morning.
f i. Its Position towards Noon.
g. Russian Corps of Grenadiers, under General Rajewsky.
g i. Its Position at Noon and in the Evening.
g ii. The grand Charge of the Russian Cuirassiers.
h. Russian and Prussian Reserves.
i i. Grand Charge of the Cossack-guards.
k. Austrian Reserves, under the Prince of Hesse-Homburg.
k i. Their March to support the Centre.
k ii. Division of General Bianchi.
k iii. Grenadiers under General Weissenwolf.
k iv. Grand Charge of Austrian Cuirassiers, under General Nostitz.
l. Hettman Count Platow and his Cossacks.

2°. The Silesian Army.
m. Position in the Morning.
n. Russian Corps under General Langeron.
o. Prussian Corps under General von York.

3°. French Army.
1. Bertrand's Corps.
2. Poniatowski's Corps.
3. A Division of Guards, as Support.
4. Victor's Corps.
5. Two Divisions of Guards, under Marshal Oudinot.
6. Lauriston's Corps.
7. Two Divisions of Guards, under Marshal Mortier.
8. Macdonald's Corps.
9. Corps of Cavalry under Sebastiani.
10. } Grand Charges of Cavalry, under Murat.
11. }
12. Marshal Marmont's Corps, and Cavalry under Marshal Arrighi.
13. Marshal Ney's Corps and Positions.
14. Position of the French Army on the Evening of the 16th.

On the 17th October.

4°. The Allied Army.
q. General Bennigsen's Army in March, on the Evening of the 17th.
r. Langeron's Corps on the Advance.
*s*3. Russian Cavalry, under Wasiltschikoff, charge the French.
t. The Crown Prince of Sweden's Army takes position in the Evening of the 17th.

Explanation of Plan No. 2, of the BATTLE of LEIPSIC (see Page 241), fought on the 18th of October 1813.

On the 18th of October.

1°. The Grand Confederate Army.

a. Columns of the right Wing, under General Bennigsen, in the Morning.

a 1. General Bennigsen's Corps, in Position at 2 o'Clock, P. M.

a 2. General Klenau's Attack upon Holzhausen.

a 3. General Ziethen's Attack upon Zucklehausen.

b. Columns of the Centre, under General Barclay de Tolly, in the Morning.

b 1. Meysdorf carried by Pirch's Brigade.

b 2. The Corps of Kleist and Wittgenstein drawn up in Line before Probstheide.

b 3. Attack upon Probstheide, at 2 o'Clock, P. M.

b 4. Russian and Prussian Guards and Grenadiers in Position.

c. Columns of the left Wing, under the Prince of Hesse-Homburg.

c 1. Their Attack upon Dölitz and Dösen.

c 2. Their Advance upon Lössnig.

c 3. Their Positions in the Evening.

d. Corps of General von Meerveldt.

e. Corps of General Giulay.

e 1. Reserves of the left Wing.

u. Platow and the Cossacks.

2°. The Northern Army.

f. Corps of General von Bülow.

f i. Taucha carried.

f 2. Paunsdorf occupied.

f 3. Sellerhausen and Stüntz carried.

g. Corps of Winzingerode.

h. Corps of Swedes.

t t. The Crown Prince of Sweden's Army in the Morning.

3°. Silesian Army.

i. Count Langeron's Corps.

i 1. Crosses the Partha.

i 2. Attack upon Schönfeld.

k. General von Sacken's Corps.

k 1. Attack upon Dombrowsky and Arrighi.

l. Corps under General von York.

4°. French Army.

1. The 4th Corps.
2. The 8th Corps.
3. The 2d Corps.
4. The 5th Corps.
6. The 11th Corps.
7. Guards in Position.
8. Guards under Marshal Oudinot, as Support.

8 I. Guards under Napoleon, as Support to the 6th Corps.

8 II. Cavalry of the Guards, under Nansouty.

9. The 3d and 6th Corps, in Position.

9 I. Their second Position.

10. The 7th Corps.

11. Position of Dombrowsky and Arrighi.

12. Napoleon's Positions in the Evening of the 18th, *marked by a blue Line.*

On the 19th of October.

The Grand Confederate Armies.

m. Austrian Divisions at 10 o'Clock, A. M.

n. Austrian Divisions.

o. Colloredo's Corps.

p. Kleist's Corps.

q. Wittgenstein's Corps.

r. Swedes, and Corps of von Bülow and Woronzow.

s. General Bennigsen's Corps.

t. Klenau's Corps.

French Army.

A. Troops posted to cover the Retreat.

B. Disorderly Flight of Napoleon's Army.

MEMOIRS,

&c.

———————

CHAPTER I.

Blücher's Memoirs—Enters into the Swedish Ser-
vice—and afterwards into the Prussian.

POSTERITY, as well as the present age, will doubt-
less be curious to know something of the biography of that consummate warrior, Field-marshal
Prince Blücher of Wahlstatt*, one of the greatest
captains of his time, and whose reputation in
military exploits can scarcely be equalled in any
period of ancient or modern history. His character is marked by a combination of rare qualities, great frankness of manner, and a popular

———————

* Knight of the grand order of the Black Eagle, of the
Red Eagle, of that of the Iron Cross, and of the order of
Merit of Prussia; of those of St. Alexander Newsky, of St.
Anne, and of St. George, of the first class, of Russia; Knight
of the order of St. Charles of Spain; and Grand Cross of the
order of Maria Theresa of Austria.

freedom of speech, which have gained him the unbounded confidence and love of his soldiers, whom, on all occasions, he calls his children, and who never speak of him, but by the appellation of father. A firmness and decision in the hour of danger, rank him with the first commanders in the world. In the heat of battle, in the tumult of an important onset, when leading his troops to an attack, his courage, intrepidity, and presence of mind, are most conspicuous. His voice always cheers the resolute, and his example animates the wavering and tardy. But nothing concurred so much to raise our hero to that pinnacle of glory which he has attained, as that singularly intuitive penetration and foresight which he displays, in counteracting the deep-laid designs and manœuvres of the enemy in the field. No movement of his adversary seems to escape his eagle-eyed precaution, and his determination is at all times as rapidly formed, as his consequent orders are executed. No distance seems too great, no impediments insurmountable, for his military genius, and the devotedness, discipline, and resolution of his troops. His discretion, prudence, and calmness, even in the hour of victory, are so happily blended with vigorous measures, that, from their combination, the happiest results are derived on all occasions, so as to preserve his conquests, and secure the full harvest of the heroic deeds of his gallant army. After the lapse of centuries, our veteran's character will, no doubt, still afford a constant theme of admiration, and be held up as a perfect model for imitation.

The illustrious subject of these memoirs, Gebhardt Leberecht von Blücher, is a descendant of a very ancient and noble family, whose barony is situated in the dutchy of Mecklenburg-Schwerin. He was born at Rostock, in that dutchy, on the 16th of December, 1742, being the youngest of six brothers. His father was a Captain of Dragoons, in the service of the Elector of Hessen-Cassel. During the memorable war carried on by, and against, Frederick the Great of Prussia, known throughout Germany by the name of the seven years' war, his parents (then residing at Rastow, in Mecklenburg-Schwerin), who were fearful of his safety amid the scenes of plunder and devastation that daily occurred, sent him with an elder brother, Ulrich Siegfried Blücher, to their son-in-law, Captain von Krackwitz, in the island of Rügen, near Stralsund, as a place less exposed to the horrors of war. He was at this period about twelve years of age. Four of his brothers were already serving in the Prussian, Russian, and Danish* armies. The Swedish Hussars, quartered in

* A son of the brother who entered the Danish service, is now Grand President of the city of Altona, in Denmark; a gentleman, whose liberality of sentiment, and philanthropy, have won him the hearts of the whole of the inhabitants. When

the island, attracted his notice so powerfully, and
gave such a bias to his youthful inclinations, that
his mind became dazzled with military glory, and,
notwithstanding the earnest remonstrances of his
sister and brother-in-law, to whom he expressed
his desire of entering as Cadet into the Swedish
regiment of Hussars, he soon after secretly left
their house, and offered himself to the Captain of
a squadron, then in quarters in the neighbourhood. This officer, however, happened to know
von Krackwitz, and he sent him notice of his
brother-in-law's intentions; young Blücher was
accordingly summoned home again, and every
argument was employed to persuade him to wait
at least a few years before he executed his project;
but all was in vain : " he would pursue his favourite propensity, he would become an officer of
hussars," he said, " and the sooner he entered the
service, the less time would be lost." In consequence, he commenced his military career, as
Cadet, in the present Swedish regiment of Mörner
Hussars, and he first drew his sword upon an
enemy, in combating that very Prussian regiment
of Black or Death's Head Hussars which he was
afterwards destined to command.

Gebhardt Leberecht von Blücher, in his se-

---

the peaceful citizens of Hamburgh were driven from their
homes by the cruelties of Davoust, the President, von Blücher,
waved every consideration, to relieve *individual distress.*

cond campaign as Cadet in the Mörner Hussars, being with his regiment at the out-posts, was sent by the commanding officer with a detachment of ten men, to occupy an advanced post, with express orders, should he be menaced by an attack from the Black Hussars of the enemy, to fall back; but, that he might depend upon having a squadron ready at hand to support him, if necessary. Twenty-four hours elapsed without any enemy showing himself. By break of day, however, a videt reported to the Cadet von Blücher, that some move-ments of the enemy were observable in the woods opposite his post, and that he presumed an attack was meditated. Our young officer rode forwards at the head of his men, to have a nearer view of the wood, which he scarcely had in sight, before an enemy's troop rushed at full gallop out of it. Blücher was too weak to attempt any opposition, and, therefore, obliged to make good his retreat, and, if possible, to join the support which had been promised him, or at least to fall in with his own troop, from which he had been detached; but that had already retreated, as well as the sup-port. He was briskly pursued by the enemy, and, after having had his horse shot under him, he fell into the hands of the Prussian Black Hussars; a private of which corps, Martin Krause by name, having ridden up to him, when fallen with his horse, and taken him prisoner. The skirmish of the day having terminated to the advantage of the Prussians under Colonel von Belling, and the squadrons that had been in action having been called over, the prisoners and booty were collected, and the former brought before the Colonel. The very juvenile appearance of Blücher particularly struck Colonel von Belling : he asked him his name, who was his father, how long he had served, and other questions of the like import. The frank and ingenuous answers of Blücher excited the admiration and wonder of the by-standers, and quite won the heart of the Colonel, who from that moment sought to gain the confidence and friendship of his youthful prisoner. His first step was to keep him about his person, previously accepting his proffered word of honour, not to leave him, on any pretence whatever, until he was regularly exchanged. A year nearly elapsed in this manner, during which time Blücher was often persuaded to enter the Prussian service ; but he always replied to every overture made to him, " I have taken my oath of allegiance to serve the King of Sweden, and I cannot on any terms forego that oath. My father, I know full well, has a high sense of the honour of an officer, and I should never dare to appear again before him, if I should now enter the Prussian service, without my being first officially dismissed the Swedish." The remonstrances which his father at this period made to him, did not a little tend to strengthen him in his resolution. A veteran Captain of the Hussars,

likewise, took some pains to instil into the mind
of young Blücher those principles of honour which
are the brightest ornament to the character of an
officer. In fine, every one that saw him with Colonel Belling felt interested in his welfare; and
his affability insensibly procured him the good-
will and friendship of all around him. In the
course of the campaign, the Death's Head Hussars, commanded by Colonel von Belling, took a
Swedish officer prisoner, that had, in a former
part of the campaign, deserted from the Prussians;
and the Swedish general, on hearing of his capture, made great interest to have him exchanged.
Colonel von Belling had determined to have him
hanged as a traitor; but, on being much importuned
to release him, he made an offer to the Swedish general, that if he could procure Blücher's formal dismission from the Swedish service, he would send
his prisoner back to head-quarters. To this proposal the Swedish Commander-in-chief consented,
and soon afterwards transmitted Blücher's discharge. It happened, that, on the very day this
arrived at Colonel Belling's quarters, Lieutenant
Helmholdt, of the Black Hussars, had been killed
in action, upon which, the Colonel proposed our
Cadet to fill the vacant lieutenantcy: it was
granted; and, that no impediment might intervene to prevent him from commencing his military career in the Prussian service with every
advantage and honour to himself, he generously

purchased for him Helmholdt's equipage, made
him a present of it, and kept him near his person, by appointing him one of his adjutants
during the remainder of the campaign. Colonel
von Belling continued to act towards Blücher as
an indulgent father, and was often heard to say,
" My young Adjutant will one day become the
ornament of the Prussian army, if his natural qualities and talents are blended with a well-digested
ground-work of military tactics." Blücher himself often mentions, that to the attentions and directions of his patron, and the veteran Captain von
Pulscharbi, his early knowledge of the theory of
military affairs is wholly owing. His gratitude
towards his benefactor raised in his heart such
an unbounded love and affection for him, that,
upon some unpleasant differences breaking out
subsequently in the regiment amongst the officers,
he, on all occasions, warmly defended Colonel
von Belling from the malicious aspersions of his
enemies. He had, about this time, been promoted
to a company in the regiment; soon after which,
Colonel von Belling, upon some occasion or other,
at the end of the Polish campaign, fell under the
displeasure of the King, was obliged to retire, and
lost his regiment. The command of it was then
given to Colonel von Lossow, a bitter antagonist
of Belling, in all those unfortunate differences
between the officers, which eventually deprived
him of the favour of his sovereign. The Major of

the regiment, von Merseberg, having died a few months after these occurrences, Captain Blücher, as senior officer, ought to have been promoted to the vacant majority; but Lossow, knowing his attachment for Belling, and disliking him on that account, proposed Captain von Jägerfeld for the vacancy, with such a brilliant display of his merits, that he obtained the majority, to the disadvantage and vexation of Blücher. Colonel Lossow, it seems, entertained a rooted antipathy to him, because of the steady friendship with which he defended the character of his benefactor in all the attacks that were secretly made against it under the connivance of Lossow. Blücher did not hesitate to inform Frederick of the injury which had been done him; but his memorials had no effect, and his petitions were rejected. On finding that all further application was entirely useless, he at last wrote a letter to the King, in the following terms:

" Permit me, with all due submission, to apprize your Majesty how insupportable it is for me to see myself superseded by an officer, who has no other essential merit whatever to boast of, than being the son of the Margrave of Swedt.

" Your Majesty will therefore be graciously pleased to permit me to resign, sooner than expose myself to the most acute sensations during every hour of my life.

" BLÜCHER."

To this letter, Frederick wrote the following laconic and characteristic note, addressed to Major
von Schulenberg, Commandant of the regiment :

" Captain von Blücher has leave to resign, and
—may go to the devil as soon as he pleases.

                                       " FREDERICK."

Blücher's disappointment was doubly painful,
because he was at this period paying his addresses
to the daughter of Colonel von Mehling, in the
Saxon service, then residing in Poland. He had
himself but little fortune ; and the amiable young
lady could boast, perhaps, of almost every good
quality but that of wealth ; yet, our honest Blücher, scorning to retract, married her soon after,
leaving the Prussian army, farmed an estate under
his father-in-law, and became a country gentleman, devoting his leisure hours to the simple occupations of husbandry, and after the lapse of
a few years, by his own personal exertions and
diligence, became possessed of considerable landed
property in Pomerania. He was afterwards chosen
High Bailiff of the province. To the honour of
Frederick the Great, many of whose actions bear
the marks of a whimsical eccentricity, it must be
mentioned, that Blücher, in his agricultural pur-
suits, received much pecuniary assistance from him,
to enable him to purchase advantageously, and im-

prove his estates. His purse was open to him, whenever he wanted it. Upon the death of Frederick the Great, which happened fifteen years after Blücher had quitted a military life, he was again restored to the Prussian army, by his successor, who appointed him Major of the second battalion of his former regiment of Black Hussars. He soon rose to the rank of Lieutenant-colonel, and within the year to that of Colonel. In 1789 he was invested with the order " Pour le Merite."

Blücher is a soldier to the full extent of the expression. The field of battle has formed him for a commander. On that theatre of heroic action, his energetic soul found scope for developement. The cavalry of the Prussian forces loved him to an excess of enthusiasm ; and, soon after this period, his popularity amongst the troops began to show itself on several memorable occasions. But, before we enter into details, we will close this portion of his biography with the following authentic sketch of the memoirs of his family, and an epitome of his own life, up to the present moment.

Death having deprived Colonel von Blücher of his first lady, he afterwards married the daughter of Mr. von Colomb, Counsellor of the Finances, and sister to Major von Colomb, in the Prussian service. By his former marriage he had three children ; two sons, Francis and Gebhardt, and one daughter ; who are all still living. Count Francis

von Blücher is, at present, Colonel-commandant
of the Brown Hussars, and distinguished himself, in the most eminent manner, during the
campaigns of 1813 and 1814 *. The second son,

---

* 1°. Major von Blücher, with a detachment of Prussian hussars, from the army of his father at Altenburg, succeeded in
surprising General Souham's advanced guard on the 19th of
April 1813, drove it sword in hand through Weimar, and made
a great number of prisoners. General Souham having pushed
forward a numerous support, the Major was obliged to retire,
after having first caused the troops of the Confederacy of the
Rhine, belonging to Weimar, Gotha, Coburg, and Hilburg-
hausen, to surrender at discretion ; and who now, with eager
hearts, assembled under the banners of Prussia, unfurled by
the hand of victory, to avenge the disgrace that had sullied the
German name.

2°. Lieutenant-colonel Francis von Blücher, being with the
rear-guard of General von Kleist's corps, when reconnoitring the
enemy near Nollendorf, on the 14th of September 1813, had
the misfortune, after an obstinate affair, to be unhorsed by the
lance of a Polish hussar, to whom he surrendered himself prisoner, after having received seven wounds. He was, without
delay, sent to the rear of the first French corps. The Pole, on
hearing his name, hastened to announce his prize to Napoleon,
who immediately ordered him into his presence, although bleeding from every wound, and in the most exhausted state. Napoleon began with his usual hasty manner of questioning:
" What's your name?" " What's your rank?" " How many
troops has the King of Prussia?" " How many can he bring
into the field?" The son of our veteran hero collected strength
enough to answer this last question with the coolness and bre-
vity worthy of his father :

" My beloved monarch, Sire, has as many soldiers as he has
loyal subjects!"—" Your answer is very haughty," rejoined

Count Gebhardt von Blücher, served as Captain, in his father's regiment, but, having resigned, now resides on the family estates in Pomerania. The daughter married Count von Schulenberg, became a widow, and, in 1814, was united to Baron von der Asseberg.

Our hero's path of glory commenced during the campaign on the Rhine in 1793. It was at the head of the Black, or "von Golz's" Hussars, that those talents for enterprise, so conspicuous in his following campaigns, first began to expand themselves. In the formation of his plans, he evinced a certain cool circumspection, a dexter-

---

Napoleon, in the hollow tone of displeasure so natural to him; and then dismissed him. The Lieutenant-colonel was conveyed to Dresden, treated with respect and attention, and obtained his liberty by the capitulation of Dresden in the October following. An eye-witness to this conference, from whom we have the anecdote, corroborated by the Count himself, here adds,—that when the Lieutenant-colonel had left Napoleon's presence, the Pole, who had taken him prisoner, stood erect, in military attitude, before his Emperor, and being unacquainted with the French language, attempted by signs to give Napoleon to understand, that he had deserved the decoration of the legion of honour. The former seemed inclined, at first, to pretend ignorance of what he meant; but, as the Pole would not stir from the spot, Napoleon suddenly exclaimed, in a tone of vexation: "He shall have it." But many of the bystanders confessed, that the gallant prisoner had acquired more honour, by his answer, than the Pole did by his acquisition of the cross of the legion of honour.

ously concealed caution, and an irresistible energy in their pursuit, which, with his peculiar talent of making his arrangements in the presence of the enemy, imperceptibly procured him, though only at the head of a corps of partisans, a considerable reputation in the army. He acquired the entire confidence of his troops also, because he was known to provide for their wants with an indefatigable care, which overlooked, at times, both limits and restraints. The young officers were particularly attached to him, it being his custom to live on terms of intimacy with them, that at once, flattered their pride and gained their esteem. The hours devoted to the table were enlivened by a conviviality on his side, which, however prominent, never, on any occasion, derogated from the dignity attached to a superior officer.

When galloping down the front of his regiment, either on parade or before the enemy, his heroic figure, his eye full of fire and energy, an inspiring voice, and a gallant chivalrous management of his horse, attract the notice of the files, fix their attention, make an indelible impression on the spectators, and seem to pledge success to the heart of every soldier, if led on by such a commander.

In the campaign of 1794, the regiment of Black, or Death's Head Hussars, was given him, as a reward for his important services; and on the 4th of June of the same year, he was promoted to the rank of Major-general, and made a Knight of the grand order of the Red Eagle. He published, at this period, a small but interesting work on a war of posts and skirmishes, with remarks on ambuscades, that may be accounted the most excellent of its kind.

Major-general Blücher was made a Lieutenant-general in 1801, took possession of Erfurth and Mühlhausen in the name of the King in 1802, and was afterwards appointed Governor of Münster.

Blücher's campaign of 1806, his brave and persevering defence of Lubeck, and his very honourable capitulation at Ratkau, near that place, will be the subject of one of the following chapters. General Blücher was exchanged for the French General Victor, and on his passing through Finkenstein, in East Prussia, on the road to the head-quarters of his Sovereign, was received by Napoleon with marked distinction.

After the peace of Tilsit, His Majesty the King of Prussia intrusted him with the care of the military affairs of Pomerania, one of the three military governments newly created.

At the opening of the campaign of 1813, his royal master gave him the chief command of the Silesian army, that army whose deeds have immortalized the name of Blücher and of Prussia, and dispersed those lowering clouds which had so long overcast the former resplendency of the

Prussian arms.   His unparalleled marches, the
prudence of his masterly manœuvres, his unceasing activity, that overthrew, in so many instances,
the mighty preparations of the most experienced
chief—his bloody and obstinate battles, his splendid victories in this and the following campaign
and the rapidity that accompanied the execution
of his deeply-concerted plans, have excited the
astonishment, admiration, and unfeigned eulo-
giums of his cotemporaries, and indeed of all Europe.

After the stupendous victory of Leipsic, our
veteran was promoted to the rank of General
Field-marshal * ; and a few days previously to his
landing on Albion's sea-girt shores, he was raised
to the dignity of Prince Blücher of Wahlstatt †,

---

* Which mark of distinction was announced to him by the
following letter :

" General Blücher,

" Your repeated victories increase the services rendered your
country, so rapidly, that I find myself deprived of the power
of following you with proofs of my gratitude.

" Accept of a fresh mark of it, by my naming you General
Field-marshal; and may you enjoy this dignity for many years,
to the satisfaction of the country, and as an example to the
army, which you have so often led to victory and glory.

" FREDERICK WILLIAM.

" *Leipsic, October 20th*, 1813."

† His Prussian Majesty wrote Blücher the following lines on
this occasion :

" You have happily and gloriously closed the struggle for the

by the most grateful, the most magnanimous, and
the best of Monarchs.

His visit to England, so fresh in the memory
of every one, resembled more the triumph of an
adored hero, than the presence of a general ac-
companying his Sovereign. Blücher's name became the watch-word of exultation with all ranks
in the metropolis ; and, wherever he appeared, he
seemed to inspire every one with love and veneration towards him.

---

honour and welfare of your native country ; but the gratitude
which the State owes you still continues ; and, as a proof of it,
I hereby raise you to the dignity of Prince Blücher of Wahlstatt *, and your heirs to peers of the realm, as Counts Blücher
of Wahlstatt. It will forthwith be my first care, in showing
my due sense of your heroic services, to grant to yourself, and
your descendants, such domains as may be best suited to support your rank.

"FREDERICK WILLIAM.

" *Head-quarters, Paris, June 3d,* 1814."

* The name of Wahlstatt is derived from the cloister and village of Wahlstatt, near Liegnitz, on the river Katzbach. This
cloister and village are famous for having been built on the
spot where a great battle was fought between the Tartars and
Henry II. Duke of Silesia, in 1241 : the Duke lost his life and
the battle ; and, in commemoration of this unfortunate event,
the cloister was built by his mother, and, to this day, a description of the battle is annually read from the pulpit, on the 9th
of April, being the anniversary of that on which the battle was
fought. The word Wahlstatt has, besides, a double significa-
tion in the German language, as it likewise implies, " a field of
battle ;" so that Blücher's title has the significant meaning—
Prince of the Field of Battles.

As a new war may break out, and rage with equal fury, and the enemy of mankind, alike ambitious, whether as sovereign prince of an island, or as emperor of a kingdom, may renew the contest for universal dominion, and the downfal of social order, morality, and religion, it is but natural to suppose, that our veteran hero is anxious to add fresh laurels to those which already grace his brow, and that he is eagerly bent on meeting his deadly foe once more, on those plains which have already witnessed his noble exploits.

CHAPTER II.

Colonel Blücher's Campaigns on the Rhine in 1793
and 1794—*The King makes him a Major-general
in* 1794, *and a Lieutenant-general in* 1801—*Is
appointed Governor of Münster in* 1802.

BLÜCHER, as Colonel of the Death's Head Hussars, was attached to the corps d'armée of General
Prince von Hohenlohe, destined to open the campaign on the Rhine, in 1793, against the French;
and he here gave such proofs of his valour and
discretion, that he was soon noticed by the Commander-in-chief.

The camp of the Prussians, near Eisoing, having
been often disturbed just before break of day, by
the riflemen of the enemy, who, under cover of
hedges and bushes, frequently succeeded in killing off the out-posts, Colonel von Blücher was
ordered to place an ambuscade, to check this petty
warfare. An opportunity offered itself, with every
prospect of success, on the 25th of July. Blücher having received authentic information that
the French intended to lie in ambush near Or-
chies, for the purpose of surprising one of the
Prussian patroles on the morning of that day, he
determined to counteract this design, by antici-
pating them; and, accordingly, about three o'clock

in the morning, when the French were seen on their march, carefully watching all the outlets as they moved onwards, a few Prussian hussars pushed into the high road, and galloped away as if retreating, while others seemed on patrole, and to withdraw on seeing superior numbers. The enemy were completely deceived by this ma-nœuvre : they eagerly pursued, flushed with the hopes of booty ; and the Prussians, bursting from their ambush, cut down all that opposed them, taking about a hundred prisoners, with much baggage and a number of horses. To Blücher's success in this enterprise the camp was indebted for a comparative state of tranquillity till it broke up.

In September 1793, the Prussians fixed their camp near Luxemburg, soon after the Austrians had left it. The French, in the vicinity, had ac-customed themselves, almost daily, to plunder the nearest villages without mercy, and seemed still inclined to continue their predatory excursions; but the vigilance of Colonel Blücher and his hus-sars soon checked their audacity. He surprised one of the enemy's principal detachments, killed and wounded a considerable number, and took fifty-seven prisoners.

To enter into a detail, however, of all the re-connoitring excursions which Blücher made in the rear and flanks of the enemy, and the num-berless skirmishes in which his brave troops came off victorious, would, from their wearisome uniformity, afford but little entertainment to the reader, and be of no importance to the historian. In fact, by a rare combination of skill, caution, and valour, he drew the eyes of the army upon him, and paved the way to that renown which has placed him on an equal footing with a Cæsar or a Marlborough.

On the opening of the campaign of 1794, Colonel Blücher had again an opportunity of acquiring the unaffected praises and congratulations of his companions in arms. He formed the plan of surprising Morsheim, a village on this side of Kirch-heim Polanden, and of driving the enemy, who were strongly posted there, out of it. A battalion of infantry under Captain Trützschler, a detachment of sixty riflemen, and two guns of the horse-artillery, were ordered to march from Alzei, and to post themselves near Oppenheim at half past twelve at night. In the mean time, to cut off the enemy's retreat, if possible, from Morsheim, Colonel Blücher caused Major von Lorenz to put himself in march with two squadrons of hussars, by the route of Pichenheim, detaching an hundred infantry and sixty riflemen through the wood to the right of Oppenheim, to get into the rear of a detachment of the enemy unobserved, who were posted on the verge of the wood; to the left, on the road to Kirch-heim, a body of two hundred infantry were ordered to

march straight forwards towards the wood, at the
same time that a hundred picked men proceeded
to the right, across the Sionshut. Colonel von
Blücher drew up the remainder of his regiment
on the high road to Morsheim. It was previously
arranged, that all the other detachments were first
to await the signal of Captain Trützschler having
commenced his attack on the small body of the
enemy in the wood, and then to press forwards,
with all the rapidity in their power, to the different points. Captain Trützschler was so far successful as to turn the enemy unobserved, and to
salute him with a volley before he was prepared.
The French detachment was thus thrown into
confusion, and being unable to retreat along the
wood, it was obliged to debouch into the plain,
which gave Colonel Blücher an opportunity to
charge upon them, and, in spite of its heavy fire,
he succeeded in either killing or wounding, or
taking prisoners, the whole detachment. Captain von Planitz, at the head of a squadron of
Black Hussars, and supported by infantry and
sharp-shooters, proceeded to the village of Morsheim; and although they were received with a
warm fire of musquetry, and the entrance into
the village was blocked up with waggons, he soon
overcame every obstacle, cleared a passage, pursued the enemy pell-mell into the village, and
completely drove them out of it at the point of
the bayonet. The enemy's cavalry, which hardly

had time to form, were furiously charged and
dispersed with heavy loss. Major von Lorenz had
already penetrated to the village, notwithstanding an abattis, across the road out of the wood,
presented some hindrance to the celerity of his
march.   Colonel von Lestocq, who turned the
village to the left, about the same time that Major
von Lorenz had turned it to the right, now succeeded in cutting off the enemy entirely, and
the few that escaped were indebted for their
safety to the ground being so much intersected
with hedges and ditches.   The fugitives that
reached Kirch-heim spread an universal alarm;
the whole expedition succeeded to the wishes of
the most sanguine, and stamped the character of
Blücher as the first partisan chief of the age.
His military reputation now rose progressively,
while the brilliant affairs that followed on the
23d of May, and 18th September, served to fix
it more firmly.

The Prince von Hohenlohe, General of the
Prussian army, having ordered an attack to be
made on the French on the 23d of May 1794,
Colonel von Blücher headed the column of the
right wing, and its operations were intrusted
wholly to him.   Accordingly, he put himself in
march, on the evening of the 22d of May, with
five squadrons of his own hussars, three battalions
of infantry, and three companies of sharp-shooters,
towards Schorleberg; and early on the morning of

the 23d continued his march to the other side of
Frankenstein, that he might be able to reach
the Neustädter road before break of day; by
which means he cut off all communication between Kaiserslautern and Neustädt. Major von
Coring was likewise detached from Schorleberg
with a battalion of grenadiers, a company of
sharp-shooters, and two squadrons of hussars, towards Ritterhof, on the road between Hochspeier
and Frankenstein. The high road towards Furk-
heim was found broken up, and a deep entrench-
ment dug across it by the French, behind which
a considerable body of the enemy's infantry had
posted themselves. Colonel von Blücher lost no
time in harassing them with a galling fire of
sharp-shooters, which forced them to retreat into
Frankenstein. The place itself being found of
too great natural strength to be taken by assault,
our prudent Colonel resolved to continue his march
across the high road, to which step he was the
more inclined, as he heard the cannonade of Prince
von Hohenlohe's army to the left, evidently on
the advance, and, as the enemy had broken up
the roads, little danger was to be apprehended to
the right of Frankenstein. In order, however,
to secure his rear, he left a strong detachment
posted on the Steige. On entering the woods
his difficulties increased. The enemy, who was
very numerous both in cavalry and infantry, obstinately defended every foot of ground, and the

number of abattis thrown across the roads materially contributed to render the contest very
sanguinary, as they were obliged to storm them
one after the other.   Our gallant Colonel, at last,
succeeded in clearing the woods and strong
grounds, of the French, and forced them to fall
back on Weidenthal, whence they were at last
driven by the riflemen and sharp-shooters.   He
now took a position on the heights near Weidenthal, close to the high road to Neustädt, his left
flank being continually harassed by the enemy's
tirailleurs.   The enemy, in the mean time, drew
up their troops, and halted on the other side of
Reidenfels.   It was impossible to pursue him
thither, from the circumstance of Frankenstein
being still occupied by the enemy.   In the course
of an hour, the out-posts reported to the Colonel, that the enemy were on the advance; it
was the French General Cisée, with two battalions,
two guns, and about a hundred horse, who, finding his retreat cut off to Lautern, by Major von
Coring's detachment, had the hardihood to attempt forcing a passage with the bayonet through
Blücher's corps.   Dearly would he have purchased
success in this enterprise, if the Colonel had not
been, at that moment, hard pressed on his left
flank by the reiterated attacks of the enemy's
columns.   Our resolute commander found himself
suddenly placed between two fires; the French
were more than treble in number; and to resist

such a superiority required no little share of intrepidity, as well as the most skilful dispositions.
By bringing some of his guns to bear on the high
road to Neustädt, and the others towards that of
Frankenstein, he kept the impetuosity of the
enemy in check, and rendered their junction a
matter of great difficulty. Here Blücher's presence of mind availed him much. He rode with
a flag of truce towards the French General Cisée,
and called out to him to surrender, as he was cut
off, and defence was useless. A general discharge of
musquetry was the only answer returned, and the
enemy's line immediately pressed forwards to assault the heights on which Blücher stood with his
brave troops, and they partly succeeded in forcing
back the detachments in advance. He did not
pause a moment in this critical juncture, but putting himself at the head of von Müffling's battalion, furiously charged the enemy with the
bayonet. The effort was crowned with success;
the impetuous French were repulsed with heavy
loss, entirely broken, and those that did not
escape into the woods, were cut in pieces by the
hussars. A considerable number of prisoners were
taken, and two pieces of artillery. Major von
Coring then occupied Frankenstein, and Colonel
von Blücher kept his position on the heights of
Weidenthal. A less vigorous and resolute conduct would have caused the total destruction of
Blücher's corps, instead of the discomfiture of the

enemy. It was the first time our gallant chief
had scope of action to display his military talents,
and the issue gave fair promise of future greatness.

A commander at the out-posts of an army,
when adored by his troops, when endowed with
skill and courage, and the rare talent of drawing
advantage from the occurrences of the passing
hour, may be said to be capable of executing
wonders, even with a handful of men. No instance more striking can be given of the just-
ness of this remark, than the conduct of our enterprising Colonel on the 28th of May 1794,
near Kirrweiler, in the Pfalz.

The French had advanced with two large bodies
of cavalry, supported by infantry and artillery,
by the way of Fenningen and Edighofen, towards Kirrweiler and Maikammer, while another
of their detachments took post between Friesbach
and Freimersheim, keeping, by this movement,
the regiment of Prussian hussars stationed near
Gemsheim and Duttweiler in check. The Prussian out-posts at Maikammer and Kirrweiler were
forced back on the main body, and the enemy
established two batteries towards Diedesfels.
Blücher's regiment of Black Hussars were drawn
up in front of Diedesfels, facing Kirrweiler. A
battalion of infantry, and two companies of
sharp-shooters, were in possession of the heights.
Another battalion of infantry, with half a battery

of horse-artillery, covered the road to Neustädt and Winzengen, by being posted on the high ground before Hambach. General von Wolfrath, with two battalions and five guns, had likewise taken up a position between Duttweiler and Kirrweiler. The enemy, with a strong force, pushed on through Kirrweiler, and their sharp-shooters spread themselves to the right and left in the corn-fields, favouring, by their incessant fire, the approach of their horse-artillery.

Colonel von Blücher at this critical moment rode forwards, to reconnoitre the enemy's dispositions. He plainly perceived that it was their intention to take up a position on this side Kirrweiler, preceded by a heavy cannonade; and, as he had only light artillery with his corps, he could not prudently accept of a contest with this arm, on such unequal terms, which would ultimately have led to the evacuation of the posts of Maikammer and Kirrweiler, to regain which, would have cost a number of brave men, if he wished to maintain his present position, or have it afterwards in his power to advance. As soon as this conviction flashed across his mind, his bold and vigorous spirit formed the resolution of immediately attacking the advancing enemy. He estimated their numbers at about six thousand, which, though far superior to himself, did not weigh much in the scale of his calculations. Orders were issued to withdraw the flanking troops,

so as to entice the enemy's sharp-shooters into the
open ground, pretending at the same time to retreat with a part of his hussars, by defiling behind some heights, unperceived by the enemy.
All his out-posts were called in, and lay quietly in
ambuscade, and our daring chief watched the approach of the favourable moment, when the
ground, and intermission of vigilance on the part
of the enemy, offered every advantage to his premeditated blow, and then, suddenly issuing from his
ambush, he furiously fell upon the flank of the
enemy's column, before the gates of Kirrweiler.
The French riflemen, on perceiving the Prussian
hussars, endeavoured to regain the town, but
were most of them cut in pieces in making the
attempt.   Blücher succeeded in breaking and dispersing the first column of the French with such
vigour and celerity, that their artillery was taken
by Lieutenant von Arnim, before they could fire
a round of grape-shot.   A part of the head of the
column tried to enter the town, and the troops
in the place were equally eager to get out of it, to
support their comrades; in short, the confusion
and disorder amongst the French were so great at
the moment, that no orders could be obeyed, or
were listened to.   Our gallant Colonel, accustomed to pursue his acquired advantages to the utmost, did not hesitate about pushing through the
place, at the head of his brave hussars, dispersing,
wounding, and taking prisoners, every troop of

the enemy that came in their way : two more guns
were added to the trophies of the affair, and, advancing to Fischlingen, the remainder of his light
troops followed him.   Some part of the success of
the day might be attributed to the enemy having
placed their artillery in line of battery, to cannonade General Wolfrath.   The enemy's second
column had retreated, and only two regiments of
heavy dragoons stood their ground in front of
Edesheim.   Colonel von Blücher, from an eminence near Fischlingen, having got a view of
their position, instantly collected the whole of
his horse, and proceeded without delay to throw
himself on their right flank, and, if possible, to
take them by surprise; he had, indeed, penetrated
within thirty yards of their flank, as one of the
enemy's regiments wheeled round with rapidity
and order, and showed an imposing and tremendous front, that might be compared to a
lofty, impenetrable wall.   Dragoons, six feet
high, with horses in proportion, presenting their
long straight swords, like so many pikes, formed a
singular contrast to the small lively animals, and
agile evolutions, of Blücher's hussars.   The sud-
denness of the enemy's movement checked the
impetuosity of the Prussians, who for a moment
stood wavering; but Blücher, ever ready at expe-
dients, suddenly called out, Halt ! and ordered detached parties to gallop down the enemy's line,
where the ground admitted of this manœuvre, to

skirmish at a distance with the enemy, and, by a
constant firing of their pistols at the horses of the
French, to cause a confusion and disorder in their
files. He accomplished his design. The commanding officer of the enemy's dragoons found,
as he thought, his position too much exposed to
the teasing attacks of the Prussian light troops,
and commanded his soldiers to wheel in column,
and to march off the ground. This was the moment for Blücher: a strong compact body of hussars, kept in reserve, now rushed with the swiftness of arrows upon the open lines as they were
forming, and instantly broke the regiment. More
than two hundred were cut in pieces, the Colonel-
commandant and a hundred men were taken prisoners, and two standards fell into the hands of
the victors. During this, the second battalion of
von Golz's hussars had attacked the enemy in
front, and happily succeeded in dispersing the remainder of the two regiments. Our indefatigable
victor pursued the enemy through Edesheim, following them up, till they got under cover of the
batteries belonging to the main body.

This brilliant affair, and gallant enterprise, cost
the enemy fifteen officers, and five hundred rank
and file, as prisoners. General Ferrino escaped
by hiding himself in a field of corn. The French
left six hundred wounded behind them, and four
hundred horses proved an acceptable booty to
Blücher's intrepid troops. No Prussian officer

was either killed or wounded, although they all
charged at the head of their men.

These splendid proofs of a bold unwearied perseverance, united with skill and foresight, met
with the most gracious acknowledgment from His
Majesty the King of Prussia; and the renowned
Colonel Blücher was promoted soon after, to the
rank of Major-general in the Prussian army.

Thus elevated, he did not fail to distinguish
himself whenever opportunity offered. An attack upon Edesheim, on the second of July, in
which the Prussian horse-artillery, in following
his dispositions, did wonderful execution, and his
hussars again broke and dispersed the enemy's
columns, served but to enhance his character in
the eyes of all military men.

The Prince von Hohenlohe, as Commander-in-
chief, makes particular and honourable mention, in
his bulletin of the 19th September, of the brave
Major-general von Blücher, ascribing the success
of the enterprise carried into execution on the 18th,
solely to-his judgment. Blücher's orders were, to
advance with his brigade of hussars, by the way of
Mohrlautern, as soon as he should receive a report,
that the attack near Hockspeier had succeeded: but
our vigilant Blücher here again acted from the spur
of the moment. He had advanced; but to have
waited for reports, he found, would give the enemy
too much time, and, with his usual energy of action,
he detached two of his squadrons to the Kaisers-

burg, to turn the flank of the flying French, marching with his other squadrons, and a regiment of
light horse, straight towards Honek: he dispersed
the enemy's light troops on all sides of him, and
brought in 600 prisoners.

Blücher's own regiment of Death's Head Hussars took 9 pieces of artillery, 2 howitzers, and
5 pair of colours from the enemy, and made 1
Lieutenant-general (Labossiere), 137 officers, 3327
rank and file prisoners; sharing a booty of 1341
horses, during the campaigns of 1793 and 1794.
The regiment never lost more than six men, as
prisoners, in the whole period.

After this campaign, Major-general von Blücher
received a command in the army of observation
stationed on the Rhine, which proved barren of
any military occurrences worthy recording.

Major-general von Blücher was made a
Lieutenant-general in 1801; and some time after
this, previously to the campaign of 1806, he was
appointed Governor of Münster.

CHAPTER III.

General Blücher's Campaign in 1806—*Battle of Jena—Capitulation of Lübeck.*

THIS campaign forms an unfortunate epoch in the military history of Prussia. It was not a campaign for conquest, or to avenge trivial injuries and transgressions, but a contention for those rights and privileges, in the enjoyment of which, nations that have a regard for social order and sound morality, place their most substantial happiness. The gigantic ambition of one man involved Prussia in misfortunes the most bitter for her Sovereign to support, and cast a foul blot upon her military character, which our intrepid hero was ordained by the wise dispensations of Providence to obliterate for ever. Blücher was not backward in assisting his royal master with salutary advice, and encountered the greatest difficulties, and braved the greatest dangers, in protecting the Prussian name from ignominy. It was *he alone* of all the Prussian generals, that scorned to yield, as long as a charge or a ball was left, to fire upon the enemy.

This short but eventful struggle produced effects that shook the Prussian monarchy to its foundations. Her army took the field, powerful, well appointed, full of confidence, and flushed with the recollection of past deeds in arms, both glorious and immortal. It returned, dispirited, nay, almost annihilated: a certain fatality, an unaccountable concurrence of unpropitious events, seemed to accompany, and to be inseparable from, every step of the government. But the villanous projects of the arch-tyrant of Europe were not at that time appreciated. The Prussian people had not then felt his rod of iron: oppression had not yet roused them to a sense of what they owed to themselves as Germans, and to their King as devoted subjects. A few years of the most painful humiliation paved the way to their acquiring, at the point of the sword, that noble independence, so worthy of themselves. Prussia's blazing star of victory shone forth once more in the distant horizon, ascending with majestic effulgence to its meridian, cheering the surrounding nations with its warmth, while prostrate Germany blessed the hour of its deliverance.

When the Prussian grand army opened the campaign in 1806, under the immediate command of its adored Monarch, General Blücher was intrusted with the right wing. At the commencement of the battle of Jena, he was ordered by the King to take upon him the command of the advanced guard of cavalry, consisting of three regiments of dragoons, twenty-five squadrons of light cavalry, and a battery of horse-artillery. The General, having advanced in front of the

grand army, to reconnoitre the enemy's movements, was prevented by a heavy fog from ascertaining their several positions. Some reports
made by his out-posts and skirmishers, induced
him to proceed towards Kosen, in hopes of surprising or meeting detachments of the enemy.
Between Poppel and Tauchwitz, Blücher encountered the French division Gaudin, which he attacked with vigour and intrepidity, making a terrible slaughter among the enemy, and pursuing
them sword in hand to the other side of Has-
senhausen. The Queen's own regiment of dragoons, the finest in the Prussian service, had
here an opportunity of distinguishing itself most
conspicuously. The enemy seemed to make a
stand, as if they had fallen in with their support,
and the Prussian artillery being brought up, began
to thunder against their supposed position, the
fog still continuing so dense, that it scarcely allowed a distance of fifty yards to be distinctly
seen. The French answered this cannonade
briskly, and with heavier metal, from their battery, for about half an hour; and it appeared by
their dispositions that a large body of troops was
debouching in line. General Blücher in consequence drew off his artillery, and formed his cavalry in columns. The infantry meant for his
support, were not yet arrived, and the fog prevented the gaining any authentic intelligence of the
actual force of the enemy. In this state of things

Blücher was obliged to remain a considerable time
inactive.   It was the Duke of Brunswick's wish,
that the whole army should be drawn up in close
order of battle, and no important step taken
until the fog had sufficiently dispersed, so that the
position and manœuvres of the enemy could be, in
some degree, ascertained.   The cautious advice of
the veteran was not followed.   Field-marshal Möllendorf insisted that no time ought to be lost,
that a rapid march forwards, must disconcert the
enemy's plans, whatever they might be, as their
corps were now all in motion, and in a probable
state of dislocation.   Vigorous measures, we
grant, could alone baffle the enemy; but vigour
without foresight, is at all times dangerous.   Möllendorf's opinion gained the ascendancy, and the
army was ordered to march in advance, incom-
moded by a mist that prevented the soldiers seeing objects within twenty yards of them.

General von Blücher did not, however, renew
his attack with the advanced guard, until this
mist had dispersed itself, opening to his view a
large body and extended line of French infantry.
His old manœuvres, of indirect charges following
each other in succession, and skirmishing on all
sides, first throwing the files into disorder, and
then, by a heavy unexpected charge, to break
through, were here found of no avail.   The new
tactics of Napoleon, of drawing up his infantry
in alternate squares, flanked by light artillery, and

connected by troops in line, frustrated all Blücher's desperate attempts to make an impression.
He felt himself foiled. On making his last charge,
he had his horse killed under him. He then drew
back his cavalry in good order towards Eckarts-
burg, and passed through Auerstädt.

It has been confidently asserted by many, that
General Blücher, in pressing too hastily forwards,
brought the army under the necessity of fighting,
and that his conduct deserved censure. But, in
answer to this reproach, we have only to remark,
that if blame ought to attach any where, it could
only fall upon Marshal Möllendorf, who turned a
deaf ear to the suggestions of the old, experienced
Duke of Brunswick, and thus evidently precipitated the army, not upon a disorganized, but upon
a prepared enemy, and that, too, under peculiar
disadvantages. Möllendorf's greatest misfortune
was that of being short-sighted, which is extremely dangerous for a general.

After the battle of Jena, General Blücher was
ordered by his Sovereign to take the command of
the Prince of Würtemberg's corps, and to conduct
it across the Oder; but, in consequence of the
capitulation of Prenzlau and Pasewalk, no other
course was left him but to direct his march towards
the Lower Elbe, and, by forming a junction with
the corps of Weimar and Lecoq, at least to relieve
Magdeburg, if not, present an imposing force to
the enemy in that quarter. This plan was the

best which human foresight could have adopted,
as it tended to divide, not only the attention, but
the forces of the enemy, and served to prevent
the whole mass of the French army from penetrating into the heart of Prussia, without any impediment in their rear or flanks ; but the vastly
superior numbers of Napoleon's forces, added to
the unusual celerity of their movements, frustrated
any good effects which the execution of the plan
might have produced, and General von Blücher
saw himself under the necessity of fighting his
way to Lübeck, instead of crossing the Elbe, or
keeping it on his flanks.   He was constantly assailed by the enemy on this retrograde march, from
all sides.   On the 16th of October, near Greussen,
he fell in with the French light troops, under General Klein.   To avoid an engagement, in the position his troops were then in, was absolutely necessary, if he would render practicable the accomplishment of his design, to reach the Lower Elbe.
Blücher's presence of mind, ever fertile of expe-
dients on the spur of the moment, assisted him
most essentially in this dilemma.   On the first
appearance of the enemy, he rode on towards
them, accompanied by a few of his staff-officers,
desiring to be conducted to the French General as
a flag of truce.   He immediately gave the General
to understand, that he had received advices from
the King of Prussia, that peace had been already
concluded, calling upon Colonel von Massenbach,

who was present, as a witness, who had read Napoleon's letter to the King, in which he had offered him peace. The French General greedily swallowed the bait, as did likewise General Lasalle, who followed with two regiments. Blücher's corps was permitted to pass unmolested; and, by a forced march, placed themselves out of all danger from that quarter. Buonaparte particularly mentions the occurrence in one of his bulletins, accompanied by a severe reprimand on the conduct of the two generals. General Kalkreuth attempted to practise the same deception upon Marshal Soult, soon afterwards, but without success.

The troops under Blücher's command, in high spirits at having deceived their wily foe, and full of confidence in their chief, now pursued their march with vigorous alacrity. They came up with a body of French, on the 27th, near Fürstenburg, and, by a gallant and well-ordered attack, succeeded in forcing through them; and, on the following day, near Lychen, they were no less successful. It was our General's intention to proceed to Prenzlow; but it being reported to him, that Prince Hohenlohe's corps had been entirely dispersed, that step became quite impossible. He therefore turned to his left towards Strelitz, being sanguine enough to hope, that, after effecting a junction with Winning's corps, he should be able to force his way to Magdeburg; or, by throwing himself across the Elbe, gain time for the fortresses of Magdeburg and Hameln to be provisioned for a siege: and then to operate, according to circumstances, in the rear of Napoleon's grand army. Engineer officers were sent to Lauenburg, to prepare materials for throwing a bridge over the Elbe at that point. At this juncture advices were received by Blücher, that Marshal Soult, at the head of a considerable force, had already passed the Elbe, and was directing his march towards him. Nothing appalled our gallant General; he continued his route towards the Elbe, firmly determined to fight his way, being flushed with his former successes, and possessing the entire devotion of his troops. A continuation of attacks now followed in rapid succession. The Prussian cavalry performed prodigies of valour, and roughly handled the enemy's horse, whenever they ventured a charge with them.

The Prince of Ponte-Corvo, commanding a strong corps of the enemy, sent a flag of truce, on the 1st of November, to General von Blücher, with a summons to capitulate, stating at the same time, that, as he was nearly surrounded by three corps of the French grand army, there was no retreat in his power. The General assured the Prince, that he never should capitulate as long as he had a cartridge left: adding, " He, for his own part, knew not the man that should prevent his marching to Berlin, or relieving Magdeburg." In the interim he was reinforced by Colonel von

Osten, who joined, with four squadrons of his own regiment, a battalion of infantry, and a company of sharp-shooters.

Amidst daily skirmishing, and simultaneous attacks, Blücher reached the neighbourhood of Schwerin, on the 3d of November. A very warm affair with the advanced guard, took place near the village of Krimitz, which continued till the evening. The Prussians beat the enemy completely out of the field, taking a considerable number of prisoners, amongst whom was a colonel, and an adjutant of the Prince of Ponte-Corvo. Partial as the advantages certainly were, that could be derived from these bloody rencontres, they were not without ultimate benefit to the Prussian service; the soldier became convinced that, upon equal terms, his strong and vigorous arm was ever an overmatch for Gallic agility.

A second summons from the Prince of Ponte-Corvo, to capitulate, was treated with the same disdain as the former, and Blücher notified his wish of declining to listen to any further overtures of the like nature.

Blücher's intended march upon Magdeburg, which, but a few days before, he had defied any one to prevent, was acknowledged, by himself as well as his staff, to have now met with obstacles that appeared but too evidently insurmountable. A continuation of forced marches had fatigued the troops to an inconceivable degree. All stragglers

fell into the hands of the French. Ammunition,
in particular, began to fail, and there were no
magazines within their reach. These considerations, maturely weighed, induced the General to
alter his plan, and to throw himself into some
city of note, by which step he could procure his
brave followers that rest they stood so much in
need of, gain time to supply them with necessaries,
and to replenish his ammunition. To avoid a
pitched battle was, however, his first and principal
care. As long as he could keep the field, or em-
ploy the French army by his marches and manœuvres, he held Napoleon in check from approaching the Oder, delayed his march on that
river, and thus gave time for the Prussian forces
to assemble and form themselves in East Prussia:
these manœuvres, also enabled the Russians, who
were actually in march, to reach the frontiers early
enough for their assistance to be of important
benefit to the kingdom.

On the evening of the 3d of November, after
reports from the out-posts had been made to Blücher, there was every reason to suppose that
Murat was marching on his left flank, Soult on
his right, and the Prince of Ponte-Corvo very
near him in front. Thus situated, by break of
day on the 4th, no other alternative was left him,
but either to fight desperately against superior
numbers, with little or no chance of success, or
to throw himself into Lübeck or Hamburgh. In

one or the other of these cities the General hoped
to maintain himself for some considerable time.
Lübeck appeared the most proper for his purpose,
as it still had remains of old fortifications. Some
Swedish troops were already in it, who, he flattered himself, might be persuaded to make a common cause with him.

If Blücher's retreat had been crowned with
success, no doubt, it would have been compared
with that of Moreau. Every attendant circumstance was well reflected upon : it was undertaken
with wisdom and foresight, and the heroic valour
of a handful of men, whose names deserve to be
recorded on the brazen tablets of history, accomplished it. What difficulties had our General not
to encounter! On his right the Baltic, and on his
left a neutral territory, was a situation not among
the least of them.

A toilsome forced march of thirty-six hours
brought Blücher and his army before the walls of
Lübeck, on the evening of the 5th of November.
The Senate refused him and his brave followers
admittance. Prussians, that have since secured
the independence of this city for ever, and saved
the German name from eternal disgrace, had the
gates shut in their faces! But the times of slug-
gish grovelling inactivity are over! Entreaties
and representations proved useless, and Blücher
ordered the gates to be forced. The General proceeded to the Senate-house, and demanded bread.

and quarters for his troops. His application was
formally protested against. The urgency of the
moment constrained him to declare, that if his
simple demands were not immediately complied
with, he should feel himself obliged to adopt coercive measures. The Senate reluctantly consented
to provide for his exhausted troops. Quarters
were appointed them, and refreshments distributed
with a liberal hand. A few hours of rest only
prepared the way for a more busy scene, and the
temporary calm was followed by a storm. Blücher's desperate defence of Lübeck gave his name
a celebrity throughout the north of Germany, and
procured him a popularity, which had lost none
of its vigour, when he again took the field, seven
years afterwards. He there fought, as every son
of Germania ought to fight, as long as a grain of
powder was in his cartridge-box. If his fame had
not been established, this intrepid conduct would
have fixed it on the firmest foundations.

General Blücher, on the following day, drew
up his little army of heroes on the Trave, leaning
his right on Lübeck, and his left on the village of
Travemünde. A corps of Danes, under General
von Ewald, were posted on their frontiers, nearly
touching Blücher's right wing. The two Generals
exchanged civilities, and the former hastened to
announce, that his orders were to defend the
frontiers against the aggressions of either party,
but to take no decided part whatever in their
operations.

At an early hour of the morning, Lübeck was invested on all sides, by three corps of the French grand army, under the Prince of Ponte-Corvo, Murat, and Soult. They made preparations to take the place by assault, and a most sanguinary conflict ensued. After the brave Prussians had expended the whole of their ammunition, and their artillery was rendered useless, from the want of powder and balls, the French, perceiving the slackening fire of our valiant General, proceeded to storm the Burg-gate of the city, at the point of the bayonet: the most dreadful slaughter ensued: the Prussians were but a handful of men, not exceeding 6000 capable of bearing arms; the French had more than 40,000 men before the place, and by dint of pouring in fresh troops through the gate, forced their way at last into the town, over the dead bodies of their comrades, that lay, by thousands, in the gateway. To withstand so great a superiority was impossible; our gallant General was obliged to yield. The French got possession of the place, and the remains of the Prussian army passed the night in their position on the Trave. Early the next morning, the Prince of Ponte-Corvo again offered General Blücher a capitulation; which, after the preliminaries were settled, was accepted by him.

General Blücher, in drawing up the terms of the capitulation, began it in the following words:

" As a capitulation has been offered me by the

Prince of Ponte-Corvo, and having accepted it, for want of every kind of ammunition, I," &c.

Objections being made to this by the French officer, who declared that it was unusual to mention the reasons of a capitulation, in stating the terms, Blücher answered abruptly, " By G—, I 'll capitulate on no other conditions whatever, let what will come of it."

It was afterwards arranged, that Blücher should be allowed to state his reason for capitulating, above and below his signature to the capitulation; and which he actually did.

Those acts of savage barbarity, those scenes of rapine, plunder, and devastation, which have always marked the blood-stained path of the followers of Napoleon, and which now took place in Lübeck, can neither be conceived nor described. Horror herself would shrink aghast at the sight, and the pen of the historian falls from his hand. The virtuous citizens of Lübeck, that venerable sister of the Hanse League, have a remembrance left them of French atrocity, that will ever rouse them to a just sense of the duties they owe to the common cause of Germany *.

---

* A corps of French troops, headed by Marshal Murat, in marching through the territories of the Prince of Lippe-Schaumburg, had stripped his stud of every horse; amongst them was a favourite animal, whose peculiar fate and extraordinary sagacity had rendered him an object of particular regard and estimation to the Prince and his family. This horse had formerly

The excesses of the French soldiery lasted three days.

General Blücher, after performing the most painful of all tasks for a warrior, that of seeing his brave men lay down their arms, wrote the following letter to His Majesty the King of Prussia:

"It is with a heart deeply wounded that I have to report to Your Majesty the gradual destruction, and fate of the corps of troops under my command, which I have had the misfortune to head, under circumstances which permitted no other alternative. The troops have, throughout,

---

belonged to an uncle of the illustrious house, and had been ridden by him when colonel of a regiment, during the campaign in Flanders, in the course of which, their relative was killed in action, and the body never found; but, before the afflicting news reached them, to their great surprise and astonishment, the horse returned alone, wounded in the neck, from the field of battle to the castle stables, a distance of at least an hundred miles. That the animal was much caressed, and a great value set upon him, no one can doubt, from the singularity of the circumstance. Every kind of application was made, and every exchange offered to the French Marshal, that this charger in particular might be restored, but without effect; a deaf ear was turned to all their entreaties, remonstrances, and representations of the causes that rendered him so great a favourite of the family. They never saw him more. Another instance of the vile principles, and selfish turpitude of sentiment, that influenced the conduct of some of the Satraps of the most execrable of tyrants.

Related by the Prince to the editor himself.

evinced a steadiness and bravery which have exceeded my expectations, and which, in any other situation, would have immortalized them. They have shown a patience under intolerable privations, and a love of discipline, that reflect eternal honour upon them. The sense of having faithfully discharged my duties to my country, affords me the only consolation I can feel, in this hour of bitter sorrow.

"Your Majesty's devoted servant,

"VON BLÜCHER."

Our distinguished General was afterwards exchanged for General Victor, and joined his King in East-Prussia.

After the peace of Tilsit, he was appointed to the military government of Pomerania.

CHAPTER IV.

Introductory Reflections—Armaments of Prussia—
Opening of the Campaign by General von Blücher,
prior to the Armistice.

THE tide of victory, like an irresistible torrent, in pursuing her tumultuous course, from the walls of Moscow to the shores of the Niemen, had burst asunder those ponderous chains of iron with which the tyranny of a despotic conqueror, to promote his ambitious views, had held the Teutonic nation enthralled. The high behests of Heaven having miraculously ordained, that Germania's sons should never again drag his triumphal car, nor do homage at his feet; it must have doubly redounded to their shame, when rescued from further disgrace, and delivered from their hated shackles, to have followed their enslaver, and, full of obsequious submission and humility, spontaneously to have offered their obedient necks, once more, to his galling and perfidious yoke. Amongst the meanest race of animals, no traces are to be found of willing slavery; and vile must be that heart, which is capable of estimating man below the brute creation.

The little Prussian army, under General von York, deserted and neglected by the flying French,

proceeded with order and firmness through the
snows and woods of Courland towards their native
soil, there to devote itself to the future service
and will of its revered master, its only fit and
honourable destination. A Russian corps had already hemmed in its line of march to the frontiers
of Prussia. The commanders, on both sides, soon
came to a good understanding with each other.
The Prussians had been driven into Russia by
force, and no other rights bound them, but those
of the stronger party. By an idle abuse of his
power, Napoleon had himself destroyed the means
of constraining others, and these self-created
rights had now evaporated into nothing. Standing thus alone, and unbiassed, the Prussians could
no longer consider themselves as enemies to the
Russians; for they had never been such in reality;
and honour forbade them to acknowledge any
commands, or fulfil any other destination, but
what the immediate orders of their lawful Sovereign might contain. The Russians, trusting to
approaching alliances with all states recovering
their freedom, derived no little advantage from
permitting the effects of the enforced coalition
between Prussia and France quietly to subside,
thus smoothing the way to a subsequent close
confederacy in the common cause of all. Avow-
ing their mutual independence, and not as enemies or allies, the two corps separated, and the
Prussians took up their neutral quarters with-

in their own territories. This reduced corps had
but just shaken off Napoleon's trammels; and no
sooner had the people beheld these arrogant vain-
glorious conquerors, returning like troops of miserable mendicants, in a state of contemptible
wretchedness (the conqueror must be ever fortunate, or else he is justly contemptible), than they
felt themselves as if led back, by the invisible
hand of Fate, to an independent existence, and
to the urgent indispensable duty of putting forth
every individual energy to maintain this independence, in a more laudable and vigorous manner
than in the year 1806. The loud and unanimous
voice of the people, and their national feelings,
were listened to, and cherished, by the Monarch
and his ministers. They confessed the necessity
of supporting the nation with all the influence of
legal authority, of improving the probable short
period of free action, to bring forward her physical strength, and then to begin the struggle anew,
for liberty and an honourable station amongst the
continental powers.

The truly unfortunate days of Jena and Auerstädt had tarnished the long-enjoyed splendour of
the arms of Prussia, and blasted her name with
scorn and dishonour. The army, on its retreat
after these defeats, had disbanded itself entirely;
the fortresses and strong-holds of the monarchy
fell most disgracefully one after the other; the
kingdom was conquered; and, after the expiration

of only four weeks, insignificant were the wrecks
of either, that were left for a beloved Sovereign to
mourn over. The few bands of faithful warriors
that afterwards joined the Russian forces, in the
Upper Prussian provinces, were too weak, and
the means of filling up their ranks too inefficient,
to attempt the recovery, at that moment, of what
had been lost. This evil was rendered greater by
the peace of Tilsit, in which, disgraceful bounds
were set to the augmentation of the Prussian
army, its strength being limited to 42,000 men;
and even the proportion of its arms to each other
was prescribed and dictated by their haughty, inflexible, and wily enemy. In the course of a year,
that brilliant and splendid military character of
Prussia, so much the admiration of every friend
to warlike and glorious achievements, and held
up as an example to all Europe, disappeared.
Reproaches from all sides followed, instead of admiration, and humiliations supplied the place of
homage.

The army was dispirited, the past afforded no
satisfaction, futurity opened no heartening prospects. A well-placed confidence in any single
commander, that might have kept alive their ardour, was no where to be found; the war of 1806
had been too short to give any one an opportunity
of raising himself to a post of eminence, and the
few that did distinguish themselves, shared the
divided approbation of popular opinion.

Owing to this spiritless situation of the army, the diminished opulence of the state, the embarrassed finances, the reduction commanded by a foreign power, and a party of lukewarm patriots at home, that opposed every energetic measure whatever, it was extremely difficult to attain those objects still kept in view. The army was to be reorganized entirely, its courage revived, its spirit reinspired, all abuses rooted out; and besides the formation and completion of the number fixed in the treaty, the foundation of a new and great military power was to be imperceptibly laid, which, at some future period, might, at a decisive moment, suddenly arise for self-defence, and retrieve the honour of the Prussian name.

The few years of peace, from 1808 to 1811, were, with unwearied solicitude, devoted to the accomplishment of these intentions.

According to the treaty with France, the army should consist of

24,000 men, infantry;
6,000 ——, cavalry;
6,000 ——, artillery;
6,000 ——, guards.
———
42,000

These were divided into six corps of all arms, called brigades, each brigade consisting of from 6 to 7000 men. Three military governments were created; namely, the Prussian, the Silesian, and

the Mark, including Pomerania. Few difficulties
occurred in completing the army to 42,000 men;
but its new formation, and particularly the rege-
nerative spirit to be inspired, found a thousand
prejudices to struggle against, together with the
ill-will and self-interest of individuals, deep-rooted
habits, an obstinate sluggishness, and an imaginary desponding helplessness ; but, in spite of all
these obstacles, seeming to present insurmountable barriers, advances were fortunately made, and
the impediments insensibly and gradually removed. In the year 1809, the army was completely reformed, had new laws and regulations, a
new exercise; and, we may say, felt itself invi-
gorated throughout. It was brought nearer the
people, and hopes were entertained that it might
become a school for the future formation of a
military national character, refined from all impure
particles.   Those obstructions met with, in the
attempt to enlarge unnoticed the new foundation
laid for the whole military power of Prussia, were
now happily overcome, and it would be but te-
dious to name them, in rehearsing the means that
were resorted to. We must be satisfied with remarking, that only unremitting exertions in employing and bringing into effect well-digested
measures, as local circumstances permitted, could
lead to the desired consummation of Prussia's
dearest wishes.

The principal objects were:

1. To be able rapidly to reinforce the army, by the continual exercising of recruits for a certain time, and then to disband them to make room for others; by which method, in less than three years, more than 150,000 men had passed the routine of military exercise and evolutions.

2. To establish workshops for the manufacturing of arms. The Berlin manufactory produced 1000 stand of arms every month; an entire new manufactory was erected and arranged at Neisse, in Silesia; and a considerable number of arms were bought up in Austria.

3. To form parks of artillery. As the whole of the field artillery was lost, it was necessary to replenish the loss out of the eight fortresses still in possession, by refounding all the heavy brass ordnance in them, and mounting iron ones in their stead. Founderies and laboratories were built at convenient places, and, in three years, the army had again complete parks of artillery for 120,000 men.

4. To arm, and furnish with supplies, the eight fortresses: as they were to be looked upon as the pillars and props of the Prussian monarchy, whose geographical situation rendering the open country so easy to be overrun by an enemy, they stood like rocks in the sea, unmoved by the passing storm. In them, the warlike strength of Prussia could be collected and preserved, in case of such

an event.   On which account, intrenched camps
were thrown up near Pillau and Colberg, and in
Silesia.   Besides the extended lines of Neisse, a
fortified camp marked out near Glatz, was intended to receive troops and military stores.   The
rough and unformed means of defence and warfare, both in men and materials, could be collected
in them, and be there modelled and formed, even
during the inroads of an invading enemy.

In 1812, these camps were all completed.   Such
unwearied exertions, and a wise economy in the
application of those means, formerly so little attended to, had placed the Prussian army on a
footing, in the course of four years, that, from
42,000 men, of which it actually consisted, it
could, in a few months, be increased to 120 or
150,000 men.

Officers, both civil and military, well versed in
the duties of their different stations, and in the
prime of life, stood at the head of the several departments.

The injurious consequences arising from a too
strict attention to seniority by promotions, were
averted, and the useful man, who had distinguished himself in battle, or made great sacrifices
to the state, was patronized and brought forward;
and thus, by degrees, a regard for the new order
of things, a renewed confidence in themselves
and in their innate value, were instilled into, and
diffused throughout the whole.

To finish the work of this new creation, the idea of a national defence, by an organized militia and levy en masse, seemed naturally to present itself. By the former, if war broke out, the army could be doubled in its numbers; and by the latter, the defence of this little kingdom could receive some degree of stability. Yet those very means that tended to reinforce the standing army with the utmost celerity, encroached on the embodying of the militia; if, by the increase of the army, all the arms in store, and the exercised and trained men, were brought into service, and none were then left to compose an efficient groundwork for the militia.

But the treaty of alliance with France, in 1812, put a stop at once to all these wise and provident preparations for erecting a firm national defence against any foreign subjugation that might be attempted. By it, the little army was robbed of half its numbers, to be employed for purposes very opposite to its original destination; and, in consequence, all attempts to attain the end proposed were paralysed; indeed, by the uncertainty how the means produced might be made use of, it would have been the extreme of folly to continue them in any shape whatever. Therefore, not only no progress was made during the year 1812, but the hope of any, seemed to be extinguished. The auxiliary corps returned at the end of the campaign into Russia, with a loss of 10,000 men, and the flower of the army was weakened, by at least a fourth.

This loss, severe as it was, might perhaps be outweighed by the military experience this little corps had acquired, by the confidence they had gained in themselves and their new formation, by the esteem with which they inspired both their allies and opponents; and, above all, by the inveterate and renewed hatred imbibed against the tyrant and oppressor of legal liberty and civic freedom *.

---

* The Emperor Alexander, a short time previously to the inroad of Napoleon into Russia, in 1812, with the view of averting the spilling of so much human blood, sent General Balaschoff to the head-quarters of Napoleon.

He was received in Napoleon's antechamber by General Duroc, who, with a feigned graciousness, entreated him to excuse the delay, but that the Emperor was breakfasting at the moment.

The door of the adjoining apartment was at length opened; the General perceived Napoleon as if just rising from his breakfast; near him were standing the King of Naples, the King of Westphalia, and the Viceroy of Italy. Upon General Balaschoff's entering the room, the Emperor called out to the *grand personages* that surrounded him, " *Allez vous en!*"

The conference lasted several hours, in the course of which, Napoleon brought forward every specious and wily argument to prove, that Russia would act the wisest part in submitting to his demands, as there was no possible chance of her being able to withstand the combined strength of France and her allies. Amongst many singular reasons adduced by Napoleon, in defence of his assertion, and to confirm it, the following may be worthy recording, as it proves what was actually the degree of estimation in which he held the German nation: " Taking

The military force of Prussia was thus situated at that epoch, when the rapid floods of discomfiture burst on the French grand army, and scattered and impelled its feeble remains, like the fragments of a shipwreck, over the plains of Germany.

The decisive moment was now arrived in which those numerous and digested plans, that had so long and anxiously occupied the Prussian government, could ripen to perfection. Although there was no possibility of attaining the desideratum of having the country defended by 250,000 men, well trained and skilled in evolutions, and it must eventually suffer some curtailment, while it is in the nature of things attempted by man to fall short of the object in view; yet, in the execution, much depended on energy, vigour, and activity, to reach the goal at a greater or less distance. The sequel has proved that this was by no means an extravagant scheme, for a few months realized the hopes cherished with so much solicitude.

To complete the regiments, and to form new corps, recruits were drawn together in Prussia,

---

for granted," he proceeded to say, " that the power of your Emperor is equal to mine, yet, you ought to reflect, that when your monarch loses five men, they are five Russians; whereas, I can only lose, in this campaign, one Frenchman and four hogs:" *(Je ne perds qu'un Français et quatre cochons.)* Meaning by *cochons*, his allies the Germans!

General Balaschoff's mission, it need hardly be added, was ineffectual.

early in January 1813, about the time that France began to raise her new levies, by a rigorous enforcement of the conscription-laws.

Within a period of rather more than two months, that is, at the end of March, the army in Silesia amounted to 25,000 men, fully equipped and well disciplined, exclusive of the garrisons, and about 20,000 men, whose formation was not yet complete. The corps of General von York arrived in the Mark, out of Prussia, about 15,000 men strong (but had more than 6000 sick). In the Mark and in Pomerania there were nearly 10,000 men, well exercised, without reckoning the garrisons, and 15,000 recruits, in an approximate state of organization.

The Prussian forces might consequently, at this time, be estimated as follows:

1. Well-disciplined, exclusive of garrisons - - - - - - - - -   50,000
2. In a state of organization   - - -   35,000
3. The sick   - - - - - - - -   10,000
4. Garrisons in the eight fortresses   -   15,000
_____
110,000

The army was therefore recruited to almost four times its former numbers. The troops were all completely disciplined towards the end of April, when hostilities commenced; but the recruits were not able as yet, to join the theatre of the war in Saxony. At the beginning of May, about the time of the battle of Lützen, the Prussian army might be placed under the following heads :

In active service, before the enemy, 70,000 men; viz.

In Saxony, at the battle of Lützen - -	35,000
Under General Kleist, at Halle - - -	4,000
Detached - - - - - - - - - - -	1,000
On the Elbe, and before the fortresses of	
Spandau, Stettin, Glogau, Wittenberg,	
&c. - - - - - - - - - - - -	30,000

Not before the enemy, 40,000 ; viz.

Reserves marching to the army - - -	15,000
Garrisons - - - - - - - - - - -	15,000
Sick - - - - - - - - - - - - -	10,000
	110,000

The militia were at this time only forming; but, according to the plan of embodying them, they were to be 150,000 men strong.

The best spirit animated all the disciplined troops; and their being divided into small brigades of 7 to 8000 men, of all arms, well provided with every equipment, was one of the best formations which troops could receive.

The commanders of the several corps were:

First Corps.

General von Blücher, General of the cavalry.

First brigade, Colonel von Klüx.

Second brigade, General von Ziethen.

Reserve brigade of infantry (guards), General von Röder.

Cavalry reserve, Colonel von Dölfs.

Second Corps.

General von York.

First brigade, Lieutenant-General von Kleist.

Second brigade, Colonel von Horn.

Third brigade, General von Hünerbein.

The series of operations in which this latter corps was engaged, since the campaign in Courland, had so changed its former organization, that at the battle of Lützen very little traces were discernible. General von York was present at the battle with 8000 men, and under him General von Hünerbein, and Colonel von Horn. General von Kleist, with a detachment of the corps, and some regiments of Russians, about 5000 men, was before Leipsic. The remainder were left to invest Spandau and Wittenberg.

Third Corps.

General von Bülow.

Under him, General von Borstel commanded all the corps before the fortresses of Magdeburg, Wittenberg, and on the Elbe.

Fourth Corps.

Lieutenant-general von Tauenzien commanded the troops blockading Stettin; General von Schulen, those before Glogau; and General von Thümen invested Spandau.

This was the state of the Prussian army, when operations commenced on the right bank of the Elbe.

Imperious circumstances unavoidably caused a

dispersion and derangement of the forces, which are usually but little taken into consideration by him, who, distant from the seat of war, attempts to calculate and weigh military occurrences in his arm-chair. Two very sufficient reasons may, however, be assigned for this dispersion: first, because a considerable number of fortified places, both of the enemy and our own, were in the rear of the line of operations: secondly, Prussia had begun the formation of her military power in the distant provinces of her dismembered monarchy, at a time when the enemy was actually occupying them; and the celerity of the movements made, would not admit of the places being relieved by the Russians, so that the whole of her active force could gradually converge to, and be concentrated at one point.

General von Blücher marched out of Silesia towards the end of March 1813, at the head of a gallant army of 25,000 men, well disciplined and equipped; and, on the 3d of April, passed the Elbe at Dresden. The Russian General Winzingerode *, with 13,000 Russians, was placed under him, and formed his corps in advance.

---

* This General being taken prisoner by accident, in October 1812, near Moscow, was brought under a guard into the presence of Napoleon, at the little town of Wereja, not far from Mojaisk. Napoleon, with a countenance inflamed with rage and passion, received him with a volley of abusive words and indecorous expressions, ending at last with:

Count Wittgenstein, General von York, and General von Borstel, with their united corps of 25,000 men, were on the right bank of the Elbe, blockading Magdeburg. The Russian detachments under Tettenborn, Dörenberg, and Czernischeff, of 6 to 7000 men altogether, had penetrated below Magdeburg, on both banks of the Elbe *.

" *I find you every where. You are a subject of the King of Westphalia, are you not? He shall punish you as a traitor.*"

Winzingerode replied with dignity; " I am born a free knight of the free German empire, and have no master to honour but Germania's Emperor. A King of Westphalia is unknown to me. When I lived in Westphalia, neither a king nor a kingdom were even thought of."

Napoleon became enraged, and hastily exclaimed, " *Away with him! His doom is fixed!*"

The General was given to understand that the King of Westphalia would have him shot, as a traitor, when arrived in his territories. But happily, on being transported, accompanied by his adjutant Prince Noischkin, towards the rear of the French army, as a prisoner of war, his escort was surprised by a party of Cossacs, belonging to Czernischeff's corps, near Minsk, in Polish Lithuania; and he regained his liberty a short time previous to the famous passage of the Beresina.

* On the 12th of March 1813, the French garrison, under the command of General Carra St. Cyr, left the city of Hamburgh, and, on the 18th, Colonel Tettenborn entered it, at the head of 2000 Russians, amidst the loud and unfeigned acclamations of the whole population. The march of the Russian detachments into the city may be compared to the triumphal entry of conquering heroes. More than a thousand citizens

The principal army of the Russians, consisting of 30,000 men, and whose advanced guard was commanded by General Miloradowitsch, stood in the

---

and inhabitants of the neighbourhood, far and near, led the cavalcade on horseback. An enthusiasm, bordering on adoration, burst forth throughout all ranks, who tumultuously pressed forward to hail their deliverers, as angels sent from heaven, with flaming swords to consume and devour their galling yokes of bitter servitude and intolerable slavery. And Hamburgh, the good city of Hamburgh, set the first glorious and bright example to the rest of suffering Germany, of an exalted spirit of independence, faithful to its country, and honouring her name. Her indignant youth, eager for revenge, panting to enter the paths of glory, formed of themselves, in a few days, a corps of volunteers, nearly 4000 strong, consisting of infantry, a regiment of light horse, and artillery, under the appellation of the Hanseatic Legion. Voluntary subscriptions, for its equipment, flowed in from all sides, and considerable were the sacrifices of gold and silver ornaments, and the little hoards of domestic thrift, offered on the shrine of Liberty, by the fair sex of all ranks. In short, no one shrunk from disclosing his sense of loyalty and patriotism.

The Hanseatic Legion, fired with the hopes of retaliation, and animated with the prospect of avenging the sufferings of their native city, were so far advanced in their discipline, by their own individual efforts, as to be able to take the field against the common enemy on the 7th of May, on which day they particularly distinguished themselves, in the affair at Wilhelmsburg, bringing in a number of prisoners. Their subsequent actions with the French and Danes, at Dannenberg, Hohen-Vicheln, Zarantin, Mustin, and in Möllenerwalde, have covered them with glory, and the far-famed character of the old Hanse Towns was maintained with undiminished splendour.

neighbourhood of Kalisch, in Poland, and towards the borders of Silesia.

The fortresses in the rear, namely, Dantsic, Thorn, Modelin, Zamocz, Stettin, Cüstrin, Glogau, and Spandau, were either formally besieged, or blockaded and invested.

Prince Poniatowsky's corps, occupying a part of Poland, was kept in check and narrowly watched by a corps of Russians.

From the frontiers of Bohemia, to the mouth of the Elbe, the aggregate force of the Allies could be estimated at 70,000 men in the field. They were in possession of no tenable point on the Elbe, as unfortified Dresden could not be considered as such, and all the bridges over the Elbe, by Dresden, Meissen, Mühlberg, and Roslau, were as yet undefended by any intrenchments or works. On the other hand, the French kept strong garrisons in Magdeburg and Wittenberg, on the same river; and in case of any misfortune, Torgau was to be considered as if held by the enemy. On the Upper Elbe the French had no troops, and Würtzburg was become the centre to which the march of all their new levies and reinforcements was directed. The Viceroy of Italy was stationed on the Middle Elbe, with a force of 50,000 men, including the garrison of Magdeburg, and the troops under d'Avoust. Towards the Lower Elbe, the French had two weak detachments under Vandamme and Morand, with which our troops in that quarter were nearly upon an equal footing.

Such was the exact situation of the hostile armies when the campaign opened by General Wittgenstein's passing the Elbe, besieging Wittenberg, and removing the seat of war to the Lower Saale.

At this period it was strongly believed, and the prejudice seemed to gain ground in public, that much negligence and tardiness were shown in not pushing on with the grand army into Thüringia and Franconia, to anticipate the enemy, and, by attacking and destroying his crude and hasty assemblage of troops in and about Würtzburg, at once to baffle and frustrate his unripe designs. But a calm retrospective view and unprepossessed comparison of the forces of the belligerent powers will offer incontrovertible proofs that it was absolutely impossible. Even if the 43,000 men under Blücher, Winzingerode, and Wittgenstein, on the Upper Elbe, had been marched forwards to Würtzburg, the enemy could not have been brought to battle before the 20th of April, and it was very improbable, according to advices and accounts from all sides, that he should not have previously collected a much superior force at that place; and the result has fully justified the foresight of the Allies, and the correctness of their intelligence. For, towards the latter end of April, from 70 to 80,000 troops arrived on the Saale out of Franconia, and which they would consequently have had

so much the sooner to encounter in Franconia itself. On the whole line of the Elbe, they did not
occupy a single strong-hold, to serve as a rallying
point: these were all in the hands of the enemy;
and the Viceroy was found to be more than equal
in strength to Count Wittgenstein, as the attack
by Möckern could by no means make the Allies
easy concerning the preponderance of these two
armies; and if Count Wittgenstein should eventually be unfortunate, the grand army in advance
from the Elbe had not only a victorious army and
a river occupied by the foe in the rear, but likewise
a very superior army of the enemy in front, being,
in fact, separated from all other armies and corps,
and without any communication with its magazines and resources.

The history of former military events clearly
proves, that to stand in such a situation before
Napoleon, would inevitably have led to results
the most pernicious for the good cause, and perhaps to complete defeat; and who could have vin-
dicated it to himself or to others, to have rested
the hopes of Europe upon the doubtful issue of
such an imprudent and short-sighted expedition?
Be that as it may, the plan of letting the grand
Russian army effect a junction with General Wittgenstein on the Upper Elbe, for the purpose of
forcing the Viceroy to abandon the Elbe entirely,
might more readily have found its advocates; but

even on that point, some previous matters required arrangement.

The field could not be taken against the Viceroy before the middle of April, Count Wittgenstein not being ready with his bridge over the Elbe, nor General von Blücher able to arrive on the Lower Saale before that time. It was about the middle of April, that the greater part of the enemy's force appeared in Thüringia, and the whole line of the Upper Elbe was then to be left uncovered, with all the bridges, and the army obliged to confine itself to the solitary bridge at Roslau, situated between two fortresses, garrisoned by the foe. This was certainly no very favourable circumstance, yet the Allies might have exposed themselves to the chance of such a critical position, if they could thus hope to gain and insure a decisive advantage over the Viceroy. But the substance of every intelligence obtained, clearly evinced the intention of the Viceroy's leaving the Saale and withdrawing into Thüringia, the moment he found himself pressed and harassed by a superior force; so that in all probability he would not have accepted battle, and the whole operation would have attained no other object than having changed the theatre of war, by forced marches. The army of Blücher and Wittgenstein would then have had the Middle Elbe in their rear, and the straight and nearest road to the Upper Elbe left open to the inroads of the enemy. Such a transference of

position was a self-evident loss, and an impair-
ment of the moral strength of the Allies. The
shortest lines of communication with their supplies and resources were to be given up, the enemy
permitted to place himself between them and the
Russian grand army on the confines of Silesia,
and they reduced to no other alternative but to take
up a position with two of the enemy's fortresses,
Magdeburg and Wittenberg, at their backs, or to
recross the Elbe.

To entangle themselves in complex operations,
upon whose favourable issue no dependence could
be securely placed, out of mere vanity and rest-
lessness of inaction, would certainly have shown
a high want of reflection.

In maturely weighing these considerations, we
are imperceptibly led to the conviction, that, until
the arrival of the main body of the Russian
army on the Elbe, by which the line of that river
could be secured, and têtes de pont thrown up
to defend and protect the bridges across it, no
further offensive operations ought to have been
undertaken.

The Russian grand army reached the Elbe on
the 26th of April, and the battle of Lützen was
fought on the 2d of May. As soon as this army
arrived on the line of operations, the army of
Blücher and Winzingerode being placed under the
immediate orders of the Commander-in-chief,
their determinations, as was before possible, could

have no influence on the whole, either one way or the other.

It has been our wish, by these representations and arguments, to convince our brother-soldiers in arms, that no reprehensible forgetfulness of what they were destined to fulfil, ever for a moment crept into the councils of the army of the Allies; and that their commanders have never neglected, through indolence and irresolution, to embrace each favourable moment of bringing up the disciplined valour and energy of the Prussian nation against the unprepared foe, whenever they presented themselves. The opinion that such a moment had occurred in the spring of 1813 was at the time generally adopted, but never combined with a clear conviction of its existence, and, as we have already proved, was both delusive and groundless.

The mighty power that gained those victories on the Moskwa and Beresina, had exhausted itself on the Elbe. The Russian army, weakened by gigantic operations till now unheard of in history, in pursuit of the beaten and discomfited enemy, and by the numerous fortresses which it had to besiege, blockade, or invest, on its glorious career, had been utterly incapable of reaching the Elbe, if it had not found in the martial strength of Prussia a most powerful ally. But even when this ally was likewise capable of bringing the Russian armies (whose operations, in the nature of things, must have ended on the Vistula), through all the fortresses that impeded their way, to the banks of the Elbe, yet the confederate forces were hardly sufficient to remove the seat of war 200 miles further in advance to the Maine; and it proves a want of common sense and understanding to forget for an instant, that the power of the enemy, the nearer he approached his resources, must increase in the same ratio as that of the Allies decreased. The months of January, February, and March afforded Napoleon time enough to draw together a force in Thüringia and on the Lower Saale, which was almost double to that of the allied army under Blücher and Wittgenstein on the Elbe, at the latter end of April. This fact was not to be controverted; nor could it be denied, whatever turn and direction might be given to the future operations of the Allies, that, with such a superiority, there was no prospect of defeating Napoleon, how disproportionate soever the armies might be in other respects.

The month of April elapsed on the Upper Elbe, in a state of inaction by no means optional. General von Blücher's army occupied Saxony, to profit by the resources of the country, in case of necessity to support General Wittgenstein, and at the same time endeavour to harass the enemy on his flanks and in his rear, by detachments of light cavalry and partisans.

Count Wittgenstein carried on the war against

the Viceroy, with as many advantages as the superior force of the latter would allow. By gaining the battle of Möckern, he protected Berlin
and the Mark from an invasion, with which they
were threatened by an enemy's army, 40,000
strong, who (according to the intercepted reports
of the enemy himself) were actually repulsed by
only 17,000 men of General Wittgenstein's army.
An irresolute timid conduct, attended with some
blunders, on the side of the enemy, and the
most inflexible courage and undaunted military
spirit on the part of the allied troops, rendered it
alone possible for the skill and intrepidity of the
Count to gain this hard-fought and honourable
victory. Prussians! you had your share of the
glory of this day!—Count Wittgenstein has himself eminently distinguished you in his dispatches.

The detachments on the Lower Elbe opened the
campaign with some success. General Dörnberg
took the French General Morand, prisoner, with his
whole division; and you, Prussians, again bore a considerable part in the glory of the contest! Six hundred Prussians bravely defended a gate and a bridge
at Lüneburgh for several hours against the whole
division of the enemy. The expeditions of the
light troops of the Allies into the forests of Thüringia were likewise equally glorious to their arms.
Major Hellwig, at the head of 120 horse, surprised

a Bavarian regiment of infantry, 1300 men strong, dispersed it, and took from it five field-pieces.

It was these acts of an exalted bravery, performed, as it were, before the eyes of the whole army, that nourished a growing confidence in itself, and proved a kind of touchstone, upon which, on trial, they discovered the sterling metal of their own prowess, while at the same time it contributed rapidly to increase the natural and real strength of the Allies. Without any marks of pride and arrogance, this confidence in themselves, and in the sacredness of the cause of their dear country, bleeding under the scourge of oppression, was conspicuous throughout the ranks, and never was an army inspired with a higher spirit.

A few days afterwards, this spirit strikingly displayed itself before all Europe on the bloody plains of Lützen.

CHAPTER V.

Battle of Lützen—Retreat to Bautzen.

As the French troops accumulated in the forests of Thüringia, and those coming from Italy approached the frontiers of Saxony, Count Wittgenstein marched from the Lower Saale towards Leipsic, and General von Blücher, who could not as yet venture to leave the high road by the way of Chemnitz to Dresden, being the shortest communication from Franconia to the Elbe, took position at Altenburg*; so that, by a quick movement

---

* General von Blücher issued from his head-quarters at this place, the following proclamation to his brave army :

" Soldiers of my army !

" Your exemplary conduct has undergone no change whatever, since you have left your native provinces, and entered the territory of Saxony. You have hitherto made no distinction between the two countries, but have held yourselves bound in duty to observe the same excellent discipline. I thank you for this proof of your noble forbearance. Such a conduct evinces the true spirit of warriors, and is best fitting us, fighting, as we are, for the most honourable and costly of all earthly possessions—our country and our freedom !

" Prove to the inhabitants of the German provinces, by the moderation of your demands, and the mildness of your treatment, that we are come, not as their oppressors, but as their brethren and preservers. Continue to act with this excellent on his right, he could easily form a junction with Count Wittgenstein.

The numbers of the French army had been carefully estimated. The several corps in march from Würtzburg to the forests of Thüringia might be calculated at from 60 to 70,000 men. The Italian divisions under General Bertrand might be 30,000 strong. It was, however, a matter of uncertainty, whether the whole would be brought up, as, according to an earlier destination, two of them were to halt on the Danube. But the strength of the Viceroy's army was better known and appreciated; for, besides the garrisons of Magdeburg and Wittenberg, and including d'Avoust's corps, it amounted to 38,000 men, of which d'Avoust had 12,000 with him. It was, therefore, justly calculated that the Viceroy would form part of the left wing of the French grand army, with about 20,000 men; the whole constituting an aggregate force of nearly 120,000 combatants.

The armies of General von Blücher and Count Wittgenstein might be estimated at 55,000 men, after having left the necessary troops on the Lower Saale, before Wittenberg, and in the tête

spirit of subordination, and should the fame of your exalted behaviour have preceded you far and near, you will be received with blessings and open arms, wherever you show yourselves, and fate may lead you."

Altenburg, April 24, 1813.

de pont of the bridge at Dessau; the Russian grand army at 30,000 men: in the whole, 85,000 well-disciplined warriors. It was, therefore, impossible, as before stated, to oppose even an equal force to the enemy in Saxony.

There was here no other alternative but either to evacuate Saxony without striking a blow, to take up a position behind the Elbe, and to defend that river, or instantly to attack the enemy as soon as he had crossed the Saale.

In defending the Elbe, the Allies could not be very sanguine in their expectations of keeping the foe long in check, he having Wittenberg, and, in case of the Allies retreating over the Elbe, most probably Torgau * in his possession, and the

---

* General Thielman was appointed Governor of Torgau on the 22d of February. The King having left Saxony, and the political state of affairs assuming a very changeable aspect, from the uncertainty of the nature of those steps His Majesty might eventually take, the General determined to observe the strictest neutrality. Marshal d'Avoust, as well as the Viceroy of Italy, were urgent in their requests, that the General might send the garrison to defend Meissen, and line the ramparts of Wittenberg with his artillery. The former even demanded permission to send French troops to garrison Torgau, but which was firmly resisted; a conduct that, at the time, met the most unreserved approbation of the Saxon Monarch. On the 5th of May Marshal Ney appeared before the gates of Torgau, and demanded entrance. General Thielman stated his want of instructions, and would not open them. On the 8th, the Marshal again presented himself before the fortress, and repeated the same pretension, which proved equally unavailing. On the 9th, a member of the

crossing of so narrow and placid a stream, presented no very insurmountable obstacles.   There
was, besides, every appearance that the Allies would
thus entangle themselves in a dangerous defensive
operation ; for nothing could be clearer, than that
it was impossible to gain sufficient time for the
Austrians to be ready to assist them in the general
cause of so large a portion of Europe ; and to continue their retrograde movement into Lusatia and
Silesia, merely to enable the Imperialists to take
the field, was evidently as little practicable, it
requiring no great foresight to calculate that such
a step would have led them to the frontiers of
Poland, and perhaps farther.   An attempt must,
therefore, be made, to give the enemy battle, and
it certainly appeared more advantageous, not voluntarily to submit to the evil impression which a
retreat in form would make upon Germany and
the army altogether, but rather boldly and da-
ringly to fall unawares upon the enemy, than to
accept the battle he might offer, or force upon the

---

intermediate commission arrived from Dresden in Torgau, demanding the opening of the gates in the name of Napoleon.

The General remained firm to his adopted neutrality till the
11th, when, at the express command of the King, he delivered
up the place to the French. He now quitted the service of
Saxony, and entered that of the Emperor of Russia, being well
convinced that, as long as French influence governed the King,
the unfading laurels of honour and glory could never grace his
brow, nor the smiles of fortune ever crown his efforts.

Allies, in any well-chosen defensive position in the rear. Many weighty and collateral reasons concurred also to render it possible that the event might prove important and decisive, both from the character of Buonaparte as a general, and the superiority of numbers which he possessed.

It still remained doubtful whether Napoleon could bring into action his 120,000 men on the day of battle*, if the Allies hastened to attack him directly on his crossing the Saale; for he would then have the steep valley of that river in his rear, and must debouch in a plain forming a fine glacis very favourable to the allied troops, as they had 25,000 cavalry with their army, and the enemy only 5000. The infantry of the Allies were indisputably better in moral value than his. Perhaps he might not expect so daring an attack; and as Napoleon and his host had never been brought to battle entirely on the defensive, there was every reason to expect, that the hostile army would be taken by surprise, and thus deprived of their usual confidence of success. In blending all these arguments together, hopes of victory, and of overthrowing at one blow Napoleon's delirious plans of conquest, might certainly be cherished,

---

* It has been since ascertained, that Napoleon had brought up all his corps into the field of battle, except the 12th corps, under Marshal Oudinot, which was a few marches in the rear, and did not come into action at all, on this side of the Elbe.

without yielding too much to illusive conjectures.

Napoleon made good his passage over the Saale at Weissenfels, on the 30th of April, with a considerable force; by which movement his supposed intention of proceeding to the plains of Leipsic was confirmed. The allied army broke up, to meet the foe without loss of time, on the plain of Lützen, to form in front of the high road to Leipsic, and, in case of beating the enemy, to force him from Weissenfels and Naumburg, by driving him towards the morasses and swampy grounds at the junction of the Elster with the Pleisse. The Prussian army was collected at Borne on the 31st of April, and on the 1st of May at Röthe; Count Wittgenstein with the Russians at Zweckau: during which, General Winzingerode observed and kept the enemy on the alert near the Flossgraben. In the night of the 1st of May the Prussian army put itself in march; and both armies united, crossed the Elster at Zweckau and Pegau.

General Miloradowitsch had taken upon him to watch the enemy on the road from Chemnitz, as the Prussians began to move to the right; and when it was ascertained that no enemy appeared from that quarter, he marched off towards Zeitz, to cover the road from Naumburg and Camberg, it being impossible, on the 1st of May, to be certain that the enemy would not push on from this point with from 20 to 30,000 men, and thus get into the rear of the army without impediment. The remaining part of the Russian grand army, consisting of guards, grenadiers, and cuirassiers, from 15 to 20,000 strong, had marched from Dresden, by the way of Röchlitz, to the Elster, and took position on the morning of the 2d of May in the rear of Wittgenstein and Blücher as reserves.

General Count Wittgenstein was Commander-in-chief of all the allied troops. The Emperor of Russia and the King of Prussia arrived on the field of battle with the reserves.

It was evident that this intrepid determination of the Allies confounded Napoleon, and took him by surprise. He was marching at this period towards Leipsic, in hopes of pushing forward from thence to Dresden, and by this rapid movement to strike a decisive and irretrievable blow at the liberties of Germany. His own bulletins express as much. He probably expected to encounter General Wittgenstein's army before his junction with General von Blücher, whom he still supposed to be at Altenburg; or he had the intention, before he attacked them, to cut them off from all communication with the Elbe, if they were united in the direction of that place.

But in these " sublime manœuvres," as the French papers termed them, he received a check ; the allied army having, at the most critical mo-

ment, fallen on his rear, and arrested his confident
and impetuous career on the plains of Lützen,
where Nature had poured forth her riches in unbounded profusion, but which the horrors of this
terrible conflict, have now covered with ruin and
desolation.

The corps of Marshal Marmont formed Napoleon's rear-guard, and occupied the villages of
Rahno, Gross-Görschen, and Klein-Görschen, to
cover the march. He had to bear the brunt of the
first shock. Napoleon immediately caused his
army to halt, and the columns already near Leipsic
were recalled.

Here it was manifest that the right point had
been chosen, both in time and place, so openly
confessed by Napoleon himself; and if we add the
important and valuable consequences that must
ensue, supposing the battle to be successful, we
may assert, without fear of contradiction, that the
bold attempt forms one of the finest military combinations to be met with in the annals of any war.

In entering into the minutiæ of the battle itself,
the author begs the particular indulgence of the
reader to this very superficial sketch. Although
the confederate warriors, for whom these sheets
are more immediately intended, must feel themselves much interested in seeing noticed, clearly
and succinctly, all the separate attacks made on
this memorable day; yet, at the present moment,
it is too difficult a task to be complete, without

again reviewing and closely examining the terrain
on which the battle was fought; the author is,
therefore, constrained to confine himself to the
general character and most striking features of
the whole.

General von Kleist being left in and near Leipsic, with 5000 men, and General Miloradowitsch, at
Zeitz, with 12,000; the allied army, 70,000 strong,
after passing the Elster, crossed the Flossgraben in
small compact columns, in close succession, to form
in line of battle, wheeling, as they deployed, rather
to the right; so that the right wing leaned on the
Flossgraben, and halted behind the heights about a
mile and a half from Gross-Görschen. It was now
noon; and the troops were absolutely in want of
some repose, the Prussians having marched without
intermission during the last six-and-thirty hours.
From these heights the gleams of hostile bayonets
were seen at a great distance, and the enemy's cavalry in full march by the way of Lützen to Leipsic; at least so it was judged by the clouds of dust
that occasionally hid them from the view of the
allied army; but it was more reasonable to suppose
that the enemy were hastily retracing their steps,
on finding their original plan disconcerted by such
a decisive and vigorous movement on the part of
the Allies. The enemy, it was perceived, occupied
the villages of Gross-Görschen, Klein-Görschen,
Rahno, and Kaja, which, lying near each other,
form of themselves a kind of irregular square:

this occupation was thought to consist of some weak out-posts, and it was therefore hoped no great resistance would be made.

The plan of the attack was, to take and occupy these villages with an advanced guard; to proceed with the front against the enemy, whose position seemed to run parallel with the high road to Weissenfels, in such a manner as to bring the principal weight of the attack against his right wing, but to undertake nothing against his left. With this concentration of force, it was the intention to throw back, if possible, his right wing, to drive Napoleon from the direct road to the Saale, and then, with the mass of the numerous cavalry of the allied army, to turn the enemy's right wing, and, by a furious charge on its flank and rear, to bear down all obstacles, and thus decide the fortune of the day.

The order of battle was as follows : the army of General von Blücher formed the first line ; that formerly belonging to Count Wittgenstein, the second ; and the corps of General Winzingerode, together with the Russian guards and grenadiers, the reserve. The Russian and Prussian reserves of cavalry were to be united. (See Plan of the battle of Lützen.) After an hour's rest, the army, so formed, marched onwards at about half past one o'clock, P. M. Colonel Klüx's brigade was ordered to attack the first village ; namely, Gross-Görschen. From three to four batteries were

erected within 800 yards, and the village heavily
cannonaded; the enemy's battalions, of which
three or more were drawn up before the village,
supported the fire with wonderful firmness for a
considerable time; the brigade then advanced, with
steadiness and discipline, to close action, and, although more troops were encountered in the village than had been expected, yet the attack was
made with such an irresistible impetuosity, that
the French were in a few minutes driven out of it
with great loss. They soon rallied, and, being reinforced, returned to the attack with redoubled
fury, and the action continued with violence without the allied troops being compelled to relinquish
a foot of ground. As the enemy continued bringing
up fresh troops every moment, General Ziethen's
brigade was ordered to advance to the right of the
village, and the Prussians soon acquired a visible
ascendancy: the enemy's infantry fought bravely,
but the two brigades still pressed forward, and carried, after an obstinate resistance, the two villages
of Rahno and Klein-Görschen, that lie about the
distance of a cannon-shot to the right and left of
Gross-Görschen. For several hours the conflict
was dubious; but the discharges of musquetry
raged with such indescribable destruction, and the
troops on both sides were so near to each other,
that the number of killed and wounded was incredible. The artillery was then gradually brought
forward, and small detachments of cavalry, of one

and two squadrons, that formed the second line of
the Prussian brigades, endeavoured to find favourable opportunities to charge: the enemy was not
remiss in bringing up his artillery and squadrons
of cavalry; and on a terrain of about one thousand
to one thousand five hundred square yards, intersected by villages, hamlets, meadows, and ditches,
the most severe and galling attacks of all arms
took place in close contact with each other, and
on which, it may be said, fell Slaughter, in all his
horrid terrors, crowned with desolation, and, pro-
digal of death, reigned triumphant.

The number of Prussians engaged amounted to
about fourteen or fifteen thousand men. The enemy, who, for the moment, acted on the offensive
in striving to regain possession of the villages,
brought up continually numerous bodies of fresh
troops into action, and at last attained a superiority
of numbers that obliged the weakened and thinned battalions of the Allies to evacuate Klein-Görschen; but, again led on and inspired by their
Generals, and profiting of some fortunate charges
of the cavalry, Napoleon was soon deprived of his
precarious advantage; and here it was demonstrably
evident, that the enemy's infantry was not, in any
respect, equal to the allied in moral value, though
superior in numbers; they displayed neither firmness nor discipline; and the unremitting, steady
fire of the Prussians in platoons, soon forced their
dismayed battalions to desert the field of battle in

disordered crowds. When it was observed on the side of the Prussians, that an important crisis presented itself to carry Kaja, but that the troops on the spot were too weak in numbers to maintain themselves in it, the reserve brigades, consisting of the guards and grenadiers, were brought into action; and these gallant files arrived on the ground at a most critical juncture. Napoleon incessantly pushed on into fire, fresh battalions from all points. The two brigades were already so thinned in their ranks, that they could only keep up a partial and irregular fire, like the open lines of a rifle-corps. The guards, however, pressed forward with incomparable bravery and order; they took Klein-Görschen, and the village of Hahalati to the right of it, by storm, driving the French before them to the other side of Kaja : in vain did the enemy endeavour to stop their progress with the bayonet; their resolution was not to be daunted : the ground over which they marched was strewed with the dead and wounded, and blood and carnage paved the way to glory. Kaja was in flames, and it was not occupied from either side.

This was the most brilliant period of the battle. It might be about six o'clock in the evening; and the Allies had gained a mile and a half in advance upon the foe, amidst a continual and murderous fire, the violence and fury of which baffle all attempts at description. This dear-bought bloody

conquest must have proved the first step towards
a most splendid victory, if, under the existing circumstances, it were to be gained in any way. But
the arranged plan for this battle, of which we have
just depicted the most important features, now
met with considerable difficulties in its execution
and continuance. The unexpected and obstinate
resistance of the enemy in the first villages, and
the number of troops he brought into the line of
battle, soon convinced the Allies that no very inconsiderable part of Napoleon's army was engaged
with them; it was, however, impossible, instantly,
on this being ascertained, to break off and decline
the combat by leaving the affair undecided, as their
adversary would have soon acted on the offensive,
had they given him time, by slackening their fire,
or revived his hopes by a retrograde movement in
the heat of action. No other option was left the
Allies, therefore, but to carry their point at all ha-
zards. It was a momentous crisis: the fate of nations seemed to depend on the issue of this sanguinary struggle, and much was to be left to the
goodness of Providence, whose omniscience mocks
the short-sighted policy of men. General von Blücher's army, that is, the whole of the first line, had
been hotly engaged with the foe, and even defeated
that body of the enemy opposed to him, though
superior in numbers; yet there was no prospect
whatever of directing the principal weight of the
attack against the enemy's right wing; and it was

therefore resolved to order up the second line, consisting of General von York's corps of 8000 men, and General von Berg's of 5000, to support General von Blücher.

With the view of attracting the attention of the enemy's right wing, and by this feint to profit of the first opening in which, perhaps, a movement of the front line of the enemy, that leaned on the village of Staarsiedel to the right, might afford their numerous cavalry a favourable opportunity to charge the hostile infantry; the Prussian cavalry in reserve, and a considerable part of the Russian heavy cavalry, were so drawn up on the plain as to support General von Blücher's left with their right wing, and to stand opposite with their left to the village of Staarsiedel. A brisk cannonade now ensued on the whole of this line. The reserves of infantry, both Russian and Prussian, were posted on the high commanding grounds in the neighbourhood, out of the range of the enemy's artillery.

At the time that the Prussian guards penetrated to Kaja, the enemy's first line being threatened on their left wing, and much annoyed by the hot fire of the artillery of the Allies, drew back from five to six hundred yards, and evacuated the village of Staarsiedel, which the want of infantry prevented them from occupying.

It was apparent that Napoleon considered the occupation and possession of the five villages already mentioned, as decisive of the fate of the battle; for he did not hesitate to bring into action more than a fourth, if not the half of his infantry, in order to retake and maintain them (namely, from forty to fifty thousand men); and thus continued an obstinate engagement for hours, in which both the Allies and the French were victorious and vanquished by turns.

The corps of General von Blücher may be rated at 20,000 men, without the cavalry in reserve : the enemy once more became his superior in numbers, and it required the most heroic exertions to preserve those points from whence he had dislodged the foe, until General von York's, and a great part of General von Berg's corps could advance to support him.   Napoleon, in bringing up his forces, spread them far to the left of the villages, thus obliging the allied troops of the second line to deploy more to the right, and, consequently, the assistance intended in aid of the first line was much weakened.   A considerable number of the first line had fallen, and many of the battalions belonging to it, reduced to inconsiderable bodies, had retired behind the villages to rally and collect themselves.

For the purpose of giving some decisive turn to this most obstinate and sanguinary contest, the General-in-chief, Count Wittgenstein, gave orders that the infantry, under the command of Prince Eugene of Wirtemburg, should fall upon the left flank of the enemy, to ensure the advantages already gained near the villages.   They were put in execution ; but the Viceroy of Italy, who had just arrived on the field with his corps from Leipsic, advanced with confidence on the Prince at this juncture ; and, instead of having it in his power to outflank the enemy, he was himself outflanked, an event which called forth all the gallantry and firmness of this young hero, and the intrepid valour of his distinguished division, to keep their position in this unequal trial.   In the mean time the allied cavalry kept up a brisk cannonade with their horse-artillery on the right wing of the enemy, which cost the life of many a brave soldier, without any important consequences ensuing.   The brilliant charges which the Prussian cavalry repeatedly made to penetrate the French ranks, were often crowned with success ; but the principal line of the Gallic infantry ever standing firm and unbroken, no object of importance could be attained by the charges of cavalry alone.

The enemy was foiled in all his repeated attempts to regain possession of those obstinately contested points of his position which the Allies had acquired during a severe action of eight hours, although the battle raged till night.

To maintain the conquered ground during the night, however, would require the advance of more reserves of infantry.   On the side of the Allies about 38,000 infantry had been engaged; and as the whole force of their foot did not exceed

53,000 men, of course, only 15,000 fresh troops of this description were in reserve. Supposing the enemy had brought from sixty to seventy thousand men into the field, which might be presumed after the arrival of the Viceroy, he had at least from forty to fifty thousand men remaining untouched. This being maturely weighed, it naturally followed that the Allies had it not in their power to keep pace with the physical strength of the enemy, on which account, it was determined to attempt, in the obscurity of the night, to surprise him by an unexpected charge of cavalry, which, if successful, might lead to very important events. With nine squadrons of the Prussian reserve cavalry that were on the spot favourable for the operation, but reduced in their efficient numbers by the murderous cannonade of eight hours' duration, the advanced troops of the enemy were undauntedly charged, broken, and hotly pursued to some distance, where, falling in with enormous masses of infantry in the rear, and owing to the darkness of the night, and a hollow way which the cavalry was obliged to pass to make another charge, they had eventually dispersed in all directions, depriving the Allies of any immediate advantages to be derived from this dashing attempt.

If the Allies would not set every thing at stake in continuing to oppose a superiority of infantry in the enemy, that nearly trebled theirs, it was incumbent on them to make good their retreat on the following day, that so they might be nearer their reinforcements, and, with as little sacrifice of position as possible, await Austria's declaration of war, and the call on Germany, to rouse her dormant spirit, to assert her liberties, and to avenge her wrongs.

The Allies had suffered no other loss in this battle, but of killed and wounded *. The enemy could scarcely have made a few hundreds prisoners ; and they had not to boast of having captured a single piece of artillery : the Allies, on the other hand, had established themselves on the

---

* The humane inhabitants of Leipsic and Altenburg, although Saxons, with a noble emulation, endeavoured to outvie each other in bringing prompt assistance to the wounded Prussians and Russians lying on the field of battle ; the country-people voluntarily lent their aid to carry them on biers, from off the ground, to the temporary hospitals, particularly to that in Altenburg, where the poor-house was hastily converted into an hospital, exclusively for the brave Allies, and in which they were nursed and attended with the tenderness of relations. The wards in the poor-house more resembled ball-rooms than the chambers of the sick ; both married and single ladies of rank and fortune, held it an honour to bring refreshments, bandages, and medicines of every description, and in many cases to distribute them themselves. Wreaths of laurel, garlands of flowers, festoons of oak, were hung round the walls, and replaced fresh and blooming every three or four days. The French were taken care of in the town-house, but not a man of them dared to put his foot within the hallowed edifice solely devoted for the relief of the gallant and adored guardians and defenders of Teutonic liberty and independence.

principal points of his position, and a few cannon
and tumbrils, with six to eight hundred prisoners,
constituted the trophies of the day.

All this was effected in a conflict with an enemy
very superior in numbers; and if we place this battle
in a point of view similar to an affair of honour, it
might be looked upon as a victory that only increased the splendour of the allied arms, and
served to convince the neutral German princes of
the zeal and unanimity that governed the councils
of the confederates *.

---

* The Emperor of Russia transmitted to our veteran General
the order of St. George, accompanied by the following gracious
letter in his own hand-writing :

" *Dresden, May the 5th,* 1813.

" General of the Cavalry, von Blücher,

" The bravery which you have evinced in the battle of
the 2d of May, the services you have done on this memorable
day, your devotion, your zeal, your eagerness to be found on
the post of danger, and your firmness in not deserting the field
of honour, although wounded ; in a word, the whole tenour of
your conduct during the battle has filled my heart with gratitude and admiration. Inspired with the desire of giving you
proofs of my sincere sentiments in this respect, I send you the
insignia of the second-class of the order of St. George. It will
remind you of a battle that must interest you in so lively a
manner by the conduct of the gallant troops you commanded,
that have so highly distinguished themselves ; and may it likewise serve as a mark of my personal attachment. As for the
rest, I pray to the Almighty that he may ever take you under
his holy protection.

" ALEXANDER."

The retreat of the allied army from the plains of Lützen, could not be considered as proceeding from the consequences of the battle; it originated solely in the evident superiority of the foe *; and if the battle had not been fought at all, would have become so much the more necessary. That these observations do not spring from an empty vaunting, or any inclination to deceive ourselves, is sufficiently proved by the conduct of Napoleon after the battle: according to his own account, he had withdrawn his corps to some distance in his rear, during the night, and did not occupy the vil-

---

* According to an official statement of the French army, under Napoleon, prior to the battle of Lützen, the corps of which it was composed, and their numbers, were as follow:

Six battalions, old guards - - } Marshal Mortier	16,000
Sixteen ditto, young guards - }	
Third corps, under Marshal Ney, consisting of five divisions - - - - - - - - - - - - - -	45,000
Sixth corps, under Marshal Marmont, consisting of three divisions - - - - - - - - - - - -	25,000
Fourth corps, under Count Bertrand, consisting of three divisions - - - - - - - - - -	25,000
Twelfth corps, under Marshal Oudinot, consisting of three divisions - - - - - - - - - - - -	25,000
Fifth corps, under Count Lauriston, consisting of two divisions - - - - - - - - - - - -	15,000
Eleventh corps, under Marshal Macdonald, consisting of two divisions - - - - - - - - - -	15,000
Cavalry of the guards under Bessières - - - - -	4,000
	170,000

lages which the Allies had left, till the noon of the following day, and then only with weak detachments ; he remained inactive during the whole of the third, and, on the fourth, put his army in motion in pursuit of the allied armies, and to follow out his plan.

On the second, the Allies marched to Borne and Altenburg ; on the fourth, to Röchlitz and Kolditz ; on the fifth, to Döbeln and Nossen ; on the sixth, to Meissen and Wilsdruf ; on the seventh they crossed the Elbe, and took the road to Bautzen on the eighth, where they hoped to be enabled to offer a second general battle to the enemy *.

---

* General von Blücher received on this day the following letter from the Emperor Alexander :

"*Dresden, May* 6, 1813.

" The Prussian troops, on the 2d of May, have, by their resolution, their firmness, and their zeal, not forgetting their distinguished bravery and discipline, excited my most unfeigned admiration, and that of the whole Russian army. I entreat you, noble General, to be the interpreter of these my sentiments towards them, which impose upon me the agreeable duty of publicly giving proofs of my esteem and gratitude to those brave men who have covered themselves with glory, on that splendid day. Therefore, General, you will have the goodness to make known to me those generals and officers who have had opportunities of doing signal services, that I may, accordingly, fix the kind of distinctions which I wish to confer upon them. In the mean time I place at your disposal three hundred crosses of the order of St. George, fifth class, to be distributed to those subalterns and privates who have the most highly distinguished themselves by brilliant deeds of arms. A chief, who

During the battle, General von Kleist, who, on the approach of the enemy's grand army, had retired from Leipsic, again occupied that city. He left it on the 3d, and passed the Elbe at Mühlburg *.

---

possesses your esteem and confidence, will deliver to you these distinctions, and, at the same time, prove to you how much I do justice to your conduct. Your fellow-soldiers in arms will hereby be convinced that they share with yourself an honorary badge, on which you place a great value, and which only the regard and devotion that prevails between you, in so high a degree, can preserve and confirm. Please to accept, noble General, the assurance of my most sincere esteem.

" ALEXANDER."

---

* 1. The French General of Division Lauri had, on the 3d of May 1813, forced the Prussian General Kleist to evacuate Leipsic. A few Cossacks had, however, loitered behind, and a patrole of eight French chasseurs à cheval rode down the Peter's Street, to clear this quarter of stragglers, and then stopped a few minutes at the Peter's gate: at this instant, a single Cossack, on a gentle trot, passed within a few yards of them, with as unconcerned an air, holding his pike balancing in his hand, as if they had been his own comrades: the writer of this, an eye-witness, was astonished at the calm manner in which he eyed the French; who, seized by an unaccountable surprise, or rather a kind of irresolute torpor, actually permitted the Cossack to advance more than fifty paces through the gate, before they bethought themselves of taking him prisoner. On galloping off after him, they fired their pistols, but the intrepid Cossack had already got clear of the gateway, and with wonderful presence of mind turned the first corner at full speed, and escaped.

2. On the same day, the French piquets being pushed forward towards Wurzen, and their patroles having scoured the

General von Bülow had, on the second of May, taken Halle by storm, capturing six pieces of artillery. This glorious exploit proclaimed, like many others, the fine spirit that animated the troops, but their results were for the moment absorbed in the unavoidable vortex of general events.

The advanced guard of the French came up with the Prussian rear-guard, on the fifth, at Kolditz, and a severe action took place, without accelerating or retarding the march of the allied columns. No further attempt was made by the enemy on this rear-guard. Against General Milo-radowitsch, who commanded the rear-guard of the Russian columns, the adversary made some attacks that led to no advantage to himself, but

---

roads on all sides, their light cavalry seemed to think all danger far distant, and began to disperse themselves in different parts of the city. Two of them rode their horses to a farrier's, in the suburb of Halle, to have them shoed; they dismounted, and hanging their bridles on the hook in front of the smith's shop, stepped in, stating their wants, and, as usual, demanding a bottle of wine, " pour passer le tems:" scarcely were they seated with their wine, on a bench before the door, when a prowling Cossack, who had been on the watch, rode up at full speed, with his pike couched towards them ; the dragoons, taken by surprise, hastily retreated into the smith's workshop, and the Cossack, little heeding them, with an agility bordering on enchantment, unhooked the bridles, and galloped off unmolested with his booty; leaving the Frenchmen to enjoy their wine at leisure, but with what relish may be easily conceived.

for which he was several times severely punished, by the success of the Russians *.

In casting a retrospective glance over this first opening of the campaign, it may be remarked, that the issue was a very natural effect of the general state of affairs in Germany. Only one of the Germanic states, and but a small part of a growing power, assisted by a moderate army of his faithful ally, fought and attempted to make head against the concentrated forces of colossal France. It was to be lamented, that, even at this eventful epoch, many German princes added their files to the host of the oppressor, that the rest of Germany was calm and torpid, and (except the bright examples of the Duke of Mecklenburg-Schwerin †, and the ancient city of Ham-

---

* The severest conflicts took place on the 12th, by Kapellenberg, near Bishoffswerda. General Miloradowitsch defended every foot of ground with incomparable bravery, and the enemy, foiled in his obstinate and repeated attempts to penetrate the lines of the rear-guard, and full of rancorous revenge at his heavy loss, plundered without mercy the pleasant country-town of Bishoffswerda to the bare walls, then set it on fire, and did not leave three houses standing.

† Mecklenburg-Schwerin was the first state that threw off the trammels imposed on it by fear and coercion, through the hated confederacy of the Rhine. No sooner had the French deserted the right bank of the Elbe, than the people, in zealous haste, anticipated the call of their Prince, and flew to arms.

History will not forget the burst of patriotism, which, on the approach of the Russians, in February, converted the faithful

burgh *) awaited with solicitude the hour of
deliverance, but wanted the courage to hasten

---

subjects of the Duke into a band of heroes. The well-appointed corps of volunteer yeomanry cavalry, headed by the Duke's
third son, Prince Gustavus, gallantly charged the Danes, on
the 10th of December 1813, at the affair on the Eider, between
Eckernförde and Flendsburg; but being unsupported by infantry, through the tardy and vacillating measures of the Crown
Prince of Sweden, their retreat was obliged to be made through
a defile defended by some battalions of the enemy. This brave
young Prince, at the head of his squadron, attempted to cut
his way through; but his horse being shot under him, and himself wounded, he was taken prisoner. On being conducted to
Prince Frederick of Hesse, who commanded the Danes, he
was released on his parole of not serving against Denmark
during the war. The Crown Prince of Sweden was very lavish
of expressions, in extolling the intrepid conduct of the worthy
descendant of the great Coburg, and appointed the Prince a
commander of the Swedish order of the Sword. A conduct to
be compared to a man's standing by, very unconcernedly, whilst
his friend is well drubbed by others, and afterwards consoling
him with proffers of friendship.

Related to the editor by Baron von K—n.

---

* A weak garrison of about 2000 men, of all arms, being left
in Hamburgh, under the command of General Carra St. Cyr,
and those troops fit to take the field having been marched to the
vicinity of Magdeburg, to join the Viceroy of Italy, but little penetration was wanting to foresee, that the spirit of Liberty, so
long enchained, would seize the first favourable moment to
burst her galling fetters. On the 24th of February 1813, when
the French authorities, both civil and military, made evident
preparations to evacuate the place, and leave it to its fate, the
populace were not backward in expressing their sentiments of
freedom and detestation of their tyrants, both vehemently and

its approach! Austria had not yet completed her
armaments; and only a brave and resolute re-

---

loudly. The arms of Napoleon were torn down, and treated
with every mark of contempt, the custom-house offices sacked
and demolished, and several other acts of popular fury were
committed. Six persons were, in consequence, arrested by
order of General Carra St. Cyr, and dragged before a military
tribunal; their trial was of the most summary kind, no witnesses
were confronted, no counsel allowed, and, after a short hour
of examination, they were sentenced to be shot as traitors, in
having aided an insurrection; and without being permitted any
communication whatever with their relatives or friends, and
even denied the solace of spiritual comfort in their last moments, they were inhumanly hurried to the place of execution,
and into eternity, unable to make their peace either with God or
man. Never were liberty, justice, and the natural rights of mankind more flagrantly violated, than in this instance. It is a la-
mentable fact, that one of the unhappy sufferers was with his
uncle in the country during the whole of the day on which the
pretended rebellion had taken place. Such are some of the infa-
mous deeds of a few of those flagitious miscreants and followers
of Napoleon, who have wantonly stained with innocent blood
every city, and every river, from the Scheldt to the Elbe, and
from the Rhine to the Danube; evincing in all their actions a
marked disdain and mockery of religion, and an avowed opposition to every thing sacred in the laws, customs, and governments
of other countries. It would not, however, be doing justice to
the French nation, to blend them indiscriminately in such remarks: contrast is the soul of description, and it is our duty
not only to present a faithful and animated picture of the actions of Napoleon's satellites, but to enrich our pages with a
narration of authentic occurrences, that may afford a fair opportunity of giving praise, and bestowing censure, wherever

sistance against the overbearing power of the conqueror, who seemed again to lift his fallen crest, could arrest his further progress, destroy his martial strength, force him to respect the Allies, inspire the rest of Europe with confidence in their arms; and, above all, diffuse and keep up that re-

---

they may be due. These considerations demand of us a case in point.

When the Crown Prince of Sweden entered Hamburgh, as Prince de Ponte-Corvo, and as commander in chief of a French-Spanish corps, the French gens d'armes, and other officers of the police, first began to exercise their functions; and it was soon discovered, that a Monsieur D——, living in Hamburgh, and author of a French and German Grammar, that had already run through five editions, had inadvertently inserted in one of the exercises the following phrase: " General Bernadotte is a good captain of banditti, but unworthy to be a marshal of France." The gens d'armes dragged him to prison, as a libel-lous emigrant; and, in a few days, he was brought into the pre-sence of the Prince, who mildly asked him, " If he were the author of the Grammar, and if he knew, from his own personal experience, the truth of the assertion he had made in it?" Upon the Prince being answered in the negative, the latter re-plied; " In your next edition, I trust, the offensive sentence will be expunged; and my now dismissing you, without punishment, will prove to you that I know how to value men of letters, when they set bounds to their opinions, taking it for granted that you have only been in an error." The author retired overwhelmed at his clemency; and if he had formerly felt indignant at the name of a republican, he had now learnt to confess, that the truly great can ever discriminate between error and premeditated malice. Would d'Avoust, Vandamme, and St. Cyr, have acted thus?—Alas, No!

liance on themselves with which their corps were already animated.

Should it be ever questioned whether this resistance was made, no Prussian need to shrink from the answer. Prussians, you may review with complacency your past deeds in arms. You have done your duty, what your country expected of you, and what God demands from the champions of a righteous and sacred cause. The nation with gratitude acknowledges your exertions, sacrifices, and privations; and the warlike spirit aroused in it, is still heightened and elevated by the innate and noble pride with which it views your glorious struggle in relieving your native land from a state of bondage, that openly violated every principle of justice, humanity, and religion. The battle of Lützen has restored the ancient splendour of the Prussian name, and quieted the perturbed shade of Frederick the Great; their cotemporaries in the field have borne witness, that, on this memorable day, the military glory of the Prussian monarchy burst forth from behind the clouds that had hid its lustre, evermore to beam in the eyes of all Europe with undiminished fervency.

The combined army went into camp on the 14th of May, in a well-chosen position, about three miles from Bautzen. The town and its environs were occupied by General Miloradowitsch, commanding the advanced guard of the army. The camp itself stretched its left wing behind Klein-

Jenkowitz, the centre was behind Gross-Jenkowitz and Baschütz, and the right wing towards
Kreckwitz.   The line of heights, situated between
the water of Klein-Bautzen and the army, and
those from Kreckwitz to Nieder-Gurke, were left
unoccupied, that the position might not become
too extended.   But when General Barclay de
Tolly, after the reduction of Thorn, joined the
army with 14,000 men, on the 17th, by the way
of Sprottau, he posted himself on the heights of
Kreckwitz to Nieder-Gurke, forming the right
wing of the army.   In the rear of Gross and
Klein Jenkowitz and Baschütz, intrenchments and
breast-works were thrown up for the artillery, that
it might have the advantage of cannonading the
enemy under cover, as a long and violent cannonade was to be foreseen.   Here the army enjoyed
a repose of eight days, of which, after so many actions and marches, and their attendant fatigues,
it stood much in need.   On the 15th, the enemy
showed himself to the piquets, but advanced
no farther than to drive them in : he pitched the
camp of his advanced guard on the opposite commanding grounds, the videttes and out-posts of
the Allies still remaining on the other edge of the
valley between them.

After the battle of Lützen the army had been
reinforced with 5000 men, under General Kleist,
14,000 under General Barclay de Tolly, 3000
of the Prussian reserve, and some thousands

of Russians. These reinforcements amounted to about 25,000 men; and if we estimate the losses of the allied army at the battle of Lützen, and subsequent affairs, at 16,000 men, its force might be fixed at 80,000 men, on the day of the battle of Bautzen. Nothing certain can be stated of the strength of Napoleon's army: his activity to recruit it was, no doubt, stretched to the utmost, during the eight days he passed before Bautzen and the intrenched camp. According to later accounts, fresh troops, in considerable numbers, had marched through Dresden, and a part of d'Avoust's corps had arrived from the Lower Elbe. The Saxon garrison of Torgau, and the King of Saxony's heavy cavalry out of Bohemia, together with Wirtemberg's contingent, had likewise joined; so that the losses of the enemy at Lützen, and in other engagements, might be considered as sufficiently replenished, and his army reinstated to its original number of 120,000 men.

Under the pressure of such a situation, in having to engage with as great a superiority of numbers as at Lützen, it would not have been advisable to give battle, if it had not formed a part of the system of the Allies to dispute every inch of ground with their opponent, to convince Europe that they had suffered no defeat in the first battle, and were neither morally nor physically in-

capable of making head against him, and moreover
to convince the Austrians that they were reso-
lutely determined not to spare their powers, nor
in fearful expectation leave the deliverance of
Germany entirely at the discretion of Austria*. The
army, strongly feeling their moral pre-eminence,
entertained no other wish but to close with their
implacable foe. The attempt of retreating farther would only have tended to dispirit the
troops, and shake their unbounded confidence in

---

* Count de Bubna, formerly Ambassador from the Imperial
Austrian Court to that of France, was intrusted by his Emperor
to deliver private proposals, and to make overtures to Napoleon
concerning a general peace ; and on the 16th of May 1813,
was, in consequence, admitted to an audience at Dresden.

The Count delivered his dispatches in person to Napoleon,
who, after reading them, abruptly observed: " Too late;" and
then turning his back to the ambassador, pretended to look
with attention out of the window.

After a short pause, the Count asked: " Sire, is that the
whole of the answer I am to bring my Emperor?—If that is the
case, permit me to demand leave of absence."

" Stop a moment," replied Napoleon, and went into another
apartment. After a few minutes had elapsed, he returned, and
addressed himself to the Count in the following terms :

" Monsieur Bubna, if your Emperor had made these proposals to me four weeks ago, I might have listened to them :
but now, after the battle of Lützen, I am become *master of
Europe*; and when I have settled affairs with the Emperor of
Russia and the King of Prussia, I may have leisure to attend
to those of your Monarch ; adieu."

their popular commanders. The face of the country about Bautzen was favourable to their arms, and it was therefore determined once more to court the smiles of fortune, and try their strength, valour, and discipline, with the superior forces of the common enemy of mankind.

On the 18th, the Allies received the intelligence, that General Lauriston, with a strong corps, probably under the supposition that the allied army was capable of no further resistance, had been detached to the Mark, and was in full march, by the way of Hoyerswerda; upon which, General Barclay de Tolly, with his corps, and that of General von York, were detached towards Hoyerswerda. They began their march in two columns on the night of the 18th: the column of the left wing, under the command of General Barclay de Tolly, fell in with General Lauriston near Konigswartha, and repulsed him after a severe contest, taking from him 2000 prisoners, and 14 pieces of cannon. The column of the right wing under General von York, about 5000 strong, encountered Marshal Ney's corps at Weissig, who intended to effect a junction and co-operate with General Lauriston; the repeated attacks made by General von York on his much more numerous enemy, prevented Marshal Ney from sending any support to General Lauriston; and these exertions, which were continued till late in the even-

ing, contributed not a little to the glorious termination of the engagement between the latter
and General Barclay de Tolly.   During the night
of the 19th, the several columns returned into
camp.

CHAPTER VI.

*Battle of Bautzen—Retreat to Schweidnitz—Blü-
cher's Ambuscade at Haynau—The Armistice.*

THE direction which the corps of Marshal Ney
and General Lauriston seemed to take towards the
right flank of the allied position at Bautzen,
plainly evinced the intention of attempting to
turn that position from the side of Glein and
Preititz, the former village lying behind the posts
of the right wing by Krekwitz. There was consequently, on the part of the confederates, a
necessity of changing their lines, and taking up
another position, which on the 20th was as follows:

The left wing now stood on a rising ground,
behind Klein-Jenkowitz. The lines in front
stretched across the villages of Gross-Jenkowitz
and Baschütz, towards Krekwitz, and from thence
in the direction of Nieder-Gurke on the Spree, on
which spot the right flank formed a curve, and
keeping the Spree in front, passed on to the wind-
mill of Glein, where it terminated.

Klein-Jenkowitz lies near a brook flowing from
the high ridges on which Hochkirch stands, and
these were in a parallel line with the left flank of

the position. The brook running from Klein-Jenkowitz to the villages of Nadelwitz, Nieder-Kayen, and Pasankwitz, to Krekwitz, and, turning more to the right by Klein-Bautzen, Preititz, and Glein, made a bend before the front, and, receding from the centre about fifteen hundred yards, formed of itself a complete segment of a circle. But at Krekwitz, the brook crossed the position, the right wing there taking in the ground between the brook and the Spree, that river running parallel with the brook about a mile and a half. At Glein the brook touched the extreme right flank of the position, from the rear, because this flank extended itself from Nieder-Gurke diagonally between the Spree and the brook, as far as Glein. In the same manner as the brook covered the front line to Krekwitz, the Spree covered the flank line from Nieder-Gurke to Glein. The space between Krekwitz and Nieder-Gurke is about fifteen hundred yards broad, and quite open, the heights forming the edge of the Spree valley, at the village of Burg, lying before it. The whole of the ground from Klein-Jenkowitz, as far as Krekwitz, might be considered as one large plain, although the left wing stood rather higher. In the rear of the position, the ground gradually rises towards Hochkirch. General von Blücher was posted with his whole corps on the commanding grounds from Krekwitz to Nieder-Gurke; the villages in front of his position, close to the Spree, were occupied by light troops. The extreme right wing, under General Barclay de Tolly, stood near Glein, and on the advantageous windmill-hill in its vicinity, having before them the defile of Klix, over the Spree, within reach of their artillery. It being necessary to establish their defence on the Spree, behind the villages of Nieder-Gurke, Doberschütz, Pliskowitz, and Malschütz, the windmill-hill afforded a strong point of defence in disputing the passage of this river below Malschütz.

On this day the troops of the whole army were posted in the following manner:

Lieutenant-general von Berg's corps, about 4000 men strong, stood on the left wing behind Jenkowitz: on his right, Lieutenant-general von York's corps, not exceeding 5000 men, extending behind Baschütz. There was an open space of two thousand yards, forming a plain from Baschütz to Krekwitz, on which no troops were placed in the first line, being covered by the reserves of cuirassiers drawn up behind it.

The front of Blücher's corps, which might be rated at 18,000 strong, besides the reserves of cuirassiers, extended from Krekwitz to Nieder-Gurke, and from thence by Doberschütz to Pliskowitz.

General Barclay de Tolly was posted at Glein, with 14,000 men. Marshy grounds, full of pools, connected with each other, and having but few passages between them, formed a line of defence from Pliskowitz, on the Spree, to Preititz, on the rivulet in front, between this corps and that of General von Blücher. General Miloradowitsch stood before this front, in and by Bautzen, with a force of 10,000 men; and on the heights by Burg, General von Kleist with 5000. The Russian Imperial Guards, and the rest of the Russian infantry, near 16,000 in the whole, stood as reserves in the rear of the left wing and centre. Partly behind these, and partly to their right, the Russian reserves of cavalry, consisting of 8000 cuirassiers, were drawn up. The front line from Klein-Jenkowitz to Krekwitz, and by Nieder-Gurke to Glein, was more than six miles in extent. —*(See Plan of the Battle of Bautzen.)*

The nature of the ground unavoidably forced the Allies to occupy too large a terrain, not very compatible with precautionary suggestions; and the obvious necessity of taking possession of the high ridges that ran parallel to the left wing towards Hochkirch, whenever the enemy advanced his columns, did not contribute to contract it. A part of the reserves, consisting of the Prince of Wirtemberg's division, and a detachment from Miloradowitsch's corps, were afterwards ordered to occupy them; by which movement the lines in front were lengthened more than three miles. The defence of the left wing in the mountains had of course many advantages. No apprehensions could be entertained, that the enemy would penetrate over the plain from Klein-Jenkowitz to Krekwitz, as the

crossing of the marshy banks of the rivulet must
be attempted under the fire of a numerous and
well-served artillery, protected by intrenchments
and breast-works, and, therefore, not easily to be
first silenced. The villages of Gross-Jenkowitz and
Baschütz were prepared for defence, strong detachments of cavalry were at hand, and that part
of the plain from Baschütz to Krekwitz was so
strongly flanked by the height of Krekwitz being
rather in advance of the position, and upon
which stood Blücher's left wing, that the enemy
could not here advance a step, without being previously in possession of Krekwitz.

General von Blücher's position was on the advantageous heights near Krekwitz and Nieder-Gurke,
having the valley of the Spree, full of meadows,
intersected with ditches, before him; his front
was, without doubt, difficult of access, but the
extension of his line to three miles from Krekwitz by Nieder-Gurke to Malschütz, might be
considered as much too great for a body of only
18,000 men; and being a mile and a half from the
grand army, if he met with a repulse, he would
be obliged to retreat through two defiles over the
boggy sides of the rivulet, to reach the main body;
he could not, therefore, spare any considerable reserve, nor, in arranging his dispositions, post less
than 12,000 men in his front.

General Barclay de Tolly had to defend a point
of the general position, that afforded in itself some

good natural bulwarks of defence; but he was
surrounded by woods, and at a greater distance
from the centre than General von Blücher.

Thus situated, towards noon of the 20th of
May, the enemy assaulted General von Kleist, on
the heights near Burg, and at the same time, General Miloradowitsch, near Bautzen; and a furious
fight for some hours was maintained with the
greatest bravery, by General von Kleist and his
intrepid corps. It seemed as if the enemy held
the possession of these heights as a necessary prelude to the battle, by his bringing up fresh columns of troops into fire, and repeating his attacks;
but five battalions from General von Blücher's
corps were ordered up in support of General von
Kleist, to keep his physical strength in equipon-
derance with that of the enemy, who, about
three o'clock in the afternoon, after suffering murderous repulses, endeavoured to turn General von
Kleist's left flank, by penetrating to Nieder-
Gurke; he was, however, baffled in the attempt,
on finding some battalions of von Ziethen's brigade and artillery posted on the heights close behind the defile, and only a brisk fire of sharp-
shooters was now kept up in the valley at this
point. These stubborn efforts of Napoleon, so
wasteful of human blood, were frustrated by the
good countenance and undaunted valour of General von Kleist's corps, to whose glory and renown, fresh and ever-blooming laurels were added

on this day. It is to the incessant assaults made by the enemy, that followed each other like the waves of a tempestuous sea, from twelve o'clock at noon till eight in the evening, with the view of overwhelming the gallant Prussians, and driving them from their impregnable position, by the mere force of numbers, that we are to ascribe the enormous loss which he suffered in the battle of Bautzen, and of which, some calculation may be formed, by the authentic and official fact of 18,000 of his wounded having been transported to Dresden. A sharp action took place with General Miloradowitsch, on the side of Bautzen, and, in the mean time, the enemy had forced back General Emanuel, with his corps of Russians, towards the mountains to the left of Bautzen, and pushed forward considerable masses of infantry; but the Russians being timely reinforced, the adversary did not succeed in breaking through any of the lines of the allied corps in advance, or in taking post on the left flank of the army, as was his evident intention. On the extreme right wing, under General Barclay de Tolly, no movements were made on either side, which might be explained, by the corps of General Lauriston and Marshal Ney not being yet in the field.

The firing began to cease at night-fall, and thus ended the action of the 20th, of which it was difficult to decide, whether it were a battle, or only the first opening of the operations; for although, on the part of the Allies, those points only were defended and maintained, that served to obstruct the advance of the enemy, and his pressing on the position itself; yet, in considering the heroic resistance and invincible courage and intrepidity of their troops, and the conduct, example, and bravery of their Generals, added to the advantages of the ground, and the severe losses already felt by the disturber of the peace of Europe, great hopes might be entertained, that, on a renewal of his attacks, discomfiture and disgrace might become his bitter portion, and the Allies, satiated with victory, might tranquilly repose on their arms, to enjoy the heart-thrilling satisfaction of having done their duty. But, it not being the intention of the Allies to make those disputed points the field of battle, in case of the enemy's acting on the offensive the next morning, while more advantages were to be drawn from the position itself; and as the expected attack on General Barclay de Tolly would cause these advanced points of the position not to be exactly adapted to the whole, the corps of General Miloradowitsch and von Kleist were withdrawn in the night, into the position : the former joined General von Berg, and the latter General von York. The allied troops passed the night under arms on the field of battle, cheering each other with gratulations of having made a gallant defence; and if there be any thing

that could ensure or prognosticate the happy success of a future day, it was the peaceful order that
every where prevailed amongst the troops, so seldom found after such inveterate and sanguinary
conflicts.

Soon after daybreak, on the 21st, the first
shots were heard along the line. The enemy, in
renewing his attacks, directed them against two
principal points of the allied position, namely,
General von Blücher's and General Barclay de
Tolly's; and after these attacks had been opened
by the sharp-shooters and artillery, he gradually
displayed his whole force down the full extent of
the allied line.

From the eminences of the allied centre they
had a full view of the enemy's columns, marching
over the heights to the right and left from Bautzen, and drawing up in heavy compact masses,
directly opposite to their position, but out of the
reach of the artillery. These masses of troops
might be estimated at from 30 to 40,000 men,
and they were scarcely drawn up in order of battle,
when pillars of smoke were seen rising from the
high grounds near Burg: this was the signal of
attack for Marshal Ney and General Lauriston,
who instantly pressed forward, with about 30,000
men, and threw themselves with great impetuosity
on General Barclay de Tolly, at Glein. A very
hot engagement ensued, which lasted till near ten
o'clock A. M. The superiority of the enemy in

numbers obliged the General to lose ground, to relinquish the strong post of the windmill-hill, and, step by step, to retreat over the rivulet in his rear, and across the Lobau water, to the commanding heights of Barutis. This side being a very vulnerable part of the position, General von Kleist was immediately ordered to his support; his corps had, however, in the bloody affair of the day before, been reduced to near 3000 effective men, and, instead of being able to drive back the enemy, in co-operating with de Tolly, they could only succeed in silencing his fire in part, and keeping him in check.

In the mean time, the conflict in the mountains had commenced with redoubled animosity, but the inflexible spirit and steady fire of the allied battalions prevented the enemy from making any progress in this quarter during the whole day. The Prince of Wirtemberg and General Milorado-witsch supported this point with their infantry, and the favourable terrain cost their obstinate foe an inconceivable number of men.

The cannonade in the centre now began, as the enemy seemed to menace an advance. General von Blücher having before him the wood on the side of the Spree, could form no judgment of the strength of his adversary, and only some trifling affairs between the rifle-corps and light troops oc-curred in the valley. This was the state of the battle about noon, as Marshal Ney and General

Lauriston pushed on columns to their right, and occupied the village of Preititz: this village lay between General von Blücher and General Barclay de Tolly, on the brook so often mentioned, close to Klein-Bautzen, consequently behind the right wing of General von Blücher. Nothing could be of more importance to this General, than the occupation of this village: if the enemy proceeded from thence to the unoccupied villages of Klein-Bautzen and Puschwitz, the General had no other line of communication with the grand army than through Krekwitz; but Krekwitz lay in front of the position, within the range of the enemy's artillery, and could, besides, only be occupied by a single battalion; the enemy were already standing in the village of Pasankwitz, close to it, and it was a matter of uncertainty whether the village of Krekwitz could finally be maintained or not. Under such dubious circumstances, General von Blücher resolved to part with the only reserve he had at his command, and therefore ordered his reserve brigade to march to the support of General Barclay de Tolly, for the sole purpose of retaking the village. He was in hopes, that, not being himself seriously engaged, this brigade would be able to give another turn to the affairs of the right wing, by falling upon the right flanks of Marshal Ney and General Lauriston. A detachment of the Prussian reserve cavalry was, at the same time, sent towards the Spree, that now

separated General von Blücher from Marshal
Ney, to observe the passages, to threaten the
enemy still more in his right flank, and to cannonade him with their horse-artillery.   These
dispositions were hardly made, and the troops
marched off, when the enemy attacked General
von Blücher himself in his whole position, first at
Pliskowitz, then at Nieder-Gurke, and at last
throughout the whole line of the Spree: a most
heavy and destructive fire of musketry was kept
up without intermission, which having lasted
about an hour, and his second line of infantry
coming into action, General von Blücher began
to discover, with that quickness of foresight so
peculiar to this military hero, how unsafe it was
to maintain his extended lines, and issued prompt
orders for the reserve brigade to return, and post
themselves ready for an emergency, at Barschütz.
But this brigade had already marched to Preititz,
and, in combination with the corps of General
von Kleist, entered at once with great vigour and
resolution into the village, and gallantly carried
it at the point of the bayonet, although with a
very heavy loss.   They kept the village occupied,
and the rest of the brigade returned according to
orders.   Such was at this period the situation of
General von Blücher's corps, that it was obliged
to present a front on three sides; namely, between
Krekwitz and Nieder-Gurke, against the enemy
advancing from the heights of Burg; from Nieder-

Gurke to Pliskowitz, to defend the low grounds
of the Spree, and from Pliskowitz to Preititz, at
the back of the pools, against the advance of
Marshal Ney. The whole of the reserve had been
detached to retake the village of Preititz, in the
rear, and thus to keep open the threatened fourth
side of the position, the only one by which reinforcements could be received, or a retreat, if necessary, be made. The action in his front had
about this time taken a very unfavourable turn;
two Russian batteries, the one by Krekwitz, the
other by Nieder-Gurke, that formed the principal
defence of these points, had expended all their
ammunition; the enemy, an over-match in numbers, had made himself master of the heights behind Nieder-Gurke, from which alone this point
could be defended, and he now marched forwards
over the low grounds between the rivulet and the
Spree; and although the brigade of Colonel von
Klüx had twice repulsed him with severe loss, by
bravely charging him with the bayonet; yet, it
was evident, the heights were not to be retaken.
General von Blücher demanded reinforcements,
and General von York was ordered up to secure
the execution of his dispositions, who immediately
marched to the village of Krekwitz, to fall on
the right flank of the advancing enemy; but the
expected succour came too late; the two brigades
of General von Blücher's front had gradually
withdrawn themselves out of their convex posi-

tion to the high grounds about Krekwitz; but
here not a spot was found adapted for further defence, and, in consequence, only one measure to
keep himself master of the terrain, remained at
his option, and that was to unite the weak battalions of the brigades with the rest of the reserve,
and, waving all other considerations, to act, with
impetuous firmness, on the offensive. No doubts
can be entertained, that, by this very rapid
movement, he would again have penetrated to the
valley of the Spree; but the brigade reserves were
at the instant not yet returned, and, besides, very
important consequences were here previously to
be regarded. If Blücher had reconquered this
ground, still the battle was not gained; the less
so, as the terrain already lost, on the extreme right
wing, was so decisive an event, that, from the moment the impossibility of moving onwards, on this
point, was perceived, the Commander-in-chief
did not expect any favourable issue to the contest
in general. General von Blücher, in hazarding
every thing to recover his former position, and
even if crowned with success, had unavoidably
dislocated his whole corps; he was unacquainted
with the advance of General von York; the battle
raged with Generals Barclay de Tolly and von
Kleist, and the maintaining of their occupied
lines was a matter of uncertainty. He therefore
resolved to undertake no operation until he had
received fresh orders, and wishing to wait the re-

turn of his reserves to Purschwitz, he directed the two other brigades engaged, to maintain themselves to the last extremity in their positions, before they retreated to Purschwitz. The reserve cavalry, being of little service on this close ground, were ordered to draw back across the defile, that the retrograde movement, if obliged to be made through it, might not meet with any impediment.

At this period the centre was yet untouched, the enemy only making demonstrations, showing and deploying his columns, and keeping up a brisk cannonade *. It was clear that their opponent

---

* The Emperor of Russia and the King of Prussia were standing together, in the rear of one of their batteries, from which a heavy fire was kept up on the enemy with great effect, who answered with a shower of shells, when one of the shells fell within ten yards of the spot where the allied Monarchs were conversing. A Prussian veteran, of the artillery, no sooner saw the shell take ground, but running up with an intrepid presence of mind, was fortunate enough to extinguish the fusee before it burst. The King of Prussia, who saw the action, called out to him, asking his name, and how long he had served. " Thou shalt be rewarded, my brave fellow," said the King; " I here on the spot promote you to the rank of an officer."— " I humbly thank your Majesty for this gracious mark of your favour," replied the man; " but I cannot accept it: I might have been a corporal years ago, if——*. Your Majesty, however, will not, I hope, be displeased, if I mention that *the pay* of an officer would make my family and myself happy for life." The

* He could not write.

feared the strength of the allied position at this point; and he, perhaps, expected that the centre of the confederate army, in sending support to the hard-pressed right wing, would be so weakened, as gradually to prepare for the favourable crisis of its attack by close action, on the event of which might depend his gaining a complete and decisive victory over the Allies.

Since the opening of the campaign, it had always been kept in view by the Allies, for very sage and political reasons, rather to break off before a battle was ended, if its tendency was doubtful or uncertain, than to expose themselves to the chance of a total defeat; and as the whole contest had actually taken an unfavourable turn, this step was here the more necessary, inasmuch as their undisputed superiority in cavalry enabled them to throw this choice into the balancing scales of their operations, whenever it was held judicious. The same causes which rendered it dubious, whether the last exertions of General von Blücher, to recover the lost ground, would prove beneficial for the whole, or not, but might place Blücher's corps in a very dangerous situation, determined the Commander-in-chief, between three and four o'clock P. M. to decline the contest on this position, and to order a retreat.

King understood him: his boon was granted, to which were added, the order of the Iron Cross from his Sovereign, and the order of St. George from the Emperor of Russia.

The retreat was made in the most perfect order and regularity in two columns. The Russian troops of the centre and left wing took the direction of Hochkirch to Lobau; the Prussians, that of Würschen to Weissenberg. General Barclay de Tolly and General Kleist, with the reserves of Prussian cavalry, drew up again in line of battle, on the advantageous heights of Gröditz, to keep Marshal Ney and General Lauriston in check, which was done the whole evening with such good success, that Generals von Blücher and von York had time to pass Weissenberg with the extremities of their columns: this measure was very requisite, the enemy being much nearer Weissenberg from Barutis, than the former were from the points of Krekwitz and Baschütz. When the centre of the Allies broke up, the enemy did not attempt to follow.

This stupendous battle afforded the enemy but few prisoners, and not a single piece of artillery fell into his hands: it must be allowed, however, that he succeeded in forcing the Allies, after a hard struggle, to relinquish a part of their strong position; but it was accomplished by such an enormous and inhuman sacrifice of men, that Napoleon's loss may be moderately estimated at double that of the Allies, they having had from 14 to 15,000 men killed and wounded, and, as already related, the enemy sent 18,000 of his wounded back to Dresden; and it has since been indu-

bitably ascertained, that the small town of Bautzen and its vicinity alone had to provide hospitals
for 7000 of his severely wounded men after the
battle.

On this vast theatre of carnage, where, but a
few hours before, the most luxuriant crops, peaceful villages, and hamlets, decked the fertile fields,
smiling in all the native graces of a fruitful spring,
every thing perished and was blasted by the un-
timely blight of wasteful war, and the dire ra-
vages of the ruthless sons of spoil, insatiate in destroying whatever could refine and embellish nature.   The horrid transactions of these French
military-barbarians are written in blood, and bear
that hideous character by which the voice of God
and nature has designated the most flagrant of human offences.   They can never be forgotten : the
affrighted inhabitants fled into the woods, and the
face of the country was suddenly transformed
into a savage, wild, and desolate wilderness.

Napoleon, in the midst of his mathematical calculations and theorems, might feel the instability
of human events, and find an error in the defini-
tion of such kind of victories as the present one.
It had been his custom totally to defeat his adversary with a very disproportionate and trifling loss
on his side, and then to extort a rash and precipitate peace.   The attributes of his station as conqueror demanded this.   And here, after having
experienced in Russia a reverse of fortune, unpa-

ralleled in history, that involved him in difficulties
scarcely surmountable, he could have nothing
more at heart than to destroy in their bud the
dawning hopes of Europe, to crush the rising spirit of liberty, now spreading far and near, and to
appal his enemies arming on all sides by rapid,
splendid, and decisive victories. It is notorious
that this was not done. Partial advantages formed
the utmost confines of his boastings, presenting,
of themselves, but a weak and tottering dam against
the irresistible rolling tide of self-confidence that
was now set in against him. Fresh calamities
awaited him in his rear, and were ready to burst
over his power and his plans. The victorious Hero
of Spain, Lord Wellington, now stood on the
frontiers of France to chastise, on his own thresh-
old, their haughty and abhorred enemy.

There was, therefore, no well-founded cause for
the Allies to complain of their situation, and they
might be convinced that order, perseverance, and
intrepidity would inevitably bring them to the desired goal, in defiance of those ostentatious accounts of victories so industriously published to
Europe by their wily antagonist.

The allied army continued on the 22d, its retro-
grade movement from Lobau and Weissenberg to
Görlitz. At Reichenbach the rear-guard had a
lively affair with their pursuers, that cost the
French army a Marshal and two Generals, and
Napoleon his most intimate friend. Buonaparte

being dissatisfied that his Generals of the advanced-guard sent in no prisoners from a supposed defeated army, undertook, in a sudden burst of in-
dignation, the command of it himself for one day,
to teach them, as he said, a more vigorous execution of his infallible orders. The rear-guard of
the Allies was posted at Reichenbach, having a
very numerous cavalry and artillery, the former
burning with impatience to try a charge upon equal
terms with the French. A sharp cannonade was
kept up, some regiments of French dragoons
actually showed themselves, and the allied horse
had an opportunity of wreaking their vengeance,
by repulsing them with heavy loss. It happened
that, during the cannonade, a fatal ball struck
General Kirschner dead, close to Napoleon, tore
open the bowels of Marshal Duroc[*], and mortally
wounded General Labruyère. Napoleon, shud-

---

[*] Marshal Duroc, Duke of Frioul, lived on a very intimate
footing with Napoleon. He was born in 1772, at Ponte-Mous-
son, and was the son of a house-painter of that place. By the
help of a relation he was educated at the military school, made
a Lieutenant in 1792, and rose to the rank of Captain in the
Artillery in 1796; at which period Napoleon became acquainted
with him, and found in him a fit person to execute, with implicit
devotion, some of his barbarous mandates. It is well known
that he assisted in poisoning the wounded French in Syria in
1799. Since which he had been sent on several diplomatic
missions to St. Petersburg and Berlin, and was afterwards, as
Marshal of the Imperial Palace, much about the person of
Buonaparte.

dering at this sudden stroke of fate, levelled so near his sacred person, turned round the head of his horse, and, without a word or exclamation escaping his lips, or altering a muscle of his countenance, rode off in agitated haste from the spot.

The pursuit was afterwards followed up in the usual manner; and the excellent and matchless cavalry of the Allies gathered fresh laurels at every rencounter.

From Görlitz the march of the allied armies was continued in two columns, by the way of Naumburg to Queisz, Bunzlau, Haynau, and through Lauban, Löwenberg, Goldberg, Striegau, to the camp of Pültzen, near Schweidnitz, where it arrived on the 1st of June.

The Prussian army marched, with the corps of General Barclay de Tolly, in the column of the right wing that proceeded through Haynau.

It being the object of the Commander-in-chief to continue the retreat as slowly and leisurely as possible, without entangling himself in any general or serious affair ; and the enemy having begun to press and harass the rear-guard very closely, a plan which General von Blücher had conceived with that boldness of genius which displayed itself on all momentous occasions, was now arranged and put in execution. An ambush was to be placed for the enemy's van-guard, to chastise them severely for their rashness, and to distress their further operations : the terrain behind Haynau seemed well fitted for this purpose.

About a mile and a half on the other side of Haynau, is situated the village of Michelsdorf, and from this spot to Doberschau, about the distance of three miles, it is quite an open and champaign country, except the villages of Pantenau and Steudnitz, which, lying in a kind of valley, form a defile. To the right of this flat open country, is a defile, formed by low grounds and copses, which, beginning at the village of Ueberschaar, continue, without any break, as far as Baudmansdorf, lying about three miles on the same level to the right of Doberschau.—(See the Plan of the Ambuscade near Haynau.)

On the 26th the Prussian army left Haynau on the high road to Liegnitz. The rear-guard followed, at a distance of twelve miles, and passed Haynau the same day.

It was General von Blücher's well-concerted plan to let the actual rear-guard, which consisted of three battalions of infantry and three regiments of light-horse, under the command of Colonel von Mutius, retreat over the plain to Steudnitz, after halting before Haynau till the enemy came out to attack ; and they should then endeavour to draw and allure the enemy after them. In the mean time, the whole of the reserve cavalry, consisting of twenty squadrons, with two batteries of horse-artillery, were placed in ambush at Schellendorf, under the command of Colonel von Dolfs. They were to advance through the defiles with all the rapidity and secrecy in their power, so as to push forward over the plain through Ueberschaar, and to fall unexpectedly on the right flank of the enemy's advanced-guard, at the moment when they were occupied in attacking Colonel von Mutius.

A windmill between Baudmansdorf and Pohls-dorf, which could be distinctly seen by both par-ties, was to be set on fire, as a signal for the re-serve cavalry in ambush to advance. General von Ziethen's brigade was drawn up as reserve behind Pantenau and Pohlsdorf, and the conduct of the whole intrusted to this General. Our veteran General von Blücher, anxious for the accomplish-ment of his premeditated surprise, remained in the neighbourhood. The enemy pursued Colonel von Mutius, in appearance with much precaution, and did not show himself out of Haynau till past three o'clock, P. M. marching slowly and warily as if in doubt. Colonel von Mutius, according to orders, retreated in seeming haste.

The division of General Maison composed this advanced-guard; and Marshal Ney, to whose corps it belonged, left it just before the attack. General Maison, as if warned by a presentiment of his danger, expressed his fears concerning the safety of his advancing into the plain, to the Marshal himself, who ridiculed them. The Marshal pro-

ceeded to another point, and General Maison
marched with a heavy heart into the plain.   He
however neglected sending detachments into the
defiles on his right, as the only way to secure
that flank in a proper manner, and prevent any
surprise.

The enemy having passed Michelsdorf about
fifteen hundred yards in advance, the reserve cavalry put itself in motion, having about a mile
and a half to march before they could be as near
to the enemy as Colonel Mutius.   They left the
ground at full trot, and General von Ziethen fired
the mill as a signal for the attack.   General
Maison, on seeing this, suspected some ambush,
and immediately ordered his troops to form in
squares; but little time was left them to perform
the evolution, for Colonel von Dolfs, leaving two
regiments as reserve, and without stopping to
make use of his artillery, seized the favourable
moment, and precipitated himself on the enemy
with the swiftness of the winds.   The French
cavalry betook themselves to flight, leaving the
disorderly masses of infantry in the act of forming, to their fate.   They were furiously charged,
and rode down in the space of a few minutes.
Those that were not cut in pieces or taken prisoners fled through the village of Michelsdorf,
towards Haynau.   The whole affair lasted but
twenty minutes; and by the quick dispersion of

the enemy, Colonel von Mutius was almost deprived of a share in the brilliant action.

The trophies that fell into the hands of the Allies, consisted of 18 pieces of cannon, their whole artillery, and the usual spoils of baggage, tumbrils, horses, and stores ; but a scarcity of harnessed horses prevented their bringing away more than 11 pieces of artillery, and from three to four hundred prisoners were taken. The allied cavalry, covered with glory, then retired to Lobentau : the rear-guard took a position there, and kept up videttes and out-posts on the plain close to Haynau. During the whole of the following day the enemy kept himself close in Haynau ; and it was not till the 28th, that the rear-guard retired to Kloster-Wahlstatt.

The cavalry obtained in this splendid engagement that renown so difficult to be acquired in modern times, owing to the superior tactics of the infantry ; it is, however, here incontestably proved that there are opportunities in which this superiority is of no avail, and cavalry can perform wonders, and cut their way through every obstacle that may oppose their progress, when disciplined valour, and the enterprise and foresight of experienced officers, are happily blended together.

The brave Colonel von Dolfs fell in gallantly leading his squadrons to the charge,

Napoleon no sooner arrived at Liegnitz with his army, and perceived that the Allies retreated towards Schweidnitz, and not to Breslau, than he immediately detached a corps of 30,000 men to the Neumark, which entered Breslau on the following day.

Prior to the battle of Bautzen, Buonaparte had himself offered an armistice *, and to enter into negotiations. These offers were now renewed, and on the part of the Allies accepted †. A preliminary armistice of thirty-six hours was first regulated, and soon after prolonged to three days.

As the allied armies were on their march to Silesia, General von Bülow, with an army of 20,000 men, had advanced from the Mark into Lower-Lusatia. A corps under General Oudinot was

---

* It was on this day that Napoleon sent a letter, written with his own hand, by a flag of truce, to the Emperor of all the Russias, in which he made, it was supposed, very flattering overtures for a cessation of arms.

His Imperial Majesty, having received it, and being pre-informed of its probable contents, demanded of the bearer, " Whether he had likewise brought a similar epistle for the King of Prussia ?" On being answered in the negative, Alexander observed : " Then I cannot open this : I can listen to no communications from the Emperor of France but in conjunction with the King of Prussia."

The flag of truce was obliged to return without fulfilling his mission, and Napoleon saw himself under the necessity of offering proposals for a cessation of arms conjointly to the two allied potentates, and which was accordingly done.

† The plenipotentiaries from both sides had a long conference on the 30th, which lasted eighteen hours, at Kloster-Wahl-statt, near Liegnitz.

detached by Napoleon to check the progress of this General, whom he found posted at Luckau, and a smart action ensued on the 4th of June, which principally turned on the possession of Luckau; the French, however, were unable to drive the Prussians out of the place, although in flames; and the enemy being at last attacked in their rear by General von Bülow's cavalry, under General Oppen, they were forced to relinquish the field of battle, with a loss of from 4 to 500 prisoners, and one gun.

The enemy's lines of communication with the Elbe were threatened to be intercepted, and a vexatious war of posts and skirmishes was now carried on with constant success against him. On both banks of the Elbe, and even to the borders of Franconia, Prussian and Russian detachments scoured the country in every direction; a considerable number of prisoners were brought in, and several of the expeditions were particularly fortunate: Captain von Colomb, our hero's brother-in-law, having passed the Elbe with a squadron of volunteer light horse, at the time the two conflicting armies were standing on its banks, had penetrated as far as the borders of Franconia, where he surprised a transport of 18 pieces of artillery, 6 howitzers, and 40 tumbrils, proceeding to the French army under the escort of Bavarian troops. He spiked the guns, blew up the tumbrils, and made from 2 to 300 prisoners. The

Russian General Czernischeff crossed the Elbe with a body of 1800 men, light troops, and near Halberstadt unexpectedly fell in with the West-phalian division of General von Ochs, with about 2500 men, 14 pieces of cannon, and a number of ammunition-waggons, of which the latter formed in haste a circular bulwark, on a rising ground near the road ; but General Czernischeff did not hesitate cannonading him with his light artillery ; and several of the ammunition-waggons having blown up, he rapidly charged the enemy with a rare intrepidity : the Cossacks succeeded in break-ing through the fortified circle, and General von Ochs, with all his infantry, about 1000 men, were taken prisoners; 14 pieces of cannon, 60 tum-brils, and 800 artillery horses, and large quantities of military stores fell into the hands of the Cos-sacks, and were conveyed in safety over the Elbe. A detachment from General Woronzoff's corps, under the command of Colonel Borizoff, had like-wise passed the Elbe ; and on the 23d of May, encountered near Cönnern, between Halle and Bernburg, a body of French cuirassiers, 400 men strong, under General Pinsot; after an obstinate conflict of two hours, the whole were either killed, wounded, or taken prisoners by the Cossacks; and a train of 19 waggons, with stores, baggage, &c. became their booty on the road to Merseberg. The Russian General Emanuel surprised a transport of artillery, between Reichenbach and Görlitz, took

2 pieces of cannon, spiked 6, and blew up 15 tumbrils. General Lasalle, another French general, and 300 men, were killed, and 600 taken prisoners. General Woronzoff having afterwards formed a junction with General Czernischeff, they both put themselves in march towards Leipsic, the Duke of Padua * being employed there in remounting depôts of French cavalry : they would have had the most brilliant success, if at this moment, intelligence of the armistice had not reached them.

Negotiations respecting the armistice had been, in the mean time, carrying on, and, on the 1st of June, it was concluded at Plaszwitz, for a period

---

* As this Duke (Arrighi), during the armistice, was carrying on his acts of oppression at Leipsic, a Russian officer arrived with a flag of truce, to treat concerning the exchange of the remains of Lützow's corps that had been so basely surprised.

From the midst of the crowd that accompanied the Russian officer to the hotel of the Duke, very lively acclamations and cheering huzzas, in compliment to the brave Russian, were distinctly heard, even under the windows of the Duke's apartments. He appeared much incensed at these marks of disrespect, and strict orders were issued to punish those culprits who could dare to be so insolent towards one of Napoleon's marshals. Rewards were even offered to apprehend the delinquents, and to those who could discover any individual guilty of so great a crime ; but the Duke's proclamations, and his threats, were equally useless ; for, lo ! they were his own soldiers that had alarmed the fancied dignity of this ape of a tyrant's despotism : some hundreds of honest Westphalians, whose breasts glowing with a true patriotic flame, could not forget the name of Herrmann, and that Teutonic blood still flowed in their veins!

of seven weeks; namely, to the 20th of July, al-
lowing a notice of six days.   On the 26th of July
it was prolonged at Neumark in Silesia, to the
10th of August.   This armistice was, in every
point of view, of a very different complexion
from those which in former times had been forced
upon, or offered by Napoleon to his adversaries.
Here no sacrifice * of territory was made ; no for-

---

* It must not be forgotten that the greatest sacrifice made
by the Confederates, was their granting the *uti possidetis* in
the 32d French military division; a measure, the policy of
which still continues enveloped in a degree of mystery, and
by which Hamburgh remained in the hands of a vengeance-
breathing despot, forcing upon him, as if in his own despite,
the means of punishing those brave spirits who had first dared
to manifest a patriotic zeal, by flying to arms and unfurling the
banners of unanimity for the deliverance of Germany, and their
own independence.   Enormous were the exactions which Napoleon imposed and levied ; cruel and relentless the robberies and
spoliations that were committed and justified by his Satraps,
so as utterly to destroy and undermine for a series of years, the
opulence and prosperity of this venerable head of the Hanse
league.   It is surely difficult to conceive any character more
odious and despicable than that of a ferocious hireling, who,
trembling at a tyrant's frown, issues the mandate that is to devote
virtuous citizens to starvation, to desolate happy and peaceful
hamlets, to wring agonizing tears from the widow and the fa-
therless !—Such is d'Avoust.   An official and moderate estimate
states the total amount of the losses caused to this city and its
environs by d'Avoust, at thirteen millions sterling.   The population was reduced from 120,000 to 40,000 souls ; more than
1500 houses were either burnt or demolished; and by d'Avoust's
unnatural, stubborn, and vindictive cruelty, more than 1600 fa-

tresses were delivered up, nor were even those besieged, to be uninvested. The French troops were
to occupy, according to the fourth article of the
armistice, a line of demarcation in Silesia *(see the
Map)*, which extended from the borders of Bohemia,
near Schreibershau, on nearly a straight line by the
way of Parchwitz, Liegnicz, Lähn, and Goldberg,
along the banks of the river Katzbach, till it falls
into the Oder. The lines of the confederate army
in Silesia, under Blücher, commenced at Ditters-
bach near the frontiers of Bohemia, passed through
Pfaffendorf and Landshut, following the course
of the Bober to Rudelstadt, and from thence to
Kanth, Bettlern, and Althof, to the left bank of
the Oder : the whole of the territory between
these lines of demarcation being declared neutral.
The 12th of June was the time fixed, on which
all the troops and detached corps were to be in
the rear of their lines of demarcation.

A body of 10,000 Danish troops had arrived in

---

milies were stripped of their bedding, furniture, and cattle,
turned out to live under the canopy of heaven, in the midst of
a severe winter, and, in short, became beggars on the high roads.
And yet, this honourable officer—this moralizing Marshal, has
the effrontery to justify his callous deeds, by asserting, they
were needful for the defence of Hamburgh : now this is an abominable falsehood ; for, after the conflagrations of the distant
villages, instead of attempting to defend the burning ruins,
they were abandoned at the first onset of the bold and hardy
Russians.

thevicinity of Hamburgh, with the supposed intention of making a common cause with the troops of
the Allies; but owing to the political discussions
of the Danish cabinet, with England and Sweden,
this design had at this period undergone a change.
The Danes suddenly declared themselves for
France, entered into the views of Vandamme *

---

* It was under the immediate command of Vandamme, that
Hamburgh was bombarded. A few authentic anecdotes of the
early part of this man's life may serve to amuse the reader.

Vandamme is the son of a citizen in humble life, of Cassel
in Flanders. After receiving a common day-school education,
he was clerk in an office for some time, but being intrusted
with a sum of money, he decamped with it, and commenced the
life of a swindler and vagabond; detection soon following, he
was publicly whipped, and set in the pillory at Bergen in Flanders. Indeed, he had received sentence of death; but through
the intercession of Mr. Schubitz, a respectable merchant of
Dunkirk, his life was saved. Soon afterwards he was sent to
the galleys at Marseilles, where he remained till he was liberated by the Jacobins in 1793. He distinguished himself by his
abominable cruelties towards the Royalists in Paris, and on this
account was made a General by the National Convention, and
sent to command a body of troops in Flanders. He began his
new career in a manner most fitting his character and Jacobin
principles: upon entering Dunkirk, he ordered his former patron and deliverer, Mr. Schubitz, to be arrested, and sent him to
Paris, denounced as a furious aristocrat and dangerous royalist.
He ended his life, of course, under the guillotine. Such a signal
instance of base ingratitude and atrocious perfidy can scarcely
be equalled in history. But are not the satellites and adherents
of Napoleon, wretches of one common stamp, a brotherhood
of butchers?

and d'Avoust, and thereby forced General von Tettenborn to evacuate Hamburgh. Thus fell for a second time, into the hands of the French, one of the most ancient free imperial cities of Germany, whose exertions in the cause of liberty made her so worthy of the freedom she aspired to, and whose loss may be esteemed one of the severest and most painful which the Allies had as yet suffered.

Two very cogent reasons may be here adduced, why it was the interest of the Allies that an armistice of seven weeks should be concluded with the enemy : the one, to restore the exhausted strength of the army by every possible reinforcement, and to prepare for a vigorous renewal of the war ; and the other, because Austria had secretly given Russia and Prussia to understand, that such a period of time was necessary to complete her armaments.

In this war undertaken against France, there were some events on which the Allies ought to have solely depended, and by which alone they could be placed in a situation to stand on an equal footing with the preponderating power of Napoleon. The Allies were either to rely on a general insurrection in Germany, the disallegiance of the Confederation of the Rhine, on partial revolts in the north of Germany, Tyrol, and Italy; or they must look to the coalition of Austria as admitting no doubt. By a continuation of the war, one of

these favourable events, if occurring to its full
extent, would yield such an accession of strength,
that the possibility of success might be confidently cherished.

Hopes were, at that time, not entirely given up,
that the northern powers, Sweden and Denmark,
might enter the league; and, indeed, Sweden had
already expressed herself in very unequivocal
terms.

Certainty being unknown in the political world,
the Allies were constrained to tranquillize themselves with a greater or less degree of probability,
that such events could be brought about. But
the sequel has proved that their calculations were
free from error. Austria did declare against
France; and the conqueror, in the zenith of his
power, soon found himself deceived in the unfail-
ing effects of his imaginary and vain-glorious
omnipotence.

What man amongst the Allies could have hoped,
in December 1812, that, in June 1813, Russia,
Prussia, and Austria, would stand on the banks
of the Oder and the Elbe, with a power both formidable and superior; forcing Buonaparte to subscribe to other laws than those of his over-ruling
will and imperious commands? Who had not
thought, on being told that Napoleon, in six
months, would again have an army of several
hundred thousand men in Germany, have fought
the Allies with an overmatch in numbers, in two
pitched battles, that the consequences must inevi-

tably have been, a general despondency prevailing amongst the Allies, a retreat far into Poland, ending in their total destruction, and Austria silenced for ever?

It is with unceasing gratitude towards Divine Providence, the Allies have to acknowledge that their hopes were more than realized. With what a sense of immeasurable benefits conferred, ought they not to be grateful, that the Emperor Alexander, trusting to Prussia and Austria, boldly pursued the enemy to the Oder; and towards the Monarch of our illustrious hero, who, unshaken by misfortune, and unbiassed by the voices of desponding cavillers, flew to arms, threw off the disgraceful yoke, to protect the honour and independence of the Prussian nation: towards the Emperor of Austria, who, disregarding the extorted tie of affinity, fearlessly declared himself as champion for the emancipation of Germany, and the liberties of Prussia!

During the period of the armistice, the efforts of the Confederates were particularly directed to the following objects:

1. The necessary reserves and reinforcements for the Russian army were accelerated on their march to join; and an army of reserve was organized in Poland of at least 100,000 men.

2. The regiments in the Prussian army were completed, and measures adopted for supplying the depôts promptly with recruits.

3. The procuring of arms and ammunition from England and Austria.

4. The preparation of all kinds of accoutrements.

5. To arm, form, and discipline the militia.

6. To provision, arm, and repair the fortresses, particularly Schweidnitz.

7. To throw up the necessary têtes de pont on the Oder.

8. The procuring and collecting of provisions for the army during the next campaign.

On the other hand, Napoleon did not relax in increasing his means of resistance in the same proportion. All the troops he could possibly form during the period of the armistice, were put in march. To fix the exact number of combatants, with which he took the field, is rather difficult. What we know as certain is, that he drew no army from Spain, but only drafted veterans and subalterns to organize the new battalions of conscripts in France. The troops that arrived from France and Italy in Germany, in the month of April, were calculated at 100,000 men, and in the month of March, at 60,000; and if we, upon an average, suppose that Napoleon formed, in the last three months, the same number of troops as in the four months previously to the armistice, namely, 160,000 men; by adding the army of 60,000 men still on the Elbe, the whole amount would then be 380,000 men; from which we are to deduct, at

least, 50,000 men for his losses in the battles of
Lützen and Bautzen, and all the other bloody encounters, and by sickness and desertion. To this,
also, must be superadded the Danish and confederate troops 70,000 men, and the aggregate number will be 400,000. The writer is, however,
convinced that this is over-rated by about 50,000
men; for, according to all subsequent accounts
which have been collected, the sum total of
350,000 men seems the nearest to truth, and to ex-
clude the reproach of any palpable exaggeration.
Here we have to observe, that these 350,000 men
found a considerable counterpoise in the combined powers of the allied army : and when we
reflect that an army of only 80,000 Allies bravely
stood their ground against 120,000 French, in two
battles, without suffering a defeat, obliged the
enemy to continue his operations with unusual
precaution, and at last made him eager to conclude
an armistice, no doubt could be entertained of a
favourable issue to the approaching campaign. If
the Allies had in part failed, the failure might be
attributed to the want of a sufficient physical
force; but, on a renewal of warfare, they had now
to contend with an army formed of heterogeneous
troops—their opponent, with an armed nation :
there could be no reason to doubt whether any
force might ensure success, as the condition of
the Allies could not be accounted desperate; Germania's sons had neither lost their courage nor

their hopes, and could look forward with confidence to still more glorious and greater exertions than those already made. If, with all the difficulties and disadvantages under which Russia and Prussia laboured at the onset and commencement of the former campaign, they achieved a certain degree of success in repelling the enemy, might they not entertain much better hopes from the issue of a second, with a whole nation in a state of military organization? In war, no one can ensure success and victory; but here, with the preconcerted resistance of a brave, powerful, enthusiastic, and well-disciplined army, the highest probability was certainly on their side.

Of all the allied powers, Prussia appears to have made the greatest exertions, in proportion to her extent of territory and comparative population. The active army was completed during the armistice to its full numbers, and the most provident and wise measures were adopted to fill up its losses in the expected campaign with promptitude. It was divided into four principal corps; and our hero, the veteran General of the cavalry, was appointed Commander-in-chief. The first corps was commanded by Lieutenant-general von York; it consisted of four brigades of infantry, one brigade of cavalry, and a due proportion of artillery: its force may be computed at 38,000 men. The second corps was headed by Lieutenant-general von Kleist, of nearly the same strength. The third

corps was under the command of Lieutenant-general von Bülow ; and the fourth, of Lieutenant-
general Count Tauenzien. The efficient strength
of the whole Prussian forces in the field, at this
period, a few days previous to the 10th of August 1813, may be calculated at nearly 150,000
regular troops. The militia counted 170,000 men
in its ranks ; and the levy en masse presented a
very formidable body for defensive operations.
General von Blücher now took the immediate
command of the Prussian army in Upper Silesia,
posted on the lines of demarcation as already mentioned.

Soon after the conclusion of the armistice, the
French army went into more extended cantonments. A part of the young guards, and the 2d,
3d, 5th, 6th, and 11th corps d'armée, remained
in Silesia, in the neighbourhood of Liegnitz, Goldberg, Bunzlau, Löwenberg, Glogau, and Grünberg.

The following dispositions were made with the
allied army of Russians and Prussians in Upper
Silesia. The Prussians were composed of the first
corps, under the command of General von York,
and the Russians, of two strong corps, under the
command of General Count von Langeron, and
General Baron von Sacken. General von Gneisenau was appointed Quarter-master-general of the
Staff to this army, which now consisted of about
70,000 men.

CHAPTER VII.

Denunciation of the Armistice—Opening of the Campaign—Blücher's Victory on the Katzbach.

THE armistice was denounced on the 10th of August. According to the convention of the 4th of June, hostilities were to commence on the 17th of August: but, as the enemy had repeatedly violated the neutral territory by imposing and enforcing requisitions of every kind, and had so basely surprised the corps of Lützow* at the commencement

---

* Major von Lützow's free corps, known by the name of the Sable Knights, or Corps of Vengeance (their uniform being black), was composed of some of the most exalted characters in Germany. Young men of the first-rate talents, of the most noble families, whose grand views of national liberty, of the privileges of citizens, and the birthrights of men, had absorbed all minor considerations, served as volunteers in its ranks. His Majesty the King of Prussia gave permission for its formation in the month of February 1813. Theodore Körner, by birth a Saxon, a promising young poet, whose works are read with delight; Mr. Göschen, son of the most famous typographer in Germany; Mr. Jahn; Mr. Humboldt; the Prince of Karolath, and a long list of gallant youths, eminently distinguished themselves. Their rapid marches in the rear of the French grand army, and the war of posts and skirmishes which they carried on so successfully, prior to the armistice, made them the terror of all French stragglers and detachments. But, above all, their he-

of the armistice, General von Blücher, by way of
reprisal, advanced with his army into the neutral

---

roic example fanned and lighted up a flame of chivalrous enthusiasm, caused an extraordinary fermentation to be excited
throughout Germania's plains, and thus materially aided the
good cause. Their ultimate fate casts an odium on the honour
and character of the Duke of Padua, which may place him on
a footing with d'Avoust and Vandamme, if not with the perpe-
trator of the massacre at Jaffa.

The intelligence of the armistice reached the corps on the
9th of June, near Hoff; and the official annunciation on the
14th, at Plauen, where they had halted, was delivered to Major Lützow by Captain Monbe, a Saxon officer, who, at the
same time, presented Captain von Jensewitz as the Saxon
officer appointed by the commanding officer of the district to
conduct the corps to the frontiers. The French General commanding at Gera invited Major von Lützow, and several other
officers of the corps, to dinner, and received them in the most
hospitable and friendly manner. On the following morning the
corps continued its march to Zeitz; and, having reached the
village of Kitzen, between Pegau and Lützen, a body of the
enemy's troops was observed on the advance towards them;
and soon after Major von Becker, with a flag of truce, appeared,
and announced to the corps that it was the Duke of Padua's
express order (who then commanded in Leipsic), that the corps
should not proceed on its march until French officers had arrived to accompany it farther. The Major instantly consented;
and soon after another flag of truce appeared, and desired the
Major to proceed with him to General Fournier, commanding
the column in advance. The Major complied, and immediately
put the question to the General, If it were his intention to act
on the offensive? which was answered in the negative; adding,
As long as the corps proceeded quietly on its march to the
frontiers.

Major

ground on the 14th, reached Breslaw the same
day, and marched towards the Katzbach on the
15th and 16th, fixed his head-quarters at Jauer on
the 17th, and employed that day in reconnoitring
the enemy's position on the Katzbach, with the
view of attacking him on the 18th; for which
every preparation was made by the Commander-
in-chief; but the enemy left the heights, on which

Major von Lützow then issued an express order, " That the
corps was to refrain from every hostile act towards the enemy's
squadrons, on pain of death." The enemy's horse now drew
up close in their rear, forming two sides of a square, and in
this state the march began. It was near nine in the evening ;
numbers were singing popular chorusses, and each pursuing his
way unsuspicious of treachery, and without a presentiment of
danger, when, suddenly, they were furiously charged by the
French in their rear, and all those, the fleetness of whose
horses did not favour their escape, were murdered in cold blood,
or taken prisoners. A few files that had time to form, and
scorning to surrender, sold their lives dearly ; but the whole
corps was dispersed on all sides, and only Major von Lützow,
with some brave companions, happily cut their way through the
treacherous French, and reached the Elbe. The Duke of
Padua sends an officer to do away all suspicion, to lull them into
security ; commands them to halt until an officer of safe conduct has arrived : the officer does arrive, and they fall as victims
of the foulest treachery, the most diabolical perfidy to be met
with in military annals.

This is an instance, amongst innumerable others that could
be adduced, that some of the Satraps of Napoleon trampled on
the most sacred pledges, without blushing and without remorse,
whenever a favourite object of their revengeful, bloodthirsty
Sultan was to be attained.

they were strongly posted, during the night, and
evacuated Liegnitz and Goldberg, which were immediately occupied by General Baron von Sacken,
after a trifling affair, not far from the latter place,
whereby the enemy lost 6 officers and 200 prisoners. The rest of the army pursued General
Lauriston on the road to Goldberg, towards Löwenberg and Bunzlau; and General von Blücher
established his head-quarters at Goldberg. General Kaisaroff had pushed on his corps at the same
time to Lahn, where he was warmly attacked by
a French brigade under General Zucchi, from the
corps of Marshal Macdonald; but he vigorously
repulsed the enemy, and took from him 160 prisoners.

At this period the positions of the several combined and confederate armies were as follows :

The united army of Russians and Prussians,
under the command of General Barclay de Tolly,
consisting of General Wittgenstein's corps of Russians, General von Kleist's corps of Prussians,
together with the Prussian and Russian reserves
under the Grand Prince Constantin and Count
Miloradowitsch, about 80,000 men strong, passed
the Bohemian frontiers on the 12th of August (on
which day Austria declared war against France),
formed a junction with the Imperialists on the
17th; and Field-marshal Prince Schwartzenberg
then took the command in chief, General Count
Radetzky being appointed Quarter-master-general.

This grand army, whose efficient numbers in the field may be calculated at 180,000 men, took up a position on the Saxon border, the head-quarters being at Prague, at which place the Emperor of Russia and the King of Prussia had arrived on the 18th, and were there met by General Moreau, who was immediately appointed General Adjutant to the Emperor of Russia.

The Swedish army of the Crown Prince of Sweden, strengthened by the Russian corps of Generals Winzingerode, von Woronzow, and von Czernischeff, an English Hanoverian corps under General Walmoden, and a Prussian corps under General von Bülow, were posted in the Mark, the Prince having his head-quarters at Charlottenburg, and from which he addressed a proclamation to his troops, full of fire and energy.

The Prussian army under General von Tauenzien, was posted so as to act in conjunction with General von Blücher, or the Crown Prince of Sweden, as circumstances might render necessary, the head-quarters being at Münchenburg.

Napoleon occupied offensive positions at all points against these corps d'armée: he threatened Berlin, Breslaw, and Prague, and moved from Dresden, as from the centre of a circle, on all sides of him. His grand army of 150,000 men, under Marshals Ney and Macdonald, and Generals Sebastiani and Lauriston, made front towards Silesia. Marshal Oudinot menaced the Mark with

90,000 men; a reserve of 60,000 men was in cantonments between Bautzen and Löwenberg; several corps of observation were stationed towards Bohemia; and his right wing was formed by d'Avoust, with 30,000 men.

It was the judiciously concerted plan of the Allies, that, if the Silesian army was attacked by a superior, overwhelming force, it should retreat, fighting, from one strong position to another; and in this manner, by drawing the principal force of the French after it, unavoidably lengthen, and at the same time weaken, Napoleon's line of operations; and thus enable the grand Bohemian army to reap important and incalculable advantages, when attempting to advance rapidly out of Bohemia upon Dresden.

On the 19th the Silesian army continued its offensive movements. The corps of General Langeron crossed the Bober at the village of Zobten, and took the village of Siebeneichen, where a division of Macdonald's corps attempted to defend the passage. The advanced-guard of the Russians, under General Rudczewitz, encountered a column of the enemy on their retreat from Lahn, took a battery, a number of prisoners, the whole of Marshal Macdonald's field-equipage, and the military chest of the paymaster-general. This daring enterprise was hardly executed, when the enemy fell upon the General with great force; but having formed his advanced-guard into a square

phalanx, and placed his rich booty in the midst,
he forced his way at the point of the bayonet,
through the opposing files of the enemy, and
reached his corps in safety.   General von York,
at the head of his corps, had taken the direction
of Löwenberg, where he found the heights in
front of the town already occupied by the advanced-guard of Lauriston's corps: General von York
ordered his up to the attack, and drove the enemy's over the Bober with inconsiderable loss.
During this affair, it was reported to General von
Blücher, who was present, that Marshal Ney, with
the cavalry of General Sebastiani, was on the
march from Haynau to Löwenberg, menacing the
flank and rear of the Prussian army.   Upon this,
General von Blücher dispatched Prince Charles
of Mecklenburg, with a brigade, to stop the progress of the enemy; but finding himself too weak
to withstand his repeated attacks, he demanded
support, which General von York complied with,
and the Prince succeeded in keeping Marshal Ney
in check, so as to enable our veteran General to
follow up his advantages at Löwenberg.   Marshal
Ney halted at Gröditz-Berg, in a woody, intersected terrain ; and General von York drew up his
forces opposite to him, at the distance of a cannon-shot, while the General-in-chief directed the
march of the other columns thither, with the intention of attacking the enemy the next morning.
General von Sacken had marched, on the same

day, towards Bunzlau, in pursuit of the enemy,
who had evacuated, in great haste, both Liegnitz
and Haynau.   It was the 6th corps, under Marshal Marmont; but the advanced-guard of General von Sacken's corps succeeded in bringing
him to action at the village of Kreibau, behind
Haynau.   He then took up a position on the hills
of Kaiserswalde, to the left of the high road towards Bautzen.   After an obstinate engagement,
which cost the enemy a great number of men, he
was obliged to relinquish his strong position, and
retreat on the road to Bunzlau.   On his march,
General Nevarofsky fell on his right flank, kept
up a heavy cannonade and galling fire of musketry, and pursuing with the cavalry to the village of Ober-Thomaswaldau, night alone put an
end to the sanguinary combat.   The corps of General von Sacken bivouacked between Wolfshain
and Thomaswaldau.

After reconnoitring the position of Marshal
Marmont, General von Sacken caused him to be
attacked on the morning of the 20th, and forced
him to abandon Thomaswaldau, and to pursue his
march to Bunzlau, under a continual succession of
severe engagements and charges.   The enemy
being driven out of the intrenchments they had
thrown up near this place by assault, and having
blown up his magazines and broken down the
bridges, the town was occupied by the troops under General Count Lieven.   Marshal Ney's corps,

and the cavalry under General Sebastiani, had
made good their retreat through Bunzlau in the
night between the 19th and 20th; General von
Blücher was, therefore, spared the necessity of attacking him, as the French had entirely abandoned
the right bank of the Bober on the 20th August.
But, on this day, Napoleon, by forced marches,
had reached Lauban with his guards and the corps
of cavalry under General Latour-Maubourg, and
hastened to make the necessary dispositions that his
retreating army might act again on the offensive.
He arrived at Löwenberg by break of day on the
21st, at the critical moment when the Silesian
army was on the point of crossing the Bober. Napoleon lost no time in throwing bridges over that
river; and General Lauriston repassed it at noon
at the head of the 5th corps, the rest of his army
following. This sudden return of the enemy's columns, and the great force they displayed, did not
escape the penetration and foresight of our veteran
General, who rightly judged that the enemy, being
reinforced, was determined on giving battle; but
to avoid doing so was absolutely necessary from
various circumstances; and he therefore concentrated his gallant army on the Gröditz-Berg,
during which his advanced-guard seized every advantage which the nature of the ground permitted,
to obstruct the progress of the enemy, and keep
him in check.

At noon, on the 22d, the Silesian army was

drawn up in order of battle between Abelsdorf
and Pilgramsdorf. The French threw themselves
on its left wing, which General von Blücher drew
back behind Goldberg, placing his army in position, with the Katzbach in front, and his left wing
extending to Liegnitz. On the 23d the French
attacked Goldberg with the 5th and 11th corps :
the advanced-guards of General Count Langeron
and von York defended the town and the heights
with the greatest bravery. General Lauriston, who
had the command of the French troops, took Wolfs-
berg, defended only by small detachments, and debouched with columns of infantry, but was repulsed
with heavy loss, three several times, during which the
Prussian cavalry made many brilliant charges with
great success. The Prince of Mecklenburg, who
fought the enemy on the left bank of the Katzbach, had to sustain the most violent and impetuous attacks ; the great superiority of the French
artillery had dismounted a part of his guns and
thinned the ranks of his columns, while twenty-
four squadrons of French horse, profiting by the
favourable moment, made a grand charge, took a
battery, and surrounded two battalions. Some
squadrons of Prussian cavalry, and the regiment
of Mecklenburg Hussars, threw themselves, at this
moment, with indescribable fury, on the enemy's
cavalry, broke their first line, forced the second
upon the third, retook the guns, and released the
battalions which had been taken prisoners. On

this memorable occasion, the gallant Prince of
Mecklenburg seized a Prussian standard, rallied
some battalions that were giving way, put himself
at their head, and led them on again into action.
This was one of the hottest affairs of the whole
campaign. Some of the battalions of the Silesian
militia highly distinguished themselves, and excited the admiration of the veterans of the army.
General von Blücher learnt, from the prisoners
that were made, that Napoleon was in the field
with the flower of the French army ; and at the
same time General von Sacken, who commanded
the right wing at Liegnitz, reported, that the
French, in considerable force (the third and sixth
corps), were on the advance against him. The
Bohemian army would, in all probability, advance
on this day, two days' march into Saxony ; it was
possible also, that the Crown Prince of Sweden,
with the northern army, would be in Lower Lusatia ; General von Blücher therefore held it
more advisable to draw off the French army farther from the Elbe, so as to prevent Napoleon
from finding time to unite his scattered forces to
a converging point. He accordingly issued orders to break off the combat, judging the contest
no longer equal, and to retreat towards Jauer.
The loss of the Silesian army, during the whole of
the engagements, from the 21st to the 23d,
amounted to 3000 men ; but that of the French

must have been far more considerable, as the vantage-ground was favourable for the allied arms.

Napoleon, on the first intelligence of the progress of the Bohemian army towards Saxony, soon perceived how necessary his presence must be on the Elbe; and scarcely had his guards arrived in Silesia, on the 22d, before they were ordered to trace their steps back again to Dresden. He followed them on the 23d, accompanied by Marshal Ney, leaving Marshal Macdonald commander-in-chief of the third, fifth, and eleventh corps. Marshal Marmont's corps, and the cavalry under General Latour-Maubourg, likewise began their retrograde march to Dresden. On the 23d, General Souham took the command of the third corps, during Marshal Ney's absence.

Nothing of importance occurred to Blücher's army on the 24th; the French were posted on the Katzbach, and the Allies at Jauer. On the 25th, the advanced-guard of the latter made a movement forwards, and the light cavalry of Sacken's corps pursued the third corps to the environs of Haynau, when the latter faced about, and again moved towards the Katzbach. Upon this, General von Blücher marched the corps of General von Sacken to Malitsch, that of von York to Jauer, and directed the corps of Langeron to take up their ground on the fine position of Hennersdorf. The fifth French corps stood in the position of Goldberg, having its advanced-guard at Prausnitz; the eleventh corps

behind Goldberg; and the third corps near Roth-
kirch, with a division posted at Liegnitz. These
corps were, however, separated in part by the Katzbach and Neisse, which, owing to the heavy rains,
had overflowed their banks, and become raging torrents. The Prussians having concentrated themselves near Jauer, could either advance on the
enemy, or take up an impregnable position on the
mountains, in the rear; but General von Blücher,
with his usual penetration, quickly perceiving that
the main spring of action, Napoleon himself, was
not in the field, and satisfied that the counter-
march of such numerous bodies could not but be
known to him, with a promptness of decision so
marked in all his resolves, determined to improve
the opportunity, and made dispositions for a general attack on the enemy, at two o'clock P. M. on
the 26th August. The three corps d'armée were to
pass the Katzbach, between Goldberg and Liegnitz; those of von York and von Sacken to attack
the third French corps with the utmost rapidity;
during which the corps of Langeron was to cover
the rear of both, towards Goldberg. The corps
of General von York, having reached the heights
of Brechtelshof, reported to the Commander-in-
chief, that the enemy was already on the advance,
and had driven in the out-posts; and particularly,
that General Langeron was briskly attacked.
Upon this, General von Blücher halted his columns, and drew them up again in ambuscade.

A most tremendous and continual rain *, and lowering sky, had so darkened the atmosphere, that every movement was rendered very difficult, and any kind of reconnoitring almost impossible. To the left of the village of Eich holz, some commanding ground became the key of the whole position *(see Plan of the Battle on the Katzbach)*, and General von Sacken was ordered to line it with his artillery, which was done with his usual promptitude and celerity; a Prussian battery, of twelve-pounders, strengthened his left, and their brisk and well-directed fire forced the enemy, in despite of himself, to deploy his columns slowly and disadvantageously, between

---

* As this memorable battle has been the peculiar boast of the Prussians, the greatest security to the province of Silesia, and the first check the ambitious power of Napoleon experienced on the plains of Germany, a detailed account of the occurrences that marked and preceded the glory of the day may not be unacceptable to the reader.

For several days previous to the battle, the confederate army had to struggle with uncommon difficulties. An incessant rain had inundated, in a great measure, the face of the country. Their marches were nothing but a continual wading, up to their knees, through innumerable rivulets, that, swollen by the rains, rolled like torrents from the mountains. Each bivouack, at night, was taken up on ground ancle-deep in mud and mire, the rain falling without any intermission. Their supplies of provisions could not be brought up, and the army suffered privations with an heroic fortitude, and calm determined resignation, that form the brightest gems in their crown of victory.

Weinberg and Eich-holz. This was the moment intended by our bold veteran for the general attack *. The advanced-guard, and von Horn's brigade, fell on the right wing of the French, at Weinberg; the Prince of Mecklenburg's brigade followed in support, that of von Hünerbein covered the left flank against Lauriston, and the brigade of Steinmetz, together with the cavalry, formed the reserve. General von Sacken caused his advanced-guard to take post to the left of the village of Eich-holz, and two regiments of Russian riflemen occupied the village, supported by two others. Lieutenant-general Nevarofsky

---

* The eyes of all Europe were, at this time, on the conduct of Blücher, and his able defence of Silesia has justly exalted him to a most elevated place in the military annals of the present day. Collected within himself, he in no instance hazarded the event of a battle by premature experiments on the enemy, but deliberately observed their approaches, and seized the important moment to make his attacks: his cool and temperate demeanour maintained that confidence with which he had inspired his troops, and his unaffected eloquence, when addressing them, did but increase their veneration. The cannonade had begun, the infantry were in column, when our veteran General rode down the lines, and stopping at intervals, harangued the troops in nearly the following words:

"My brave lads; this day decides! Prove to your King and to your country, that your courage is equal to your fidelity. Prove it, I say, at the point of your bayonets. Look yonder, there's the enemy. March, show yourselves as gallant Prussians." Reiterated huzzas, and cries of " The King for ever!" resounded from all sides, with bursts of enthusiasm.

formed the first line, and General Count Lieven the second line of the advanced-guard. There
being an evident possibility of turning the left
flank of the enemy, General von Sacken ordered
Major-general von Lanskoy with the cavalry,
General Karpoff with the Cossacks, and General
Wassiltschikoff with the Achkirsch hussars, to
leave Eich-holz to their left, and to attempt to
fall on the enemy's left flank. In this position
the attack began. General Lanskoy took the
French in flank, and General Wassiltschikoff,
supported by the Prussian cavalry, attacked them
in front; Lieutenant-general Nevarofsky supported these fierce charges with the whole of his infantry, followed by General Lieven, who advanced
into the first line. With an impetuosity and a
defiance of danger that baffles all description, as
if animated by one soul, and impelled by one
spring of action, the whole line of battle now
precipitated itself on the enemy *. The incessant

---

* It was the second battalion of the Brandenburg regiment
of infantry, that formed the head of the column which made
the first onset. Cool, steady, and compact, the battalion advanced to storm three batteries, protected by two squares of
infantry of the enemy's centre. The cannon-balls plunged
into the ranks, mowing down whole files. The Prussian column,
silent as death, moved on unshaken. A galling fire of grape-
shot now thinned their ranks. No one looked either to the
right or left, and shouts of " Forwards! forwards!" stifled the
cries of the wounded and the dying. Whole sections fell, and

rain, pouring down in torrents the whole day, had
rendered fire-arms useless; not a musket would
go off, when, with loud shouts and reiterated
huzzas, a conflict with the bayonet took place,
the most sanguinary, desperate, and destructive
that is to be met with in the history of battles.
Whole columns of Frenchmen were in a few minutes overpowered by the physical enthusiastic
strength of the Allies, and suddenly transformed
into frightful heaps of wounded, dead, and
dying; not a soul escaped; no one thought of
taking prisoners; " Forwards! forwards! Go on!
go on !" were the watch-words, and Death stalked
in hideous majesty before the impenetrable files of
the Prussians and Russians; from the gleams of
whose bayonets their appalled enemies shrunk
aghast with horror and confusion. The Prussian

---

the dauntless survivors did but press on the more vehemently
to use the bayonet.   Closing with the enemy, a dreadful pause
of irresolute suspense seemed to intervene, when, as the officers
shouted, " Down upon them! down upon them !" a furious
murderous charge with the bayonet ensued.   In the heat of the
attack no quarter was given, and scarcely ten minutes elapsed
before the enemy's phalanx was transformed into a pyramid of
ghastly corpses.   The other square, shuddering at the fate of
their advance, broke, and took to their heels.   The tumult and
confusion in the French centre were so great, that two regiments of French horse, which advanced at full gallop to cover
the fugitives, passed the Prussian column at this moment, mis-
taking them for their comrades,

cavalry charged at intervals, in single squadrons, and took several pieces of artillery.

On the left wing, General Langeron had to sustain the most furious attacks; twice did General Lauriston succeed in carrying the heights of the Russian position, and twice was he driven from them, at the point of the bayonet. French impetuosity here found its overmatch in the adamantine steadiness of Russian bravery and devotion. Marshal Macdonald's efforts were at last in vain; the French could no longer withstand the determined resolution of the Allies; he attempted, as a forlorn hope, a grand charge of cavalry, but this was repulsed with severe loss, and he was obliged to relinquish the field of battle, leaving a great part of his artillery behind him, and seek his safety, and that of his routed army, across the foaming torrents of the Katzbach and the Neisse, which, swollen as they were by unceasing rains, could not be done but with great danger and difficulty. They were here pressed hard by the Allies, and driven down the steep precipices of their banks into the raging floods beneath *. This decisive

---

* Who shall venture to describe the extatick feelings arising from the consciousness of having gained a signal victory over an implacable foe ? Veterans, soldiers by profession, gratify their passion for honour on such an occasion. It is honour they seek, it is honour they gain : but the heart of the patriot, when taking the field to save that country so dear to him, to

battle, by which the gigantic plans of Napoleon received a fresh check, and the foundation was laid for the emancipation of Germany, and the peace of Europe, commenced about three o'clock P. M. lasted till night was far advanced, and ended on the Katzbach. In the night, when all firing and pursuit had ceased, an enemy's reserve, with sixteen pieces of cannon, advanced on the road from Liegnitz, with the intention of harassing the right wing, to draw off its attention, and thus enable the discomfited army to retreat unmolested; but it was warmly received by the Generals von Lieven and Nevarofsky, and quickly repulsed with heavy loss; after which attack this hard-fought contest ceased entirely. Sixteen pieces of artillery were captured, sword in hand, by the conquerors; but there was no possibility, on this day, to ascertain the exact number of guns and prisoners taken; among the latter was, how-

---

preserve the glory of that King so beloved and adored, over-flows with an excess of rapturous delight, an indescribable charm, that beggars all description : such, however, was the feeling that pervaded the Prussian army on the eve of this day. Each column, each company, was eager (like children with their play-things) to show their comrades the prisoners they had taken, the trophies they could boast of. Blücher listened to the tales each had to relate with the indulgence of paternal partiality: " Well, my lads," he would say, " the French will think of us; they 'll remember our bayonets, I warrant them." —" Hear me, father Blücher," the soldiers would answer : " This day is a day of days; if we go on so, who 's afraid?"

ever, the French General van der Suden. The
loss of the combined army was by no means considerable. On the 27th, the advanced-guard of
General Count von Langeron attacked the corps
of Lauriston, retreating towards Goldberg. General Kapezewitz caused the Generals Partschoulid-
seff and Denischeff to attack an enemy's square
mass of infantry, of three battalions, and flanked
by four guns; the intrepid Russians did not let a
man escape, they were all either killed, wounded,
or taken prisoners; and this severe loss so dis-
couraged the rest of Lauriston's corps, that, being
briskly pursued, and losing eighteen guns, they
evacuated Goldberg, and General Langeron occupied it the same day. Blücher paused not a moment: on the 28th, the victorious Silesian army
crossed the Katzbach at Liegnitz and Goldberg,
during which the several advanced-guards continued without intermission to follow up the
enemy towards Löwenberg and Bunzlau, hourly
capturing prisoners in every direction. The rain,
falling in torrents, had swollen every rivulet to an
outrageous stream, which had broken down every
bridge, so that the whole country was in a state
of inundation; there was in consequence no way
of passing the Bober, but at Bunzlau, and to this
point all the French columns were obliged to
direct their march.

General Puthod had been detached, on the 26th
of August, to manœuvre in the rear of the allied

army, by the way of Schönau and Jauer. The
intelligence of the battle being lost had reached
him; it was not however in his power, on
account of the waters being out, to repass the
Bober; he made the attempt at Hirschberg, but
not succeeding, he marched down the right bank
of the Bober, towards Löwenberg, and passed the
night of the 28th at Zobten. On the 29th, he
directed his steps to Löwenberg, where he made
several unavailing attempts to replace the bridge
over the Bober. This delay gave General von
Langeron time to gain a march upon him, having
received advice of his movements; and as General
Puthod saw the danger he was in of being attacked
at a disadvantage, he endeavoured to regain the
high road to Bunzlau; but General Rudzewicz,
commanding the advanced-guard of Langeron's
corps, having cut off his retreat on this road, he
bent his march towards Zobten once again, which
being reported to General von Korff and Prince
Czerbatow, who had followed the advanced-guard
with cavalry, as support, they threw themselves
on this route by a forced march, and General
Puthod, finding himself hemmed in on all sides,
drew up his corps on the heights near Plagwitz,
by Löwenberg, and prepared for a desperate defence. General Czerbatow, in consequence, directed the march of his division to this point, and
General von Korff followed along the banks of
the Bober, with his cavalry. The Prince arriving

on the commanding ground opposite the enemy's position, established a battery of light artillery, that began to play briskly on the French columns, and detached four regiments of riflemen to attack and gall the enemy on his right flank. The French were not slow in making the most vigorous resistance, and their batteries did great execution; but at this moment, their left flank being hard pressed by General Rudzewicz, Prince Czerbatow commanded an assault to be made with the bayonet on their right flank; it was carried, and the French driven pell-mell from the heights into the roaring Bober, and all were made prisoners that did not precipitate themselves into the river. The trophies of this signal victory over Puthod's corps were glorious to the allied arms. General Puthod, more than 100 officers, and 8000 men, were taken prisoners; 16 pieces of cannon, 2 eagles of the 146th and 148th French regiments of the line, and the whole of the artillery park, fell into the hands of the gallant confederates. The Brigade General Siblet, a colonel, many officers and privates, were drowned in the rapid stream of the Bober. The whole loss of Langeron's corps did not exceed 200 men*.

---

* A praiseworthy emulation spurred on the troops, and, under the blessing of an all-ruling Providence, the success of this great day may be justly attributed to the invincible courage and intrepidity of the confederate Silesian army: General von Blücher never lost sight of the enemy, and attacked him almost

On the 30th of August, General von Blücher transferred his head-quarters to Holstein, near Löwenberg, and continued to pursue the enemy in the most active manner. General von Bennigsen entered Breslaw on the 30th of August, with his Polish army of reserve, and proceeded from thence to Liegnitz, marching on the same line with Blücher. In bivouack, at the village of Kielingswalde, between Naumburg and Görlitz, General von Blücher addressed a proclamation to his army *. The insignia of the grand order of St.

---

daily. In the course of eight days he had fought him in eight bloody encounters, not to mention trifling affairs ; beat him completely in a pitched battle, and directly afterwards made three serious attacks upon him. We may venture to affirm, that, in modern military annals, no example of such a succession of bloody and eventful days is to be found as those between the 18th and 29th August 1813.

---

* *Blücher's Proclamation to his Soldiers, after the Battle on the Katzbach.*
" Silesia is cleared of the enemy. Brave soldiers, of the Russian and Prussian army under my command, it is to your vigorous exertions and resolution, to your patience in supporting fatigues and privations, that I owe the good fortune of having wrested this fine province out of the hands of a greedy and rapacious enemy. The implacable foe, with haughty defiance, met you on the Katzbach. You issued with the rapidity of lightning, from behind the heights. You disdained to attack him with the distant fire of musketry, but advanced upon him without pausing. Your bayonets, and the nervous strength of your arm, drove him down the steeps of the raging Neisse and the Katzbach. You have since waded through torrents and

Andrew, which the Emperor of Russia transmitted to General von Blücher, after the battle on the Katzbach, was accompanied by the following note, in the Emperor's own hand-writing :

" GENERAL,

" Amongst the most agreeable moments of the campaign, I reckon those, in which I can give you proofs of the peculiar satisfaction I feel, in doing justice to your brilliant courage, the activity of your operations, and the effect of your unparalleled movements.

---

rivers; you have passed the nights in storms, without shelter, short of provisions, and struggling with every want; but you murmured not, you pursued with promptitude and energy the flying enemy. I return you thanks for your exalted, praiseworthy conduct. He alone is a true soldier that possesses such qualities.

" One hundred and three pieces of cannon, 250 tumbrils, the camp-hospital of the enemy, his provisions, a general of division, 2 generals of brigade, a great number of colonels, staff and other officers, 18,000 prisoners, 2 eagles, and other trophies, have fallen into your hands. The remainder of those who opposed you on the Katzbach, terrified at the sight of your bayonets, have taken to flight. The roads and the fields between the Katzbach and the Bober bear the unequivocal marks of the confusion and dismay of the enemy. Let us sing praises to the Lord of Hosts, by whose help you have overthrown your enemies, and return him thanks, in the hour of prayer, for the victory he has given into our hands. Three volleys shall be fired in honour of the day, and terminate your devotions. And then, once more, seek the enemy in the field.

" VON BLÜCHER."

" In the hour in which we, on our side, have gained a signal victory *, I send you the insignia of the order of St. Andrew, which I have myself worn. I do not suppose that this circumstance will enhance the value of this mark of my pleasure, but it will at least prove to you, that I have lost not a moment in assuring you, and those brave men under your command, of the singular gratification your fortunate progress has afforded me.

" The glory of a commander is reflected upon his soldiers, as that of the soldiers upon their commander. Tell them how highly I rate their deeds, and accept the assurances of my best wishes.

" ALEXANDER."

Töplitz,
the 30th of August 1813.

General von Blücher received, from his grateful Sovereign, the grand cross of the order of the Iron Cross.

After a warm affair between the brigade of von Horn and the rear-guard of the enemy, at Bunzlau, very honourable to the former, although attended with considerable loss, the French evacuated Silesia entirely. They left the banks of the Bober on the 31st of August, and, on the 1st of September, the country was cleared of them,

---

* Of Culm.

and the wrecks of Macdonald's army fled through Lusatia. General von Blücher's advanced-guard crossed the Queisse the same day, which was distinguished by a brilliant operation: Major von Falkenhausen, and Captain von Swanenfeld, surprised with two squadrons of hussars, between Görlitz and Bautzen, four companies of French artillery, a squadron of chasseurs, and a company of infantry, entirely dispersed them, and took from them the last cannon saved from the wreck of the battle on the Katzbach.

CHAPTER VIII.

*Our Veteran's masterly Manœuvres in Silesia—
Battle of Dresden—Progress of the allied Armies
—Blücher crosses the Elbe—Battle of Warten-
berg.*

THE remains of Marshal Macdonald's corps now
sheltered themselves behind the Queisse, and endeavoured to recover from the universal panic that
had seized them. On the 2d of September the
advanced-guard of the Silesian army passed the
Neisse, and the main body followed. The retreating and beaten French stood, on the 3d of
September, near the Löbau pools, and on the
4th pursued their retrograde march to Bautzen:
they had already abandoned Hochkirch, when
suddenly their columns halted and bivouacked on
the nearest heights. Napoleon having, no doubt,
received intelligence of the defeat of Macdonald, had, it seems, hastened, by forced marches,
with a part of his guards from Dresden to his
support; and the corps of Poniatowsky, from 12
to 15,000 strong, at the same time advanced from
Zittau. The retrograde march of the grand allied
army into Bohemia, having given Napoleon the
power of enlarging his circle of action, he left

Dresden on the 3d of September, accompanied by
Marshal Murat, passed the night at Harthau,
arrived in the vicinity of Hochkirch on the 4th,
and immediately issued orders for the retreating
army to halt. It was soon reported to General
von Blücher, that Napoleon, with his guards, the
sixth corps, and the cavalry under General Latour-
Maubourg, were now in the field against him;
upon which he withdrew his advanced-guard under General Wassiltschikoff, behind the Löbau-
water, and concentrated his army in the rear of
Landeskrone. In this position he remained to ascertain whether Napoleon would be contented
with merely gathering up the shattered remains of
Macdonald's army, or offer battle.

On the 5th, Napoleon deployed a numerous
force in front of Reichenbach, and vigorously attacked Blücher's army. The General-in-chief,
true to his system, did not hold it advisable to accept battle at this critical moment, but passed the
Neisse and Queisse with his army in the most
complete order, leaving a rear-guard on the right
bank of the Neisse, to watch the enemy's movements and demonstrations of advancing into Silesia. Nothing could be more evident than that
the farther the enemy could be drawn from Dresden, the more decisive the operations of the allied
army in Bohemia must eventually prove. But
Blücher's patience was in vain tried on the 6th
and 7th; the foe made no attempt to advance.

Napoleon felt the whole danger of his situation; and the Bohemian army having again threatened Dresden, he saw himself kept in constant check, and obliged once more to trace his steps back to Dresden with the reinforcements he had brought with him, where he arrived on the 6th, in the evening. In the course of these operations detachments of cavalry from Blücher's army harassed the rear of the French army, and caused it a considerable loss. The Russian General, Prince Madatoff, surprised, on the 2d of September, a corps of French at Wurschen, consisting of 1 colonel, 5 captains, 18 lieutenants, 2 adjutants, and 677 privates, and made the whole of them prisoners. On the 4th, the same Prince attacked the escort of a large transport of ammunition, took them prisoners, and blew up more than 100 tumbrils. Our veteran hero, on finding the enemy less impetuous, put his army again in motion on the 8th. The corps of General St. Priest crossed the Neisse at Ostritz; that of Count Langeron followed. According to Blücher's plan of operations, General St. Priest was suddenly to attack Löbau; during which, General von York was to fall on the rear and flank of the enemy's corps at Görlitz, in the direction of Landskrone, so as to cut it off, if possible, from Reichenbach. General St. Priest was prompt and vigorous in his attack on the 8th Polish corps, concentrated at Löbau, and drove it out of Mittel-Hartwigsdorf, Ebersdorf, and Löbau; but it was not possible to execute the attack on Görlitz, as the enemy, well aware of the peril that menaced him, had made such a precipitate retreat from the place, that the Cossacks, sent in pursuit, were not even able to overtake him. General von Blücher learnt from an adjutant, taken prisoner, bearing dispatches to the Prince of Neufchatel (Berthier), from Prince Poniatowsky, that his corps had lost 23 officers and 500 men in the affair of Löbau. Macdonald's army continued its retreat to Bautzen. On the 10th, the advanced guard of Blücher's army occupied Hochkirch, the Cossacks surrounded Bautzen, and General Blücher fixed his head-quarters at Herrnhut. A division of the Austrian army, 8000 strong, under General Count Bubna, formed a junction with the Silesian army on this day, having, till then, been posted in the vicinity of Gabel, on the frontiers of Bohemia, to observe the corps of Poniatowsky.

The decided superiority of force, which our hero now possessed, urged him to move onwards; and, on the 11th, Generals St. Priest and Kapczewicz forced the passage of the Spree, and General Count Bubna advanced towards Neustadt. The French troops evacuated, by break of day, on the 12th, both Bautzen and Neustadt, and retired behind Bishopswerda and Stolpe: here they were only a day's march from Dresden, and, by the way of Pirna, in direct communication with the right wing of the grand French army. On the 14th,

General St. Priest marched in advance, and charged a column of infantry with his cavalry, near Bishopswerda, taking about 100 men prisoners. The following days were employed in narrowing the positions of the French near Dresden, and cutting off their supplies. According to the accounts of deserters, forage and provisions of all kinds were beginning to fall short in the place. General von Blücher having received intelligence that Marshal Marmont intended to make a diversion on the side of Grossenhain with the 6th corps under his command, ordered General von Sacken to advance to Camenz; and his advanced-guard, under General Fiegner, after skirmishing with the enemy the whole of the 15th, obliged him to retrace his steps to Dresden on the 16th.

In the position of Bishopswerda the Silesian army remained in a state of comparative inaction till the 22d: there seemed to be a cessation of offensive operations on the part of the army; but the great plan of the Allies was only ripening, and the main object, of acting on the flanks of Napoleon's army, was never lost sight of. Our veteran General, whether on the offensive or defensive, seemed equally successful; and no commander had, as yet, distinguished himself in a more eminent or even equal degree. His talent of daring enterprise, and his consummate prudence, carried him through triumphantly, in situations the most difficult to be conceived; and his conduct at the approaching crisis established him for ever, in the opinion of Europe, as one of the first of commanders.

Napoleon having returned to Dresden on the 21st of September from his unfortunate expedition into Bohemia, and finding himself hemmed in and compressed within narrow limits by Blücher, who stood in position almost within sight of the walls of Dresden, thought it expedient to attempt disengaging himself from so troublesome a neighbour. For this purpose he proceeded to Harthau on the 22d, causing the 11th, 3d, and 5th corps of his grand army to march in the direction of Bishopswerda, occupied by Blücher's advanced-guard under General Rudzewicz and Colonel von Katzler. Although attacked by superior numbers, the gallant Confederates maintained the unequal contest nearly the whole of the day in this position, before they yielded a foot of ground. On the 23d, Napoleon renewed his attack, and the advanced-guard abandoned the woods and heights near Bishopswerda; but no sooner did the French debouch out of the wood, into a favourable terrain for cavalry, than the Allies faced about, and the Russian cavalry under Generals Count Witt and Emanuel, and the Prussian, under Colonel von Katzler, charged them with intrepidity, and drove them, with heavy loss, back into the wood; on which occasion 10 officers and 300 privates of the guards were taken prisoners. Napoleon, nevertheless, by dint of numerical superiority, succeeded in penetrating to Gödau, where the face of the country gradually opens, and is less intersected by woods; while, towards Bautzen, an extensive plain presents itself, of singular advantage for the operations of cavalry. Our veteran General here endeavoured, with his wonted decision and alacrity, to entrap Napoleon in an ambuscade. General von Sacken was ordered to lie in ambush, with his whole corps, in such a position, that, when the enemy renewed his attacks on the 24th, he could fall unperceived upon his flank and rear; but the French remained perfectly quiet the whole of the 24th; upon which, General von Blücher directed General von Sacken to act on the offensive against the left flank of the enemy. The near approach of night prevented any movement being made in his rear; and the decisive attack and execution of Blücher's daring plan was obliged to be postponed till break of day of the 25th. Napoleon, however, as if having a presentiment of what awaited him, retired in all haste, during the night, upon Bishopswerda. In this manner was he constrained to renounce, for the third time, acting upon the offensive against the intrepid, calculating Blücher and his Silesian army, and returned to Dresden for the tenth time since the armistice, beset on every side by his enemies: and, although his concentrated position enabled him, by shifting his troops and corps from one point to the other, to make front on all sides of

him, with an imposing force ; yet this severe succession of partial losses dispirited his troops, and
threw whole corps into a state of absolute disor-
ganization. The 8th corps, under Prince Poniatowski, passed over to the left bank of the Elbe,
and marched to Penig. Marshal Victor had taken
position at Freiburg, and the 1st and 14th corps
were encamped at Gieshubel and Pirna. On the
27th, the French army evacuated Grossenhain, and
began to pass the Elbe at Meissen. Lieutenant-
general Count Tauenzien followed sword in hand,
and threw some detachments over the river to
harass the enemy. This General now formed a
junction with the army of General von Blücher,
having his head-quarters, on the 27th, at Elsterwerda ; General Baron von Sacken was posted at
Grossenhain, his advanced-guard before Meissen ;
General von York at Gröbeln ; General Count
Langeron likewise at Elsterwerda ; General Count
St. Priest in Ostrandt, and his advanced-guard towards Königsbrück ; the whole of the corps forming and establishing a link, by which the various
confederate armies were at this time connected together, and surrounding and baiting the ravenous
tiger in his den.

Nothing of material importance occurred to
the Silesian army during the last days of September, the fury with which Napoleon had endeavoured to break through or enlarge the narrowing
boundary that formed the area of his operations,

having, to appearance, nearly spent itself; and his efforts to extricate himself from his perilous situation had proved fruitless at all points. We will now present our readers with a succinct but clear detail of the operations of the grand confederate army since the denunciation of the armistice, and the coalition of the Austrians in the good cause; taking a view, at the same time, of the progress of the Crown Prince of Sweden, and the Prussian armies of Generals Tauenzien and Bülow. This digression is the more necessary, from the impossibility, without it, of forming a just conception of that stupendous manœuvre of our hero, so soon to be executed, in passing the Elbe in the face of the enemy, and throwing himself, by a series of forced marches unparalleled in the records of history, and out of the supposed sphere of man's physical powers, into the rear of Napoleon's line of operations—a manœuvre that caused every subsequent revolution of the wheel of fortune to be favourable to the Allies, and formed a pedestal to the most imperishable monument of military fame that ever was erected to the honour of one commander.

The Emperor of Austria declared war against France on the same day that the denunciation of the armistice took place. The Austrian army, which assembled in and near Prague, under the command of Field-marshal Prince von Schwartzenberg, consisted of three divisions. The Russian-Prussian army under General Barclay de Tolly, consisting of the corps of General Count Wittgenstein, General von Kleist, and the reserves under the Grand Prince Constantin and Count Miloradowitsch, marched out of Silesia on the 12th of August, and formed a junction with the Austrian troops in Bohemia on the 17th of August. This army was henceforth called the grand confederate army, Field-marshal Prince Schwartzenberg being appointed Commander-in-chief, and having his head-quarters at Prague. The several armies of the Allies were posted in the following manner: the army of the Crown Prince of Sweden, called the northern army, formed the right wing, and took up a position between Mecklenburg and the Elbe, having his head-quarters at Oranienburg, and holding communication with the army of General von Tauenzien, in position to observe the fortresses on the Elbe and Oder. General von Blücher stood in Silesia. The efficient numbers of these armies may be estimated at 350,000 men. *(See Map of the Seat of War.)*—The Bohemian army advanced towards the Elbe on the 18th, in four columns, and passed the defiles in the Saxon mountains on the 22d, after some partial advantages over small detached corps of the enemy. The severity of the weather, and the consequent bad state of the roads, prevented the Confederates from arriving before Dresden earlier than the 25th in the evening. *(See Plan of the Battle of Dresden.)*—A general assault was made upon Dresden on the following day, a redoubt was stormed, and the French driven into the body of the place.   In the interim Napoleon had arrived, by forced marches, with the flower of his army out of Silesia.   He reached Dresden at nine o'clock, A. M. on the 26th.   Under such circumstances the Allies deemed it prudent to relinquish the attempt of taking Dresden by assault, and, in consequence, the confederate army was ordered to take up a position on the heights in the vicinity of that city.   Napoleon, with his usual impetuosity, attacked the positions of the confederate troops early on the 27th, and a bloody but indecisive conflict ensued.   It having been reported to the Commander-in-chief from General von Oesterman, commanding a corps of observation near Königstein, that General Vandamme had crossed the Elbe at that place in considerable force, taking the road to Pirna, and by this movement, threatening the rear of the combined grand army, it was obviously necessary for the Confederates to withdraw again into Bohemia: besides, the principal object of these offensive operations was absolutely obtained, although the results, under more favourable circumstances, might have been of greater importance ; for Blücher, as well as the Crown Prince, had thus acquired an enlarged power of acting with energy upon the flanks and the rear of Napoleon's army. The Allies, therefore, set themselves in march towards Bohemia, in the night of the 27th, and reached the frontiers on the 29th, slowly and cautiously pursued by the French.

General Vandamme had arrived at Hollendorf with his corps on the 28th, and advanced to Peterswalde on the 29th, briskly pursuing the small corps of General von Oesterman, five times his inferior in numbers, who nevertheless contested every foot of ground with determined bravery and obstinate repulses. General von Oesterman was, however, obliged to retreat to Töplitz; Vandamme followed with eager impetuosity, and came down into the valley with eight or ten battalions; he attacked him near Töplitz, but the gallantry of the Russian troops supplied the place of numbers; General Vandamme could make no impression with his ten battalions, and insensibly drew his whole corps down into the plain. To have withstood this disproportion of numbers would have been utterly impossible for General von Oesterman, if at this critical juncture a division of Russian guards had not arrived in the field, and a brigade of Russian grenadiers dispatched as a reinforcement by General Prince von Schwartzenberg, had not come into action. General von Oesterman now attacked in his turn, and his troops fought like lions. The Russian guards showed an intrepidity on this occasion, which will long serve as an example worthy of imitation by all the defenders of the good cause. The Russian General succeeded in repulsing the enemy, and forcing him to retreat, at the close of the day, to Karwitz

and Pirsten. The happy success of this affair was
of the most vital importance to the allied arms.
The grand Bohemian army now returning from
Dresden, was on the point of repairing to Töplitz,
after the most fatiguing marches across the mountains, to enjoy some days of repose. If Vandamme's project had been crowned with success,
the most disastrous consequences must have re-
sulted to the combined forces. The good countenance of the Russians, and the brilliant valour of
their chief, decided the combat in favour of the
allied arms, and the execution of the dispositions
for the following day was thus rendered possible.
Vandamme, intoxicated with the distant prospect
of striking a decisive blow, with his single arm,
against the operations of the confederate army, hurried forwards with his whole corps into the valley,
and took post at Culm (see *Plan of the Battle of
Culm*), instead of keeping himself firm in position on
the mountains, as was his orders, or leaving a strong
detachment to occupy the passes. On the 30th, in
the morning, Prince Schwartzenberg made the
following dispositions to annihilate Vandamme's
corps. Besides the troops already engaged, the corps
of Count Colloredo, and the divisions of Bianchi
and Prince von Hessen-Homburg, were ordered
into line, the latter forming the right wing in
front, having Bianchi's division for support. The
corps of Russians formed the left wing, and the
Russian guards were posted in reserve at Soboch-

leben. Count Colloredo was ordered to manœuvre with the enemy, and, supported by General
Knorring's division, to endeavour to turn their
left wing. The far-famed battle of Culm commenced by Colloredo's storming the heights occupied by the enemy's left wing, with an irresistible
impetuosity, and in the most brilliant manner
driving the French before him out of Neu-
dorf. General Knorring, at the head of his cavalry, charged at the same time the enemy's battery, and took it, sword in hand; during which,
the right wing and front of Vandamme's army
were kept fully occupied by the Austrians and
Russians. At this crisis, the corps of General
von Kleist showed themselves on the heights of
Nollendorf, having marched from Glashütte to
gain the high road by Nollendorf. This discern-
ing general quickly appreciated the value of his
presence on the scene of action, and collecting
the whole of his troops in advance, rapidly descended into the plain, and burst like a tremendous hurricane upon the rear of Vandamme's position. This latter general attempted to make
front against Kleist; yet, baited as he was on every
side, the result must at all events prove disastrous, and leave him nothing but the fury of despair. Retreat was cut off, and no chance of
escape at hand. In fine, Vandamme's corps suffered a complete and signal defeat, and only a
few squadrons of cavalry found means of gaining

the road to Eule. The field of battle was covered
with the dead. Vandamme himself, and several
other generals, were taken; and 8000 prisoners,
87 pieces of cannon, and 2 eagles, constituted the
immortal trophies of this glorious day. Its consequences blighted the opening blossoms of Napoleon's imaginary advantages over the Allies at
Dresden. This happy event, in combination with
Blücher's victory on the Katzbach, on the 26th,
and the important advantages gained by General
Bülow on the 22d, at Gross-Beeren, excited
throughout the confederate army the most confident hopes, and elated each heart with the proud
sense of victory and well-earned glory. After
the battle, the allied troops took up a position in
the neighbourhood of Töplitz; their head-quarters, and those of the three august Monarchs,
being in the place. The French corps sent in pursuit of the confederate army, proceeded but
slowly in advance on the 30th and 31st. The
example of Vandamme's terrible fate before their
eyes, Blücher's progress, and the severe check
which Oudinot had experienced, impelled Napoleon to shelter himself once more in his pestilen-
tial den at Dresden; and the allied Bohemian army
remained in a state of repose till the 5th of September. Their ulterior movements shall be referred
to in due course; and we shall now turn to those
operations of the northern army under the command
of the Crown Prince of Sweden, that led to the im-

portant victories of Gross-Beeren and Dennewitz, whose co-operating effects formed a part of those toils, now spread, and drawing closer around the implacable Tyrant, rendered so furious by repeated disappointments.

The Crown Prince of Sweden having received intelligence that the armistice was denounced, concentrated his army between Spandau and Berlin, and took up his head-quarters at Charlottenburg, on the 17th of August. Napoleon, who was anxious to open the campaign with an enterprise of some eclat, pondered upon the project of getting Berlin into his power, and fed his ambitious hopes with thereby plunging all Europe into a stupor of astonishment at his success. For this purpose, Marshal Oudinot was charged with the command of the 4th, 7th, and 12th corps, and the body of cavalry under the Duke of Padua, forming an army of about 80,000 men, which was assembled in the environs of Baruth, on the 18th of August. Some partial affairs occurred, and the advanced posts of the northern army were driven out of Jüterbock, Belzig, and Zerbst. On the 21st, the Crown Prince removed his head-quarters to Potsdam; and as the enemy did not advance, he ordered his army to take up positions on a more extended line. General Winzingerode was posted at Saarmund; General von Bülow, between Phillipsthal and Sputendorf; General von Borstel, near Mittenwalde. The Swedish infantry occupied Potsdam, the cavalry bivouacked near Dahlen; and General von Tauenzien stood on the heights of Marienhof and Tempelhof, in front of Berlin. On the 21st, the French advanced in two columns upon Willmersdorf, and, at five o'clock in the evening, drove in the Prussian out-posts at Trebbin and Nunsdorf, taking up a position between Cliestow and Schubzendorf. By break of day on the 22d, the Crown Prince drew up his army in the following order of battle *(see Plan of the Battle of Gross-Beeren):* General von Bülow was posted near Saarmund. General von Tauenzien concentrated his corps near Blankenfelde. The Swedish army was posted at Ruhlsdorf. General Czernischeff occupied Belitz and Treuenbrietzen with his Cossacks. General von Hirschfeldt, by a forced march from the environs of Magdeburg, reached Potsdam early on the 22d. Towards noon, General von Bülow was attacked in his position, and forced back upon Heinersdorf, where he joined General von Tauenzien. The enemy having advanced to Jühnsdorf, General von Tauenzien pushed forward his corps to Blankenfelde. General von Borstel, still in position at Mittenwalde, was now ordered to form a junction with General von Bülow, in the direction of Brusendorf. Night put a stop to further operations. On the 23d, Marshal Oudinot commanded the 4th corps, under Bertrand, to advance and attack General von Tauenzien, who was immediately supported by the march of General von Bülow to the left towards Lichtenrade, to fall into line with General von Borstel near Mittenwalde. The impetuous and rapid attacks of Bertrand were repulsed at all points, and the bravery of the Prussians under Tauenzien foiled all his attempts to make any impression on their line. In the mean time, the 7th French corps, under General Reynier, had succeeded in forcing General von Bülow's detachment to evacuate Gross-Beeren; but this brave and sagacious general did not hesitate resolving to attack Reynier with his whole corps, and to drive his right wing out of Gross-Beeren. It was six o'clock in the evening, and an incessant rain had fallen the whole day. He formed the battalions in square masses, and with fixed bayonets moved onwards to carry the enemy's batteries by assault, and to close with their columns. In defiance of the showers of grape-shot, and heavy cannonade of the French, the undaunted Prussians bore down all before them: a most dreadful carnage ensued; Gross-Beeren was retaken; whole battalions of Frenchmen were bayonetted; batteries were stormed; and the cavalry, charging with equal impetuosity, effectually prevented the infantry of the enemy from rallying at any point. General von Bülow's conduct in this trying hour is above all praise: the Prussian name acquired fresh lustre under his dispositions, and the gallant band that fought with him are immortalized in the annals of Prussia *. It was only after his arrangements were made, and the men were pressing forward into action, that he received orders from the Crown Prince to attack. Prompt measures are ever the forerunner of success, and, when combined with prudence and steady perseverance, never fail to plant unfading laurels on the brows of the victors. General von Borstel, having penetrated through Klein-Beeren, and cannonaded the enemy's right flank, contributed not a little to the fortunate issue of this bloody conflict. In possession of Gross-Beeren, General von Bülow ordered the reserve, under General von Thümen, to come into line, and the cavalry to turn the enemy's right wing. The Swedish and Russian corps were drawn up, at this moment, in order of battle. General Count von Winzingerode was at the head of 10,000 horse. General Count von Woronzow commanded the Russian infantry. The village of Ruhlsdorf, but weakly occupied by

---

* Some of the Prussian battalions of infantry suffered an enormous, and almost incredible loss, very disproportionate to that of their allies ; but they were determined to conquer or die ; as for instance :

The Colberg regiment of infantry lost 26 officers, and 763 privates.

The 9th regiment of reserve, 10 officers, and 572 privates.

The 1st regiment of Neumarkt militia, 34 officers, and 551 privates.

the Swedes, to keep up a communication with Bülow's corps, was attacked by the enemy's sharp-
shooters; but the Crown Prince having ordered up
some reinforcements, the French were soon obliged to retire. Victory was, however, decided
principally by the rapid assault of the Prussians
under Bülow. The corps of Reynier was broken
and dispersed on all sides, and opened a chasm in
the French line of attack, which all the efforts of
Oudinot and Bertrand could not fill up. The retreat of the French was directed to Trebbin, and
the Cossacks harassed them without intermission.
Up to the 24th at noon, the trophies of the day
consisted of 26 pieces of artillery, 60 tumbrils, a
large quantity of stores and baggage, 40 officers,
and 1500 prisoners. The 25th was occupied in
pursuing the enemy to the Elbe; and a considerable number of prisoners fell into the hands of the
light troops. General von Bülow took up his
head-quarters on the 26th at Trebbin. The
Swedes marched to Saarmund, and the Russians
to Treuenbrietzen. Pending these events, the
French general Girard, with 10,000 men, of the
garrison of Magdeburgh, somewhat emboldened
by the absence of General Hirschfeldt, passed the
Elbe, and moved towards Berlin, by the way of
Ziesar. He was kept in check four days by the
Prussian general von Puttlitz, with some battalions
of militia; by which delay, Oudinot was already
defeated before Girard could reach him. On the

25th, General Girard made a vain attempt to dislodge the Cossacks under Czernischeff, out of
Belzig, and then took position near Lübnitz.
General von Hirschfeldt, after the battle of Gross-
Beeren, had marched with his corps back to Brandenburg, where he arrived on the 24th. Early in
the morning of the 27th, General von Hirschfeldt
reconnoitred the enemy's position at Lübnitz, and
immediately determined on an attack. The heights
were taken and retaken several times : the gallant
Prussians maintained themselves on them at last,
and Czernischeff, with his Cossacks, having come
into action from Belzig, the French were completely routed. General Girard was wounded, 8
pieces of cannon, 140 officers, 3500 prisoners, a
number of tumbrils, and all the baggage of the
enemy, fell into the hands of the victors. The
whole plan of Marshal Oudinot's operations was
in this manner rendered abortive. His intended
combinations were frustrated, and Napoleon's arrogant pride of omnipotence felt a severe abate-
ment.

General von Bülow entered Elsholz on the
27th; General von Tauenzien was posted at Baruth, and sent General von Wobeser, with his
division, to take the town of Luckau, where the
French had intrenched themselves. After a brisk
cannonade, the French commandant capitulated ;
and 9 pieces of artillery, and 1000 prisoners,
were the fruits of this enterprise. General von

Woronzow, at the head of the advanced-guard
of the Northern army, dislodged the enemy, after
an obstinate engagement, out of Jüterbock, which
they had again occupied on the 27th; and the
Crown Prince of Sweden thereupon removed his
head-quarters to Belitz. General von Bülow advanced to Treuenbrietzen, and took an advantageous position between that place and the village
of Nicheln. The head-quarters of the Northern
army were, on the 30th, at Buchholz, and on the
31st at Treuenbrietzen. On the 1st of September,
General von Bülow took post at Frohnsdorf, the
French rear-guard retreating to Thiesen. The
out-posts of General von Borstel occupied the defiles of Köppenig, and the brigade of Krafft
marched to the heights of Kropstädt : at the same
time, General von Tauenzien made himself master
of the high grounds in front of Zahne, keeping
up a communication with General von Borstel.
The remainder of von Bülow's corps took position
at Marzahne. The Russian corps drew up near
Pflighof. The French, who, from the side of
Coswig, endeavoured to penetrate their lines,
were repulsed with heavy loss by General Woronzow. On the 4th of September, the Crown Prince
of Sweden fixed his head-quarters at Rabenstein.
His Highness now directed the whole of his attention to the necessary preparations for crossing the
Elbe, by throwing over a bridge at Roslau, with

the corps of Swedes and Russians under his command, and to march to Leipsic.

Napoleon, obstinately bent upon having his favourite plan against Berlin put in execution, and but little dispirited by Marshal Oudinot's miscarriage, fancied that the failure of the first attempt proceeded from the want of good dispositions. He accordingly gave Marshal Ney the command of the 4th, 7th, and 12th corps, and the cavalry under the Duke of Padua; who, since their very recent defeat, had sought protection under the walls of Wittenburg, to collect and organize their remains. Marshal Ney joined his army on the 3d of September, and on the 4th he began those offensive operations that served as a prelude to the signal victory of Dennewitz.

In the afternoon of this day General Dobschutz was briskly attacked, by a superior force, near Zahne; but this General defended his position with such bravery and prudence, that the French, after many fruitless attempts to force him, were repulsed, and driven back into their intrenchments near Wittenburg. The whole of the 12th French corps renewed their attack on General Dobschutz, on the 5th, in the morning, and, after a bloody combat, and acts of heroic bravery on the side of the Prussians, they got possession of the position*.

---

* A young Prussian officer being taken prisoner in the early part of the action, he was conveyed in all haste to the rear,

Upon which, General von Tauenzien * was attacked at Seyda, dislodged by superior numbers, and the French occupied the post. The Crown Prince. of Sweden occupied, on the 6th, the heights of Lobessen. General von Bülow, upon

---

and brought, without any preparatory intimation whatever, into the presence of Napoleon, at Dahme; who, in his usual hurrying manner, first asked him questions, concerning his name, rank in the army, and the regiment to which he belonged, and then abruptly demanded:

" Where is Bernadotte?"

" I do not know such a person," answered the officer.

" Well, well; I mean the Prince of Ponte-Corvo."

" I know just as little about him."

" Bah! where is the Crown Prince of Sweden?"

" O! I know him very well:—he is—I do not know where he is exactly; but—he is every where, I believe——!"

Napoleon turned his back on the officer, with a furious frown, and dismissed him.

* General Tauenzien was with the Crown Prince of Sweden, on the 5th, at his head-quarters at Rabenstein, to be present at a conference held concerning the measures to be adopted. In the evening, on his return to his corps at Seyda, being unacquainted with the result of this affair, he struck into the wrong road, and soon found himself surrounded by parties of the enemy. Firmness and presence of mind saved him. On being challenged by the enemy's patroles, the General and his adjutants represented themselves as Saxon officers of the regiment of Prince Anthony, and were accordingly suffered to pass on unmolested; they happily reached the General's corps, which, together with the advanced-guard, under General von Dobschutz, had in the mean time made a retrograde movement to Jüterbock.

its being reported to him, that the French army
was in motion, in the direction of Zahne, with his
usual promptitude and decision determined on
falling upon the rear and left flank of the enemy's
army; and in consequence issued orders for his
troops to concentrate themselves, near Kurz-
Lippsdorf and Kaltenborn. *(See Plan of the Battle
of Dennewitz.)*—In the evening of the 5th, the
French corps were drawn up in the vicinity of
Naundorf, Seehausen, and Seyda. By break of
day, on the 6th, Marshal Ney began his operations. The 4th corps, under Bertrand, marched
by the way of Naundorf to Jüterbock; the
7th corps, under Reynier, to Rohrbeck; and
the 12th, under Oudinot, towards Oehna. As
a feint, the 4th corps was to turn Jüterbock,
to mask the march of the two others corps. The
enemy knew nothing of General von Bülow's
movement, he having ordered no watch-fires to be
lighted during the night. The division Morand,
forming the advanced-guard of Bertrand's corps,
fell with impetuosity on General von Tauenzien's
advanced-guard; but the moment the intentions
of the enemy were developed by this attack, General von Bülow put himself in march with his
corps, to attack the left flank of the French, re-
porting his intention to the Crown Prince, and
desiring General von Borstel might be sent, to
form his support. In the mean time, General von
Tauenzien bore the brunt of Bertrand's impetuous

attempts to force him from his position, and gallantly stood his ground. General von Bülow brought up in haste his artillery, and briskly cannonaded the enemy, to afford General von Tauenzien some advantage from his demonstration. An obstinate conflict, attended with various success, now took place, in the course of which General von Thümen's division stormed the village of Nieder-Gersdorf, and made a great slaughter of the enemy. For four hours the battle raged with indescribable fury. The enemy, driven from Nieder-Gersdorf, still made a most lively resistance. Marshal Ney had sent the 7th corps to support the hard-pressed 4th, and with it menaced Bülow's right flank. The great superiority of the enemy's force, particularly of artillery, obliged the divisions of Bülow's right wing to take up a more advantageous position in the rear; and although the reserves were evidently sufficient to preserve the position taken, yet the prospect of being able to act on the offensive was, at this juncture, very doubtful. In this important moment General von Borstel* arrived on the ground

---

* That this battle terminated so gloriously for the Prussian arms, and so disastrously to the French, may be attributed in part to the prompt support afforded to General Tauenzien's right wing by the bold movement of General von Borstel. This latter General was in line with the Swedish army till eleven o'clock A. M. on the 6th, when he received orders to march with his corps of Prussians to Eckmannsdorf; but having had

with his corps. This excellent General, by a forced march, and overlooking trivial formalities, has, by his vigorous conduct on this occasion, established his fame, and added another name to the list of Prussian worthies. By immediately storming the high grounds to the right of Gehlsdorf, at the head of his brigade, he broke the enemy's line, and paved the way to the glorious conclusion of the battle of Dennewitz. During these events, General Tauenzien kept firm in his position. A charge of French cavalry was repulsed with heavy loss, and driven upon their own infantry. General von Thümen's brigade forced the enemy upon Dennewitz, which, after an obstinate resistance, was taken by storm.

It was in this manner that the second Prussian corps of Bülow and Tauenzien, with the most rare intrepidity and exalted bravery, kept the

---

the precaution to send an adjutant forward to Lieutenant-general von Bülow for intelligence, he gained, at this crisis, the important information how necessary the presence of his corps was to support the right of General Tauenzien's position; and, giving way to the gallant feeling of succouring his brethren in arms, he changed his line of march to Gehlsdorf, sending a report of his movement to the right, to the Crown Prince, and, happily arriving on the ground at the most dubious period of the conflict, he drew up his troops to the right of General von Krafft's division; and, by an impetuous onset with the bayonet, took Gehlsdorf, and the heights near it, by storm, almost instantaneously; which bold and prompt attack materially contributed to the ultimate success of this brilliant day.

whole French army, 70,000 men strong, in check for several hours, withstood the shock of all their fierce onsets, repulsed their reiterated charges at the point of the bayonet, and placed the crown of victory on the brows of their adored Monarch so firmly, as never more to be wrested from him by any earthly power whatever.

The Crown Prince of Sweden, who, upon the first intelligence of General Tauenzien being attacked, had put himself in march from Lobessen to Eckmannsdorf, now came into action. Four thousand Swedish and Russian cavalry, with horse-artillery, attacked the French corps. At the sight of such numerous reinforcements Marshal Ney immediately beat a retreat, pursued by 70 battalions and 10,000 cavalry, of the Allies, that had not been in action. After the French were driven out of the woods near Dennewitz, their retreat was turned into a complete rout. The French 7th corps first gave way, and drew with it part of the 4th. Marshal Ney led on his reserves into fire, but a panic terror seemed to have seized the whole French army, and this General could not bring them to stand. The cavalry of the Confederates charged, with an impetuosity bordering on fury, the horse of the enemy, that covered their retreat, and broke it entirely. The fugitives rode over their own infantry ; the confusion became general, and each sought his individual safety in flight. The 4th corps, and the cavalry under Ney, retreated to Dahme, and the 7th and 12th took the road to Schweidnitz.

The loss of the French, in this battle, was immense. More than 10,000 prisoners, 80 pieces of cannon, 400 tumbrils, 3 pair of colours, and 1 standard, fell into the hands of the victors.

On the 7th General von Wobeser attacked Dahme, carried it, and made 2500 prisoners. The rest of the French corps fled towards Annaberg.

That heroic example, which the Prussians gave the world on this day, will be handed down to future ages, in the remembrance of every warrior, whose breast glows with the pure flame of patriotism; and will serve to animate, in after-times, all those whose sacred duties may call them to fight for the civic freedom and independence of Germany.

Marshal Ney, with the disorganized wrecks of his army, crossed the Elbe at Torgau, and fixed his head-quarters at Eilenburg, on the 9th; and his troops went into cantonments in Leipsic and its vicinity. Here he employed himself till the 25th, in recruiting and reinstating his shattered corps. The Crown Prince of Sweden, with the main body of the Northern army, moved down the right bank of the Elbe, towards Roslau, where he commanded considerable works to be thrown up, to serve as a tête de pont to a bridge, which he intended to throw across the Elbe at that place. A swarm of Cossacks was sent over

the Elbe, towards Dessau and Cöthen. General
von Bülow was posted before Wittenburg. The
advanced-guard of General Tauenzien occupied
Elsterwerda and Hoyerswerda. General Wobeser
stood at Falkenburg. The Russian light troops
blockaded Torgau. Detachments from the Northern army now scoured the country in all directions in the rear of the French grand army, with
constant success. General von Bülow bombarded
Wittenburg, in the night of the 25th. Marshal
Ney, having at this time recovered from his panic,
and foreseeing how pernicious the threatened
passage of the Northern army over the Elbe at
Roslau, might prove to the French grand army,
if it should experience any reverses, now made
demonstrations to attack the grand army of the
Crown Prince, and to destroy the bridge at Roslau; but he was repulsed in several partial affairs,
and the month of September ended very honour-
ably to the Swedish arms.

Quitting the Northern army for the present,
we will follow the operations of the Bohemian
army.

The grand Bohemian army, having derived every
advantage from its short breathing-time, soon
found itself in a renewed state of vigour, to enter
the lists again with Napoleon. Having received
reports that Napoleon was in motion towards Silesia, the advanced-guards passed the frontiers,
and the light cavalry, on the 5th and 6th, appeared

before Dresden. General Count von Wittgenstein arrived, on the 8th, at Dohna. Napoleon made a demonstration towards Bohemia, and General von Wittgenstein retired upon the grand army. On the 12th, Napoleon, with a considerable part of his army, was at Bärenstein. It was in vain that the Confederates waited for him with nearly 150,000 men, in the same position which had proved so fatal to Vandamme. Napoleon appeared irresolute, and drew in his advanced posts; the Allies followed step by step; and he returned to Dresden on the 13th, his army taking the following position towards Bohemia. Count Lobau was posted with the 1st corps at Nollendorf; Marshal St. Cyr occupied the heights of Borna, and the defiles of Fürstenwalde; Marshal Victor stood in position at Altenburg, with the 2d corps; and Marshal Mortier was in camp at Pirna, with the young guards.

It was deemed proper to reconnoitre the whole of the enemy's line on the 14th; and, for this purpose, several corps were pushed on in advance, who succeeded in obtaining some advantages. Napoleon, in judging that the Allies meditated a grand attack, left Dresden on the 15th, and advanced, with his whole disposable force, on the route to Bohemia. On the 17th, he reached Nollendorf; some partial affairs were favourable to the allied arms, and he was repulsed with loss, to the heights near that place. It not lying in the plan of operations laid down by the Confederates, to pursue Napoleon through the defiles of the Saxon mountains, he was permitted to retrace his steps to Dresden, where he arrived once more on the 21st of September, from his unfortunate expeditions into Bohemia. The proximity of Blücher's army urged him to leave it again on the 22d; and his return, on the 24th, was accompanied by no laurels, no arrogant bulletin, and no one mark proclaiming the presence of the conqueror of Europe, and " the first captain of the age *."

The affairs of the Confederates assumed, at this epoch, the beginning of October, the most favourable aspect at all points; and from their ulterior operations during this month, the most fortunate results might be with confidence expected.

---

* Early in the month of October, Napoleon held a council of war at Dresden, at which all his Marshals and Generals of Engineers in the field assisted. After some very unimportant matters had been discussed, he demanded their undisguised opinions on the state of things, the positions of the enemy, and the situation of his army.

They all unanimously gave him the advice to withdraw, with the grand body of his army, behind the barriers of the Rhine, to organize it anew, and then to face the Confederates in the field.

On hearing this, Napoleon started up in a rage, vowing that, if they had lost all confidence in him, they might of themselves seek their way back to France; but he should, for his part, find means, in despite of them, to crush the enemy himself.

A convention was signed, on the 8th of October, between Prince Reuss and General von Wrede, by virtue of which Bavaria made a common cause with the allied powers; and her powerful co-operation for the independence of Germany, might be daily expected. We hasten, in consequence, to give a detailed description of those military events which will ever render this month memorable in history, and endeavour to facilitate the perception of those stratocratic manœuvres, that have immortalized the name of Blücher and the august Allies, by stating the exact position of all the allied armies on the 1st of October, 1813.

The grand Bohemian army was still in its position near Töplitz; some detachments of its light troops had penetrated through the defiles of the mountains into Saxony. General von Bennigsen had arrived with his army, and taken post on the right wing.

The Silesian army occupied the right bank of the Elbe, from Stolpe to Elsterwerda, and had its advanced-posts close to Dresden. The headquarters were at Elsterwerda.

The Northern army observed the right bank of the Elbe, from Hertzberg to Zerbst, kept up a direct communication with the Silesian army, and detached light troops on the left bank of the Elbe.

The French army was in a manner surrounded and hedged in by these three armies. Napoleon was at Dresden with his guards, and the 1st,

3d, 5th, 11th, and the shattered remains of the 12th corps of his army. The 2d corps stood near Frelburg; the 8th, together with the cavalry, under Lefebvre-Desnouettes, near Penig and Altenburg; the cavalry of the Duke of Padua at Leipsic; and the 6th corps was on its march thither, where it arrived on the 2d of October. Marshal Ney was with the 4th and 7th corps, near Dessau; and Marshal Augereau, who had left Würzburg on the 26th of September, was on his march to Jena, having orders to join the grand army with the greatest celerity : his corps was estimated at 16,000 men.

It was easy to perceive that a simultaneous and combined operation, on the part of the allied armies, verging to one point, must very shortly produce a decisive blow.

At this important period, the whole of Europe felt within herself a shuddering fear, an anxious state of incertitude, that kept expectation wound up to the highest pitch, and set at nought the issues of cool reasoning and deliberate reflection. It was clear to the comprehension of every man, that a mighty conflict, at once decisive and destructive, must be approaching. The Teutonic nation, miserable and oppressed, disgraced in their honour, and humiliated in their name, longed for the hour of retribution, and consequent liberty, that they might return to the enjoyment of those happy times, when, blessed with independence, no foreign foe dared attempt to rob them of their birth-rights. The prior events of this campaign had caused a considerable agitation in the minds of the people in Germany. Patriotic zeal had bloomed afresh, and the ancient deadly hate towards the French had taken deeper root than ever: sources from whence that enthusiasm mainly sprung, which proved so disastrous, in its effects, to the fortunes of the cruel and unrelenting Despot on the plains of Leipsic.

The forces of the Confederates, by the arrival of General Bennigsen with the Polish-Russian army of 40,000 men, had been considerably augmented, and the plan of the Allies, of crossing the Elbe with their several armies in conjunction, could now be carried into execution.

Bennigsen could occupy Prince Schwartzenberg's position in Bohemia, and the latter march his army into Saxony in the direction of Leipsic, to form a junction with Blücher and the Crown Prince, who were to come from the right bank of the Elbe; and, by this combined manœuvre, converge the whole mass of their effective strength in the rear of the French army, and thus compel Napoleon to quit his strong position at Dresden, and constrain him to a general decisive battle.

A more daring promptness, vigour, and alacrity, in carrying on an operation with an army, than our bold, enterprising Hero showed, when effecting

his passage over the Elbe, were surely never exhibited in any former exploits of the like nature.

General von Blücher, at the head of the gallant
Silesian army, broke up from Elsterwerda and its
vicinity, on the 1st of October, and was the first to
commence offensive operations, by a sudden, rapid,
and unexpected march, that completely confounded
the enemy. After leaving the two corps of Generals
Count Bubna and Prince Czerbatow, before Dresden, he reached Herzberg on the 1st of October,
and Jessen on the 2d, with his whole army; and,
though clogged with the conveyance of two
bridges of pontoons, he marched with such astonishing rapidity, as to reach Elster, a village situated between Annaburgh and Wittenberg, near
the confluence of the river Elster with the
Elbe, on the evening of the 2d, and succeeded in
throwing two bridges of pontoons over the Elbe
the same night, in the face of the enemy; and
early in the morning of the 3d, the Silesian army
began to defile over them. (See *Plan of the Battle
of Dennewitz.)*—General Count Bertrand, who had
departed from Dessau in the night of the 1st of
October, had already taken up an almost impregnable position, with about 20,000 men, near Wartenberg, on the left bank of the Elbe. The corps
of General von York was the first to pass the
bridges, and they soon encountered the enemy,
who in vain endeavoured to prevent or obstruct
their deploying over. Prince Charles of Meck-

lenburg was detached, by General von Blücher, to
turn the enemy's right flank, in the direction of
Bleddin; during which operation, Blücher himself
attacked the front of the enemy's position. Prince
Charles had a warm affair, and the French retarded
his advance nearly two hours; but the village of
Bleddin was stormed, and the enemy driven from
his position.

At two o'clock, P. M. the Silesian army had gained a complete victory, although only von York's
corps had come into fire, the Russian troops having followed later, and been drawn up as reserve.
The enemy fled towards Kemberg and Wittenberg,
and was hotly pursued, sword in hand, at all points.
The trophies consisted of 11 pieces of artillery,
50 tumbrils, and above 1000 prisoners. In consequence of this fortunate combat, General von Blücher moved his head-quarters to Düben on the
5th of October *.

---

* Blücher received, soon after this victory, the following autograph letter from his Sovereign:

" General von Blücher,   *Töplitz, Oct.* 8, 1813.

     " The manner in which you have forced the passage
of the 1st corps d'armée over the Elbe, and the advantages you
have gained over the enemy near Wartenberg, have exalted
your fame still higher, and laid fresh claims to my thanks. In
expressing them to you, I add the wish that you may therein
find the greatest proof of my satisfaction, combined with my
intention of making them publicly known to you.
                         " FREDERICK WILLIAM."

No sooner had the news of this grand movement of Blücher's reached the head-quarters of the
Crown Prince of Sweden, than, with a readiness
that reflects upon him great honour, and solely
bent on a powerful and immediate co-operation,
he marched the whole Northern army, under his
command, over the Elbe at Roslau and Acken, on
the 4th and 5th of October. Several other corps
passed the Elbe at this period. General Count
Tauenzien marched to Halle. The Crown Prince
took up his head-quarters at Dessau, and pushing
forward his advanced-posts to Raguhn and Jesnitz,
opened a communication with Blücher's army;
and on the 7th, the Crown Prince and General von
Blücher formed a junction with Prince William of
Prussia, at Mühlbeck, on the Mulda. The joint
forces of the two armies, amounting to 125,000
men, had taken a firm footing on the left bank
of the Elbe. None but the most active measures
were now adopted. In the interim, Napoleon had
left Dresden, marched on the 9th to Eilenburg,
and on the 10th, to Düben; he seemed to have
the intention of attacking the Silesian army, and
to entertain hopes of meeting it singly in the field;
but our veteran General had foreseen his movements, and, in conjunction with the Crown Prince,
left his position on the Mulda, marched onwards,
and passed the Saale. The Silesian army marched
to Halle, and the Northern army to Rothenburg
and Bernburg. The Crown Prince ordered Gene-

rai von Tauenzien to proceed to Dessau, to observe the passage of the Mulda, to cover the bridge at Roslau, and, if necessary, to collect all the detachments on the right bank of the Elbe, and, according to circumstances, to cover the Marches of Brandenburg from the enemy. This corps concentrated itself at Dessau on the 10th of October, and the General pushed his advanced-posts to Oranienbaum and Wörlitz.

This bold march of the Silesian army astonished Napoleon; nay, it almost confounded him : he little expected such manœuvres, so well conceived, and a combination of movements, however complex in appearance, yet so simplified in their rapid execution. He found the two armies drawn up in battle array on the Saale, and wisely desisted from any attack.

Frustrated in his plan of fighting Blücher separately, Napoleon seems to have suddenly changed his line of operations, and to have intended making Magdeburg the centre of his ulterior enterprises. To follow out this plan, General Reynier was ordered to march to Wittenberg, and to act on the right bank of the Elbe ; and Marshal Ney was to proceed to Dessau, and occupy that place. These movements were executed on the 11th of October. General Count von Tauenzien, on the first report of these events, felt, very strongly, the possibility of his being attacked by superior numbers, and therefore determined to withdraw over the Elbe, to call in all detachments, and, in conjunction with General von Thümen before Wittenberg, take up a defensive position to cover Berlin. After some partial affairs with the enemy, the two Generals marched to Zerbst on the 12th, and from thence to Potsdam ; in the mean time, General Reynier, with the 7th corps, had only made a demonstration, and had returned to Wittenberg. This operation, however, of Napoleon, at the moment, induced the Crown Prince of Sweden to suppose that he had the intention of throwing himself towards Magdeburg, in the direction of Wittenberg, down the right bank of the Elbe; and to paralyze, as much as possible, the effects of this manœuvre, his Highness made his army repass the Saale, and march towards Cöthen. This was a very judicious step, and proclaimed the military talents and penetration of the Crown Prince in a very eminent degree, forming a striking contrast to those tardy, vacillating measures that, subsequently, in so unaccountable a manner, directed the operations of the Swedish army : for, if Napoleon really intended to reach Magdeburg by the way of Wittenberg, the Crown Prince could thus encounter him at Zerbst, and force him to give up his plan, or else to fight; in which case the Silesian army might act with success in Napoleon's rear. Early on the 14th, the 7th French corps was at Wittenberg ; the 3d, at Dessau ; the 6th, at Delitsch ; and the imperial guards at Dü-

4

ben. In direct opposition, however, to all these
seeming intentions of reaching Magdeburg, Napoleon, on this day, caused all his corps d'armée to
face about, and, by forced marches, to direct their
route to Leipsic, where he arrived at noon the same
day with his guards, taking up his quarters at
Reudnitz*, a short distance from that place. The
sound policy of this march is ever to be doubted,
and it will always remain a problem why Napoleon did not prefer the fine position behind the
Saale, so easily in his power to take, rather than, by

---

* On the 14th of October, Napoleon took up his head-quarters at the country-house of a banker of Leipsic, at Reudnitz,
near that place. The apartment he occupied was hung round
with a few excellent English prints, representing some of the
last melancholy scenes of the life of the unfortunate Lewis XVI.
The prints must have arrested his attention; and what an impression must they not have made upon him! what serious reflections must they not have created in his mind! The same
throne from which he had shaken half the governments of Europe to their foundations, was stained with the blood of him
who here, in the last moments of his sufferings, seemed to remind him how fleeting and evanescent is human greatness. No
blood, unjustly shed, filled *him* with remorse in the hour of
death, who was once beloved to enthusiasm by the same people
now groaning under Napoleon's iron sceptre.

To have observed the emotions of this gloomy man, when he
glanced his eye over these mementoes of fallen, degraded majesty, might, to many, have been invaluable; and it may be presumed that these faint resemblances of the departed victims of
popular fury made a deeper impression on the tyrant than the hosts
of vengeance-breathing adversaries that then surrounded him.

marching to Leipsic, suffer himself to be surrounded by the allied armies, and no choice left him
but to give battle whenever the Confederates
pleased. The Crown Prince marched his army to
Halle on the 15th, and General von Blücher advanced the same day, with the Silesian army, to
Skeuditz.

We will now turn our attention to the proceed-
ings of the grand Bohemian army, since the 1st
of October, that our readers may be prepared to
form a clear idea of that unequalled scene which
was preparing to be acted on the wide field of
carnage around the city of Leipsic.

The grand Bohemian army had put itself in motion in the beginning of October, and, in the direction of Commotau, proceeded in several heavy
columns to Saxony. Prince Schwartzenberg left
Töplitz on the 4th of October, and arrived at Marienburg on the 5th. The Emperor of Russia, the
Emperor of Austria, and the King of Prussia, likewise followed the route of the grand army. On
the 5th of October it occupied the following positions : the Austrian Field-marshal Crenneville was
posted, with the light troops, at Zweckau; General Meerveldt's corps at Marienburg; General Klenau's corps at Chemnitz ; the Russian and Prussian corps, under General Barclay de Tolly, and
the reserves under the Grand Duke Constantin,
stood likewise in position near Zweckau; General
von Bennigsen, and Count Colloredo, with their

several corps, reoccupied the positions of the
grand army near Töplitz. It being known that
Napoleon was still in Dresden with the major part
of his army, this precaution was indispensably
necessary to cover Bohemia from any irruption on
this side.

General Prince von Lichstenstein was ordered,
with a corps of light troops, to advance, by the
way of Eger, Hof, and Schleitz, and, in co-operation with General Thieleman, to retard the march
of Augereau's corps upon Leipsic.

Some partial engagements took place by the advance of the several corps during the 6th. General Count Wittgenstein marched with his corps,
on the 7th, to Altenburg; and General Klenau ordered General Mohr to occupy Penig, which, after
a smart action with the enemy, was taken possession of. The head-quarters of the Commander-in-
chief, Prince Schwartzenberg, were transferred to
Chemnitz on the 8th. The advanced-guard of
General Mohr drove the French from the heights
near Penig, and forced them to fall back upon
Rochlitz on the 9th. General Count Platow
scoured the country in the vicinity of Leipsic, and
endeavoured to open a communication with the
Crown Prince.

The offensive movements of the allied powers,
now undertaken on a scale bold, grand, and energetic, are not, perhaps, to be equalled by any military operations recorded in modern history. The

Confederates, by their execution, exposed their richest provinces to the inroads of the enemy, and, by attempting to throw themselves between Napoleon and France, left close in their rear an army of 200,000 men *, headed by an enterprising

* According to dispatches, which afterwards fell into the hands of the Confederates, it appears, from the Muster-master-general's return, that the French army, prior to the battle of Leipsic, consisted of the following corps and effective numbers:

	Men.
Old guards - - - - - - - - - - - - - - -	4,000
Young guards - - - - - - - - - , - - -	24,000
Cavalry of the guards - - - - - - - - -	6,000
1st Corps d'armée—Mouton-Lobau - ·· - - - -	6,000
2d - - - - - Victor - - - - - - -	18,000
3d - - - - - Ney - - - - - - - -	22,000
4th - - - - - Bertrand - - - - - - -	14,000
5th - - - - - Lauriston - - - - - -	10,000
6th - - - - - Marmont - - - - - -	20,000
7th - - - - - Reynier - - - - - - -	8,000
8th - - - - - Poniatowsky - - - - -	10,000
11th - - - - Macdonald - - - - - -	14,000
14th - - - - Gouvion St. Cyr - - - - -	20,000
- - - - - - Augereau - - - - - -	10,000
1st Division of cavalry—Latour-Maubourg - - - -	6,000
2d - - - - - - Sebastiani - - - - -	6,000
3d - - - - - - Padua - - - - - -	3,000
4th - - - - - - Valmy - - - - - - -	4,000
5th - - - - - - Milhaud - - - - - -	3,000
	208,000

The 1st and 14th corps remained in Dresden.

The

military genius, and a number of strong holds well garrisoned, while they themselves had no fortified place to serve them as a rallying point, or as a position to rest upon. But the superiority of numbers which the Allies now possessed, the glow of patriotism that pervaded the country into which they had entered, and an unbounded confidence in themselves, placed them out of all danger, as to the consequences, however exceptionable such measures might be, when judged by military rules. Napoleon, meanwhile, hastily left Dresden, with the King of Saxony, on the 7th, to prevent his being completely cut off; and arrived at Wurzen on the 8th, accompanied by the 3d, 5th, and 11th corps, and his guards. To mask, in some measure, his march, Marshal Macdonald, with a small corps, attacked General Bubna near Stolpen, but was repulsed with loss. On the 8th, General Bubna pursued his advantages, and stormed the tête de pont at Pirna.

On the 9th, the advanced-guards of the grand

The confederate army, at this period, has been estimated as follows :

		Men.
1. Grand army, under Schwartzenberg - - - -		140,000
2. Northern army, under the Crown Prince - - -		50,000
3. Silesian army, under Blücher - - - - - -		50,000
4. Russian-Polish army, under Bennigsen - - -		40,000
		280,000

Bohemian army drove back the enemy at different points, near Mittweyda and Walheim, and took a number of prisoners.

General Prince von Lichtenstein, in conjunction with General Thieleman, attacked Augereau on the 10th, near Naumburg; and, after an obstinate conflict, in which the French lost 1500 men, the Allies were, at last, obliged to yield to the superiority of numbers, and to retreat to Zeitz.

The advanced-guard of General Count Wittgenstein, under the command of General Count Pahlen, had a warm affair on the 10th with the cavalry of Marshal Murat. The latter made a vigorous resistance, but was, at the close of the affair, taken in flank, and obliged to fall back to the advantageous position of Eylau.

The grand Bohemian army, during these events, made progressive advances. Prince Schwartzenberg's head-quarters were removed to Altenburg on the 11th; General Count Wittgenstein and Lieutenant-general von Kleist were at Borna, and Count Bubna at Pillnitz. The general of artillery, Count von Giulay, marched, on the 12th, with his corps, to Weissenfels, surprised Naumburg on the night of the 12th, made a number of prisoners, and liberated 8 officers and 150 men, which the French had taken in the affair at Wethau on the 10th.

The advanced-guards of Generals Count Wittgenstein and Klenau were engaged in several warm

attacks on the 12th and 13th, repulsed the enemy,
and took from him 800 prisoners; pending which,
the grand confederate army advanced upon Leipsic, narrowing, at every step, its circle of operations.

It being held highly important, under the present circumstances, that the Commander-in-chief,
Prince Schwartzenberg, should know the exact
strength of the enemy, General Count Wittgenstein was ordered, on the 14th, in combination
with General Count Klenau, to reconnoitre the
enemy's positions. The French had evacuated
Gröbern and Gossa early in the morning, showing
themselves in great force on the heights of Wachau and Liebertwolkwitz. As soon as the advanced-guard, under General Count Pahlen, supported
by General Wittgenstein's cavalry, had penetrated
beyond Gröbern and Gossa, the Russian horse-
artillery cannonaded the enemy's masses of infantry with great effect; the allied infantry following, drawn up in echelons.

General Count Klenau directed his march to
Liebertwolkwitz; and, on finding the enemy had
thrown a considerable body of infantry into the
place, he stormed it at the head of the Archduke
Charles's regiment*. The enemy, in consequence,

---

* It seems very probable that Napoleon, on the 14th of
October, was taken by surprise through the offensive operations of the Confederates from the side of Liebertwolk-

drew up their cavalry, near 8000 strong, into a solid, compact body of great depth, supported by a numerous and heavy artillery, and were led to the charge by Marshal Murat in person *. The first lines of Count Pahlen's cavalry were obliged to give way to such superior numbers, and a furious and bloody conflict with cavalry ensued on

---

witz. He was at his bivouack, near the gallows, not far from Leipsic, when he ordered one of his adjutants to inquire of a Saxon officer, in what part of the country the terrain of the field of battle lay. The Saxon officer having given in his details, he was again asked to be very particular and exact in his description, as the Emperor was anxious for information on which he could depend.

---

* It is almost needless to observe, that much has already been before the public concerning the origin of Murat; but whether well-founded or otherwise, we will not determine; we shall content ourselves with stating that, from sources, the authenticity of which we have no reason to doubt, it has been ascertained that Murat is the son of a very rich landholder in Provence, and was sent by his father to Toulouse to study theology, being intended for the church. Young Murat, early and deeply imbued with an attachment to military studies, devoted the occasional leisure afforded him, during his residence in Toulouse, to the cultivation of the art of war. After regularly finishing his theological studies, he, it seems, entered, without his father's consent, as a common soldier, in the Ardenne rifle-corps. In the year 1792, we find him a Lieutenant in the constitutional guards of Louis XVI. which were soon after disbanded. And in 1793 he served in the army of the West as a violent republican, against the Royalists; from which period Fortune has been unusually lavish towards him in the distribution of her fickle favours,

the plains of Wachau.   The Russian horse, in
their usual brilliant style, charged the enemy on
all sides, and repulsed him.   The French cavalry
rallied four times, returning each time with redoubled fury to the charge; but the Prussian cuirassiers and dragoons, under General Klenau, with
conspicuous bravery resisted their impetuous attacks, repulsed them, and finally put them to the
rout.   Five hundred of the enemy lay dead on the
field of battle; and several hundred prisoners fell
into the hands of the victors.   General Count
Wittgenstein, having now gained certain information that the 2d, 5th, 8th, and Augereau's
corps, under the immediate command of Marshal
Murat, were in the field before him, ceased all
further attacks, and a heavy cannonade was now
kept up till night was far advanced.

Prince Schwartzenberg's head-quarters were
transferred to Pegau on the 15th of October, and
the Austrian army likewise advanced in the same
direction.

These positions of the respective armies rendered a battle inevitable; and it was resolved upon,
at the head-quarters of the Confederates, that the
general attack should be made on the morrow.—
(See Plan of the Battle of Leipsic, No. I.)

To present a faithful and striking picture of this
gigantic battle of nations, fought in the environs
of Leipsic, may be accounted the most difficult
task that ever was imposed upon a writer.   This

mighty conflict seeks in vain for its equal in history; its political consequences will extend through
remote ages; and all the dreadful evils that had
been engendered out of the detested French revolution, and the diffusion of Jacobin principles, during a period of twenty-five years, were, at one
blow, reduced to nothing.

CHAPTER IX.

*Victory near Möckern—Battle of Leipsic—Progress
of the Allies.*

Our veteran General, at the head of the Silesian
army, left his position near Skeuditz, early on the
16th, to attack the enemy posted at Möckern.
Marshal Marmont *, with the 6th corps, occupied

---

* During the first week in October, Marshal Marmont
had taken up his quarters at the country-seat of ——, at
Schönfeld, near Leipsic. The Serjeant, who one day commanded the guard before the house, had, by his insinuating address, gained the confidence of the steward left in charge of
the premises, to whom he appeared an amiable, well-informed
young man. In the course of a conversation with him, he gave
him to understand that his parents were people of substance in
Marseilles, and he was a student at the University, when the strict
enforcing of the conscription-laws had obliged him to march,
although his father had already paid for a substitute. He had
devoted his time, he said, to the arts and sciences ; but, like
many thousands of his countrymen, had been compelled at last to
make a campaign. " Ah, thus we are treated by our Emperor!
—thus we are driven to be slaughtered by his insatiable ambition !" he exclaimed in a tone of despair—" How often have I
not sustained hunger ! what privations and fatigue have I not
endured !" A long string of degrading epithets against Napoleon then followed with great volubility. The apparent frankness of his heart, and his youth, excited pity ; and he was kindly

the position of Möckern and Eutritsch, having strong detachments at Lindenthal and Radefeld. Marshal Ney, with the 3d corps, had stood on the right wing of the 6th corps as a support; but observing, at ten o'clock, A. M. that no enemy appeared on this side, he had marched his corps off the ground in the direction of Cönnewitz. General von York advanced on the road from Skeuditz to Leipsic, and General Langeron took the route of Landsberg to the same place; General von Sacken followed with the reserves. On Ge-

---

treated with wine and a hearty meal by the good-natured, unsuspecting steward.

The next morning early, the Marshal left the house with his suite. Soon after, the whole of the poultry was missed from the yard; not a hen was left. In the course of the day, the Marshal happened to return, with his troops, to the neighbourhood, and sent one of his adjutants to bespeak a good dinner at his old quarters. The robbery was immediately pleaded as an excuse for the impossibility of serving the table with poultry to the French taste. Marshal Marmont seemed much exasperated that such delicacies should have escaped him, and ordered the guard of the day before to be searched, when, lo! seven of the purloined cocks and hens were found, without their heads, in the possession of this young student of the arts and sciences. He received a sound flogging; and was placed at the gate, with a sentinel over him, for three hours, exposed to the taunts and bitter jokes of his comrades.

If every criminal and act of this kind in the French army. had received such a punishment, that, and the whole army of the Confederates together, had hardly furnished sentinels in sufficient number.

neral Langeron approaching Radefeld, he fell in
with the enemy at Freyroda; and after a sharp
engagement drove them out of both places, continuing his march to Gross-Wetteritsch, by the
way of Breitenfeld. General von York pushed
forwards his light troops, close to the river Elster,
and dislodged the enemy, after a feeble resistance,
from the villages of Stameln and Wahren; during
which, General von York marched, with the main
body of his corps, to Lindenthal, carried the village, and drove the enemy towards Leipsic. Between Eutritsch and Möckern, General von York
encountered Marmont's army, drawn up in order
of battle. General von Blücher ordered an immediate attack, about two o'clock, p. m.; and a warm
contest ensued. Marshal Marmont supported his
infantry by a battery of forty pieces of artillery,
and General von York's whole corps came into fire;
pending which, General Langeron, upon the left
wing, had taken, lost, and retaken, alternately, the
villages of Gross and Klein Wetteritsch, and Marshal Ney had advanced again in support. The
combat having continued for some time with dubious fortune, General von Blücher caused the reserves under General von Sacken to come into
line; but before they could arrive on the ground,
the two gallant corps already engaged had decided
the day. The enemy were completely beaten near
Möckern, driven out of this village, and compelled to quit every point of their position; the

allied cavalry broke into their masses of infantry, and sorely pressed them as far as Eutritsch and Gorlis, when night put an end to the pursuit. Marshal Ney had arrived as support, but came too late to renew the battle with any prospect of success; and, as General Langeron pushed on with vigour from Wetteritsch, Marshals Ney and Marmont caused their two corps to cross the river Partha at Schönfeld, leaving the villages of Gohlis, Eutritsch, and Mockau but weakly occupied, and taking up their head-quarters at the manor-house of Schönfeld. The Duke of Padua and General Dombrowsky had withdrawn their corps to Pfaffendorf, and a part of their troops occupied the suburbs of Leipsic. The trophies that fell into the hands of the dauntless Silesian army on this day, consisted of 1 eagle, 2 standards, 43 pieces of cannon, 30 tumbrils, and above 2000 prisoners. It was at a critical moment of this battle that the brave General von York put himself at the head of his cavalry, and rushing, with the overwhelming force of an imprisoned flood, upon the enemy's battery, charged and carried it, taking thirty pieces of artillery, with all their appendages, in the space of a few minutes. The invincible courage and intrepidity of the Prussian cavalry were never more eminently displayed than on this day. The conflict was murderous in the extreme; but the advantages, so dearly purchased, paved the way to that victory of victories which afterwards crowned the allied arms on the plains of Leipsic. General von Blücher's head-quarters were, on the 17th, at Lindenthal, near Breitenfeld; General Langeron made a movement with his corps towards the right wing of the enemy, drawn up in the rear of Eutritsch. There being every reason to suppose that the Silesian army, in having so closely pressed upon the enemy's line, would be attacked in the course of this day by the united strength of Marmont's and Ney's corps, aided by reinforcements, the Crown Prince of Sweden was urged to hasten his march from Landsberg to Breitenfeld, to serve as a support. The Northern army, in consequence, formed a junction with the left wing of the Silesian army, late in the evening of the 17th *. Lieutenant-general Wassiltschikoff,

---

* The Northern army, under the command of the Crown Prince of Sweden, had marched, in the morning of the 17th, from its position near Landsberg, and bivouacked at noon on the heights of Breitenfeld. It was pretty generally known at head-quarters, that, when the Confederates resolved to renew the attack on the positions of Napoleon, near Leipsic, on the 18th, the Crown Prince of Sweden was adverse to the measure, and started many difficulties and objections. On this coming to the ears of our veteran General von Blücher, feeling anxious for the events of the day, he determined to talk to the Prince himself, and therefore entreated Prince William of Prussia to accompany him to the Crown Prince, as he spoke no French, and understood the language but imperfectly. Accordingly, very early in the morning of the 18th, they proceeded to His Royal Highness's head-quarters, at Breitenfeld.

Upon

with a body of Cossacks and four regiments of
cavalry, menaced the enemy's line between Eutritsch and Schönfeld; a heavy cannonade ensued;

Upon Prince William's opening the object of their visit, men-
tioning that the attack must at all events take place, and General Blücher's wish for his powerful and decisive co-operation;
the Crown Prince, in a hurried and hasty tone, exclaimed:
" *Do but consider that you have to act against the ferocious
untameable spirit of a tiger! Reflect, that it is with Napoleon
you enter the lists, who has never as yet lost a battle!*"

Our veteran eagerly inquired what the Prince said, and, on
being informed, replied in his usual firm manner:—" *Tell His
Highness I shall attack the enemy wherever I find him, this
morning, and shall beat him too; let who will support me. Delay is all we have to fear. Indecision can alone undo us.*"

The Crown Prince, however, still continued to state and
repeat his difficulties and doubts: upon which Prince William
of Prussia declared, in the name of the Allies, " *That although they could not prevent His Highness from adopting those
measures which he might judge most favourable to the issue of the
campaign; yet, as the general attack was determined upon, they
should, on his refusal to co-operate in this momentous hour, be
obliged to leave His Highness no other troops to command than
his own Swedes.*"

Hereupon the Crown Prince, with much warmth, replied:—
" *What is it you mean? How am I to construe this language?
Napoleon himself never dared to utter such abrupt remarks towards me, as Marshal of France, which your Highness now thinks
proper to make to me, as Crown Prince of Sweden.*"

Blücher, on these observations being explained to him, rejoined, with evident irritation and impatience:—" *If His Highness is afraid—if he does not think himself strong enough, I'll let
him have Langeron's corps* (which he actually did); *but by G—
I shall make a greater impression on the foe, with my handful*

and the French having drawn up their cavalry
on their right wing, they were instantly charged
sword in hand, and driven with irresistible impetuosity into the rear of their own infantry, from
whence they fled as far as the suburbs of Leipsic.
Here they were overtaken, the major part of them
cut in pieces, and the rest made prisoners. The
enemy's masses of infantry remained immoveable,
during this brilliant and bold attack in their rear,
and only kept up an irregular cannonade. The
Prussian hussars brought back their prisoners and
five pieces of artillery, in safety, to the main body,
though galled in their retreat by a heavy fire of
musketry. The enemy then made a retrograde
movement behind the Partha, drawing themselves
closer round the city of Leipsic. Thus even the
events of the 17th proved glorious to the Silesian
army. We will now revert to the operations of
the grand army of the Confederates since the 15th.

The Commander-in-chief, Prince Schwartzenberg, issued, on the 15th of October, the following order of the day to his troops, from his head-
quarters at Pegau :

---

of men, than the Prince, as I see, will with his tens of thousands.
Procrastination will play the devil with us. Here, I observe, we
may lose time. Let us be gone." As Blücher spoke these last
words, the cannonade of the Bohemian army was distinctly
heard. The Crown Prince did attack, but his artillery was, by
his tardy movements, still too much in the rear to be up in
time.

Related to the editor by Baron von K—n.

" Brave warriors! The most important epoch of this sacred struggle is arrived. The decisive hour is striking: prepare for the fight! That tie which binds puissant nations together for one and the same object, will be drawn closer on the field of battle. Russians! Prussians! Austrians! you combat for the same cause, you combat for the liberty of Europe, for the independence of your country, for the honour and immortality of your name.

" One for all! All for one! Let this be your rallying cry, when rushing to battle. Be faithful to it in the decisive moment, and victory is yours.

" CHARLES,
Prince of Schwartzenberg,
Field-marshal."

This energetic appeal could not fail of exciting the greatest enthusiasm in the army, which eventually gave victory to the allied arms, and liberty and independence to the Teutonic nation.

On the morning of the 16th, the confederate army took up the following positions: *(See Plan of the Battle of Leipsic, No. I.)*

The 3d Austrian corps, under the command of General Count Giulay, was posted on the left bank of the Elster, near Klein-Zschocher, and had orders to attack the 4th French corps, stationed near Lindenau.

The 2d Austrian corps, under the command of General Count Meerveldt, was placed on the left bank of the Pleisse, having orders to force the passage of this river, in the rear of the enemy's right wing.

The Austrian reserves, under the command of the Hereditary Prince of Hesse-Homburg, were drawn up between the Pleisse and the Elster, near Zobigker and Prödel.

The Russian corps d'armée under the command of General Count von Wittgenstein, in conjunction with the first Prussian corps, under General von Kleist, took a position in the direction of Gröbern, Gossa, and Störmthal. The left wing of this combined corps was posted in the rear of the village of Gröbern, under the immediate orders of General von Kleist. Two divisions formed the centre, posted behind Gossa; and two divisions of Russian grenadiers, under General von Rajewsky, were drawn up as reserves in their rear.

The 4th Austrian corps, under the command of General Count Klenau, with a brigade of Prussians, under General von Ziethen, formed the right wing, and occupied Gross-Pössna. Those fine corps of Russian and Prussian guards, both foot and horse, with three divisions of Russian cuirassiers, formed the reserves of the whole grand army, and were drawn up near Magdeborn; the cavalry under the Grand Duke Constantin, and the infantry under the orders of General Count Miloradowitsch.

The whole of the Russian and Prussian troops

were commanded by the General-in-chief Count Barclay de Tolly.

The troops were all under arms at six o'clock in the morning, and the attack commenced at eight.

Lieutenant-general Count Kleist made the first movement, by advancing by Gröbern and Croste-witz towards Markkleeberg, opening upon the enemy a smart cannonade, and brisk fire of sharp-shooters. They were soon dislodged from the village, and, in spite of repeated attacks, he continued to maintain himself in it throughout the day. At the same time, the corps of the Prince of Würtemberg moved upon Wachau, attacked the village and the wood near it, carried them both, and forced the enemy to retire. The Prince of Gorczakow advanced from Störmthal upon Liebertwolkwitz, but arrived later on account of the distance. The right wing, under Count Klenau, marched by the way of Gross-Pössna, and took post upon the heights to the right of this village, menacing, by this movement, the flank of the enemy's position at Liebertwolkwitz.

The 2d corps of Austrians, posted on the extremity of the left wing of the grand army, commenced likewise the attack, by opening a lively fire of riflemen, from the low woods on the left bank of the Pleisse; but the ground presented so many insurmountable obstacles to the bringing up of artillery, that the plan conceived by the

Field-marshal Prince of Schwartzenberg, could not be promptly executed.

Napoleon was not wanting in making his dispositions, on the first approach of the confederate columns. The whole of the 8th corps, under Prince Poniatowsky, received orders to defend the village of Dosen, and the passages of the Pleisse, from Cönnewitz to Markkleeberg. Marshal Victor, with the 2d corps, defended Wachau; and General Lauriston, with the 5th corps, the little town of Liebertwolkwitz. The whole of his guards were marched from Reudnitz to Probstheide, forming the reserves of his army. The 11th corps, commanded by Marshal Macdonald, advanced from Stötteritz towards Holzhausen.

The cannonade and fire of musketry continued with unabated fury, on both sides, from ten o'clock till near eleven. At this period Marshal Macdonald showed himself in advance before Holzhausen, and, in conjunction with General Lauriston, succeeded in forcing General Count Klenau to evacuate the position he had occupied; two divisions of the young French guards, under Marshal Mortier, having been detached by Napoleon to serve as supports.

Count Klenau took up a fresh position between Gross-Pössna and Seifertshayn, and ordered a succession of attacks to be made on the wood occupied by the enemy: these posts were taken and

retaken several times, with variable success; and
on this wing the issue of the combat remained undecided, as, towards the evening, both parties had
kept their positions. An attack of cavalry, under
General Sebastiani, who, by dint of superior
numbers, had forced the Austrian horse to retire,
was repulsed by two regiments of Prussian cuirassiers, with their wonted bravery and dauntless
intrepidity.

On the side of Wachau too, the enemy, aided
by fresh troops, began to press forward about
eleven o'clock. Napoleon had sent Marshal Oudinot, with the two other divisions of his guards,
to this important point, as support for Marshal
Victor, together with General Drouet, with
the whole of his reserve artillery. These considerable reinforcements rendered it necessary
for the Prince of Würtemberg to order a retrograde movement, his flank being thereby menaced; but he made a lively and obstinate resistance; and as General von Kleist had kept his
position near Markkleeberg, he was promptly supported, some fortunate attacks held the enemy
in check, and five pieces of artillery were taken
from him.

Perceiving the advantages which the enemy
had, in some measure, gained at this point, General Barclay de Tolly detached General von Rajewsky, with two divisions of grenadiers, and the
third division of Russian cuirassiers, to the sup-

port of the Prince of Würtemberg. The attack of the cuirassiers proved unsuccessful, but the brave grenadiers stood their ground against the enemy with firmness, and the efforts of Napoleon to follow up his temporary successes proved ineffectual.

As soon as Prince Schwartzenberg was apprised that Napoleon was throwing the whole of his reserves upon Wachau and Liebertwolkwitz, and was straining every nerve to break through at these points, he immediately ordered up into line the whole of the Austrian reserves, under Prince von Hessen-Homburg, that were posted at Zöbigker. At the moment that the head of the Austrian reserve cavalry, under General Count Nostitz, was debouching in advance of Gröbern (about one o'clock, P. M.), the French dragoon guards and Polish cavalry, under General Letort, had already penetrated to the vicinity of Gröbern, and many of their battalions of infantry, drawn up in square masses, were following in close order. General Count Nostitz, with inimitable promptitude, charged the enemy's cavalry, at the head of three regiments of Austrian cuirassiers, broke and dispersed them on all sides, cutting in pieces several squares of the French guards, or putting them entirely to the rout. The division of Bianchi had debouched out of Gröbern, in following the cavalry, and now advanced to Markkleeberg, where they relieved the troops under General von Kleist.

General Bianchi cannonaded the flank of the enemy's advance, towards Wachau, repulsed them with heavy loss, and took eight pieces of cannon.

The enemy, on finding all his attempts to gain ground, at this point, frustrated, now turned into a new path of operations, by repeating his attacks upon the corps of the Prince of Würtemberg; for which purpose the corps of cavalry under General Latour-Maubourg, headed by Marshal Murat, was brought into action. The French infantry was much superior in number to that of the Russians, and there were only ten squadrons of their light cavalry on the spot. The enemy, favoured in part by the terrain, advanced to the charge with impetuosity, and were actually on the point of breaking through the centre of the confederate army, and cutting it off from the right wing, when the Emperor Alexander, ever at the post of danger, ordered, at this decisive moment, the regiment of Cossack-guards to charge the enemy. That charge was irresistible, the French horse were broken and dispersed, and 24 pieces of artillery, out of 26, lost but a few minutes before, were retaken.

Animated by these transient successes, the enemy's columns again pressed onwards to the left of Wachau; but the Russian grenadiers fought with unshaken resolution, vigorously repulsed every attack, and at last drove the enemy from off the field, at the point of the bayonet.

Towards three o'clock, P. M. the whole of the

Austrian reserves had arrived at the different points assigned them, and the Russian and Prussian reserves, posted at Magdeborn, were drawn nearer. Prince Schwartzenberg now ordered a general movement to take place in advance, to put himself in absolute possession of the glacis of Wachau. The Russian guards and the division of Austrian grenadiers, under General Weissenwolf, were posted in the centre, to serve as supports wherever they might prove necessary, during this renewed attack. In the mean time, Napoleon was not remiss in reassembling his troops. He concentrated his cavalry at Liebert-wolkwitz, and occupied the heights in front of Gossa, on which he planted a numerous artillery. Towards five o'clock, some strong columns of the enemy's infantry attempted to take this village by assault; they had already entered it, but the Prussian brigade under General von Pirch, drove them out again. The enemy continued to form fresh columns of attack, and advanced once more with fury to the assault. In the mean time, Lieutenant-general Jermoloff, at the head of the Russian foot-guards, had advanced to support the position, and the artillery belonging to the Russian and Prussian guards, were placed on an eminence, to the left of Gossa. Their fire was tremendous, and produced the greatest effects; the enemy lost an enormous number of men, were repulsed, and driven into their first position, while the Allies gallantly maintained themselves at all points in and near Gossa. At the termination of this bloody conflict, the night was far advanced. Although the desperate and sanguinary charge of Murat had not been unsuccessful, and he actually did, in some measure, succeed in breaking the centre of the confederate army, yet it effected no material change in favour of Napoleon's positions, and the Allies could with confidence feel that no diminution of their relative strength was the result.

We have already observed, that General Count Meerveldt, on the extreme left wing, had encountered almost insurmountable difficulties, in executing his orders of forcing the Pleisse, with the intention of turning the enemy. An attack in the front of Cönnewitz was rendered impossible, by the enemy having broken down the bridges, and well lined the dams with infantry and artillery. Several attempts to pass the river, at Dölitz and Lössnig, had proved unsuccessful. Towards the evening, General Meerveldt succeeded in forcing a passage at the head of a battalion; but, being attacked by a great superiority of numbers, was obliged to fall back. On this occasion, General von Meerveldt was unfortunately taken prisoner, his horse being shot under him, and himself slightly wounded*. Thus ended the battle

---

* The Count was immediately hurried, though wounded and bleeding, into the presence of Napoleon. A series of abrupt

of the 16th, on the right banks of the Elster and
Pleisse. Pending these events, the corps under
the command of General Count Giulay, posted
on the left bank of the former river, did not remain inactive. General Bertrand's corps had
taken a position in front of Lindenau and Plagwitz. He was, however, so vigorously attacked by
General Giulay, that he was obliged, at one, P. M.
to evacuate Plagwitz, and soon after Lindenau,
leaving two pieces of cannon in the hands of the
victors. Bertrand retreated behind the Kuhthurm,
drawing up his infantry in squares, and keeping
a brisk cannonade on the advance of General
Giulay's corps, that now occupied the left bank
of the Luppe, near Lindenau. Napoleon having
sent strong reinforcements of cavalry, from the
side of Leipsic, General Bertrand again moved
onwards, and, after suffering a very heavy loss
of men, carried the village of Lindenau*. Ge-

---

questions opened the conference. Under the pretence of commiserating the Count's situation, Napoleon liberated him on
his word of honour, but likewise commissioned him to make
splendid proposals for an armistice to the allied powers. The
principal conditions were:

    1. An uninterrupted retreat for his army over the Saale.

    2. The evacuation of all the fortresses on the line of the
Vistula and the Oder.

    3. And then to negotiate for a peace.

---

    * At this period of the battle, Napoleon sent off a courier to
the King of Saxony, at Leipsic, with a note, written by himself, containing the following words:

neral Giulay then took up his old ground, near
Klein-Zschocher.

Such were the results of all those bloody combats that marked a circle of many miles in circum-

---

" *Nous avons du succes ; on m'attaque du côté de Lindenau,*
mais on se cassera le nez.
                                    " NAPOLEON."

The courier, who was nothing less than a German Prince,
much attached to Buonaparte, made many additions to the
contents, during his audience of the King, so as almost to persuade His Majesty that victory was certain. The Duke of
Bassano, who had accompanied the King from Dresden, was at
this period continually with him, on pretence of imparting the
most auspicious news of the battle; but, after the retreat of the
French army was in some measure arranged, his visits were
discontinued, with excuses of ill health, and great fatigue.

On the morning of the 19th, the King sent Colonel Ryssel
to the Emperor of Russia, with the offer of a capitulation, to
save the city, *at a time too,* when the Duke of Padua demanded
of the magistrates, with imperious threats, a hellish requisition
of fifteen cwt. of pitch and tar, that he might set the suburbs on
fire with greater celerity: had this been done, the conflagration
would have been ascribed to the Confederates; but this base act
of perfidy was prevented from perpetration, by the firmness of
the magistrates, in refusing the delivery.

The Crown Prince of Sweden paid the King a visit, soon
after he entered Leipsic, and a long, and, to appearance, very
friendly conference, was interrupted by the report that the
Emperor Alexander was riding towards the King's quarters.
The Emperor did alight in the square opposite, and the Crown
Prince, after the exchange of a few compliments, proceeded to
his hotel. On the same evening, the Emperor Alexander had
an hour's conversation with the Queen of Saxony alone, in her
own apartment. The next morning the King returned the

ference, and of which Leipsic may be said to have formed the centre. It cannot be affirmed that they were altogether so favourable, or so decisive for the allied arms, as the hopes of the most sanguine might suggest; yet Napoleon could by no means boast of a victory in any shape, although it must be confessed that the French troops fought, on this day, with singular bravery. Those momentary advantages, acquired by their courage, were however productive of no important consequences; for they did but lose again, in a few moments afterwards, what they had obtained by a horrible and inconceivable prodigality and wanton waste of human blood *. The heart of man

---

Crown Prince's visit, but had no conference whatever with the other three Potentates, having only written a few lines to the Emperor of Austria, at Rotha. The King of Prussia, on the following day, caused His Majesty to be informed, he might choose any place of residence, more agreeable to himself, than either Leipsic or Dresden could possibly be.

---

* We may venture to state, from the authority of many officers, who have been eye-witnesses to the fact, that Napoleon, at all times after a battle, showed considerable asperity and ill-humour, whenever a regiment filed off before him, that had been in fire, and lost but few men. He would scarcely deign to look at it, or speak a word to the commanding officer; even though the regiment had been posted where it had had no opportunity to distinguish itself. If a regiment, on the other hand, had lost half its complement of men, he was instantly in good-humour, did justice to the merit of the officers, and particularized them by name, even as low as captains. But, when

must ever shudder at the recollection. The right
wing of Napoleon's army had lost the important
terrain of Markkleeberg. The centre of the confederate army had remained in possession of the
position it had taken at the commencement of
the battle. Marshal Marmont had also been
completely beaten. Consequently, the Allies
might boldly appropriate to themselves the palm
of victory, and calmly leave the question to posterity, how far Napoleon could be justified in vain-
gloriously boasting to the world, that he had
wrested it out of their hands, at a time when the
battle was not even ended, much less decided.

The Crown Prince of Sweden, on finding that
the movement of General Reynier towards Wittenberg had only turned out a simple demonstration, filed off his army from Halle to Landsberg.
General Count Bennigsen, having left a considerable corps, under the orders of General Tolstoy,
before Dresden, had put himself in march to join
the grand confederate army, and was to arrive, on
the 16th, at Colditz. General Colloredo, who
had marched for the same purpose, in the direc-

---

he saw the remains of a regiment, returning out of battle, not
exceeding the strength of a company, his transports seemed
without bounds. He would graciously condescend to speak to
some of the privates personally, generally ending with these
expressions : " *You are now worthy of me! Your regiment has
experienced an enviable fate, which every brave soldier must wish
for !*"

tion of Freyberg and Chemnitz, could only reach
Borna.

The grand army of the Confederates, in expectation of a general attack from the side of the
French, was drawn up in order of battle, by break
of day on the 17th.   The out-posts were, in many
places, only a musket-shot's distance from each
other.   On the heights in front of Gossa, the
enemy had formed large masses of infantry ; and,
in the vicinity of Liebertwolkwitz, a long line of
cavalry presented itself.   After some useless demonstrations, by marching and counter-marching
his troops, Napoleon still showed but little inclination to attack at any point.   Prince Schwartzenberg, being willing to wait the arrival of Generals Bennigsen and Colloredo in the line of
operations, likewise, on his part, deferred the
attack.

A grand council of war, at which Prince
Schwartzenberg presided, was held in the afternoon, at the village of Sestowitz.   It being reported that General Bennigsen could not reach
Naundorf before the evening; that General Count
Colloredo was in march from Borna ; and that the
arrival of the Crown Prince of Sweden, to support
General von Blücher, was still uncertain ; it was
unanimously resolved to defer the attack until the
18th; it being taken into consideration that, on
the morrow, the army of the Allies would be reinforced by nearly 100,000 men, and thereby ensure

with greater certainty the most brilliant results.
The power of acting on the offensive had at least
undergone no material alteration since the 15th;
and a wise General could, without fear, adopt, for
the present emergency, the reverse of that policy
which might then have been thought advisable.

General Bennigsen effected his junction with
the allied forces, at Naundorf, in the evening;
and General Colloredo took up a position near
Gröbern, at about four o'clock in the afternoon.
The Crown Prince of Sweden quitted Landsberg
at two o'clock, A. M. on the 17th, and encamped
with his whole army at Breitenfeld. General
Winzingerode occupied Taucha.

In this manner Napoleon permitted the 17th of
October to pass away in a state of inaction, that
proved to him an irreparable loss of time. His
motives appear the more inconceivable, as it may
be presumed that he could not be ignorant of the
approaching accession of strength which the Allies
were on the point of receiving, and which, when
once united, must eventually annihilate his army,
already half beaten. It is equally beyond conception, why this great captain did not occupy the
line of the Saale, on the 17th and 18th, when no
obstruction whatever lay in his way.

The reinforcements which the Confederates had
received, and the menacing attitude of their position, which threatened a vigorous attack on all

sides, in the course of the following day, acted as powerful inducements for Napoleon to narrow the vast circle of terrain which his army occupied on the 16th and 17th, and indirectly forced him to take up a more concentrated position. He, in consequence, caused all the advanced corps to fall back in the night of the 17th, and, early in the morning of the 18th, posted his army as follows · (*See Plan of the Battle of Leipsic, No. II.*)

The 8th, 2d, and 5th corps, under the special orders of Murat, took post near Cönnewitz; the right wing being commanded by Prince Poniatowsky; the centre, at Probstheide, under Marshal Victor; and the left wing, under General Lauriston, near Stötteritz. Several detachments were placed in advance of the line, occupying the villages of Dölitz, Dösen, and Zuckelhausen, and the shepherd's house at Meysdorf. Marshal Macdonald took up a position, with the 11th corps, near Holzhausen, keeping up a communication with the left wing of the army under Ney. The guards were drawn up in solid square masses, on the Thonberg, near the tobacco-mill, where Napoleon remained a great part of the day. The old guards formed four columns, ready to advance upon any four points that might be threatened. Marshal Oudinot was afterwards ordered to support Prince Poniatowsky with two divisions of the young guards, and Marshal Mortier was charged by Napoleon to guard the passes to Leipsic.

The allied army was under arms by break of day, occupying nearly their former positions, except that, on the right wing, the advanced-guard of the corps under General Bennigsen had taken post at Seyfartshayn.

As soon as it was reported to Prince Schwartzenberg, that the enemy had filed off from Wachau and Liebertwolkwitz, he immediately caused the necessary dispositions to be made for a vigorous assault. The whole of the grand army of the Confederates, under his command, was divided into three separate columns. The first column, under the command of General Count Bennigsen, was composed of his own corps, that of General Count Klenau, and the brigade of von Ziethen, and received orders to proceed from Seyfartshayn and Gross-Pössna, in the direction of Holzhausen. The second column, under the command of General Barclay de Tolly, was formed of the corps of General Count Wittgenstein and Lieutenant-general von Kleist, having for reserves all the Russian and Prussian guards, and being destined to advance against the heights of Wachau. The third column, under the orders of General Prince von Hessen-Homburg, was composed of the divisions of Bianchi, Prince Aloys Lichtenstein, Count Weissenwolf, and the reserve cavalry, under General Count Nostitz; the corps of Count Collo-

redo forming its reserve. The division Lederer,
from the 2d Austrian corps, remained on the left
bank of the Pleisse, opposite Cönnewitz, as the
third column advanced upon Dösen and Dolitz.
(See Plan of the Battle of Leipsic, No. II.)

The first column, subdivided into three divisions, began to advance at about eight o'clock,
A. M. The corps of Russians, and the Austrian
division under Bubna, filed off in the direction of
Zweinauendorf, by which movement Macdonald's
corps was out-flanked, and forced to retire to Stötteritz. General von Bennigsen, meeting with
mere detachments to oppose his progress, advanced rapidly, and drove the enemy back to Mölkau.
The 4th Austrian corps, under General Klenau,
marched upon Holzhausen, and carried the village
after a warm action. General von Ziethen's brigade, destined to keep up the communication between the corps of Bennigsen and Klenau, and
the centre column, pushed forwards at the same
time to Zuckelhausen, and took the village after
some resistance.

The second column, commanded by General Barclay de Tolly, was assembled near Gossa; the Prussian corps, under General von Kleist, formed its advanced-guard. These generals began to put their
troops in march about eight o'clock, but found
Wachau deserted by the enemy. The village was
occupied, and two brigades were advanced between Wachau and Liebertwolkwitz, that soon

repulsed some detachments left there by the enemy. The brigade of von Pirch found the shepherd's house at Meysdorf still occupied by the French, who retreated on perceiving preparations were making for a serious attack. The reserve cavalry kept open the communication with the left wing and the third column. The corps of Russians under Count Wittgenstein followed close upon the rear of Kleist's corps, and the two corps drew up in battle array, not far distant from Probst-heide. The Russian and Prussian guards took post as reserves near the brick-kilns, where they remained throughout the day.

It was towards two o'clock, P. M. that the two brigades, headed by Prince Augustus of Prussia, and General von Pirch, belonging to Kleist's corps, received orders to storm the village of Probstheide. This village formed, in some measure, the centre of Napoleon's position, and might, indeed, be accounted the key to it. No wonder, then, that Napoleon not only occupied it with a large force, consisting of the 2d corps under Marshal Victor, and a part of the 5th, but likewise threw in from time to time considerable reinforcements from his guards in reserve. To carry this position, so defended, was certainly no very easy undertaking. The place itself was defended by more than 8000 infantry; and batteries on both sides of the village, spread death and destruction all around. But nothing appalled the gallant

Prussians; and the two brigades above mentioned, stormed and carried it at the point of the bayonet. The French, backed by reinforcements, soon returned to the charge, and the Prussians were forced to yield to superior numbers, and retreat to the end of the village. A corps of the enemy attempted at this moment to take them in flank, but a regiment of West-Prussians repulsed them with loss. This advantage enabled the two brigades to storm and carry the village a second time; and for the second time, the enemy, by the mere force of numerical strength, again succeeded in driving the Prussians out of it. The brigades rallied at a short distance, in the most gallant manner, and, assisted by a detachment of Count Wittgenstein's corps, commenced a heavy cannonade on the solid masses of the enemy's infantry, debouching out of the village. Their loss was enormous; and every attempt the French made to advance was repulsed by a most destructive and murderous fire of grape-shot, that lasted till late at night.

The third column, under the orders of the Prince of Hessen-Homburg, advanced likewise about eight o'clock, A. M. on the right bank of the Pleisse, and took possession of the glacis between Dösen and Lössnig. The enemy's detachments in those villages were either dispersed or driven in; and this column then moved forwards in line with the second or centre column. The Prince

was wounded in Dösen, and the command de-
volved on General Bianchi. This general, being
shortly afterwards hard pressed by the enemy, was
supported by the corps under Count Colloredo,
and the position was not only maintained, but
the enemy repulsed to Cönnewitz.

Prodigious as were the efforts made on this day
by the confederate army, to make an impression
on Napoleon's line of positions, yet the conflict
was marked by no particular feature. Striking vi-
cissitudes on either side were not experienced, nor
did any one bold manœuvre turn the fortune of the
day. But a series of regular assaults, bloody and
obstinate, seemed to form the general character of
the battle on this side of Leipsic.

Whilst the allied army were acquiring these advantages, the Silesian army, under our veteran Hero,
and the Northern army, commanded by the Crown
Prince of Sweden, did not remain inactive; the
latter being now much further advanced, the
main attack was made by him. The Northern
army left their camp at Breitenfeld at eight o'clock,
A. M. and filed off towards Taucha, where, following the dispositions laid down, they were to
pass the Partha, in conjunction with General Langeron's corps, so as to unite their left wing with
General Bennigsen's army. The cavalry under
General Winzingerode, and the corps of Lieutenant-general Bülow, that formed the extreme left
wing, marched off in the direction of Taucha,

General Baron von Pahlen made a most brilliant attack on the place, got possession of it, and made a battalion of Saxons that defended the town, prisoners. General Woronzow, with a corps of Russians, passed the Partha at Grasdorff. The corps of General Langeron was to pass the Partha at Taucha; but General von Blücher, judging, by the position of the enemy, that there would be no difficulty in forcing the passage at Mockau, which step would much facilitate the debouching of the Northern army by Taucha, gave orders to attack at that point. The enemy made but little resistance, and General Langeron's corps passed the Partha, and advanced upon Leipsic.

Marshal Ney was soon aware that his position behind the Partha was forced at all points, by the Northern army moving forwards from Taucha, and immediately changed his order of battle, by posting the three corps under his command, in a line between Schönfeld, Sellerhausen, and Stüntz. The 7th corps was drawn up in two lines near Paunsdorf. The brigade of cavalry belonging to this corps, the light artillery, and a battalion of light infantry (all Saxons), as likewise a brigade of Würtemberg cavalry, under General Normann, were posted between Paunsdorf and Taucha. These troops were upon the point of being charged by the Russian cavalry, when they marched hastily forwards, the infantry shouldering their firelocks, and the cavalry sheathing their swords,

and came over to the Allies. The Saxon corps *
posted in Paunsdorf, no sooner heard of this
event, than they took the same resolution; and
although the Saxon General, von Zeschau, endeavoured to prevent them, yet the whole of the 1st
brigade, consisting of eleven battalions of infantry, three squadrons of cavalry, and three
complete batteries of heavy artillery, followed
the noble example of their brethren in arms,
and made the cause of the Confederates their
own. General Platow received them with every
mark of joy and enthusiasm, and detached some
regiments of Cossacks, to keep the French horse
in check, that endeavoured to impede the march
of the Saxons and faithful Germans, on the right
road of honour. The Sovereigns of these troops
were, no doubt, fighting on the side of France;
but the love of liberty and independence, and a
feeling of genuine patriotism, animated their

---

* On the 18th, at Paunsdorf, one of Congreve's rockets fell
before the front of a battalion of Saxons; but the fusee burning out by accident, before it burst, it produced no effect.
Some of the men, on examining it, and discovering it to be one
of the English rockets, of which they had heard such a terrible
description, began to crack their jokes on this new-created
harmless messenger; but in the midst of their merriment, a second happening to fall in the ranks, spreading destruction and
dismay all around, the whole battalion, as if seized with a sudden
panic, broke and dispersed itself instantaneously, nor could the
officers, with all their authority and threats, collect and rally the
men again, to bring them into the line.

From an eye-witness.

hearts, and fired their imaginations, with the glory that would await them, if, in the hour of victory, their swords were found drawn for the deliverance of their adored country, and the downfall of the oppressor of mankind.

During these important events, that so unexpectedly promoted the success of the day, General Count Langeron had advanced upon Schönfeld, where he encountered the enemy prepared to meet him. A violent cannonade ensued: the village was carried at the point of the bayonet, after a bloody resistance, and the enemy, on evacuating it, set it on fire. The cavalry of the Northern army was at last come into line, and effected their junction with the advanced-guard of Bennigsen's corps, and the Cossacks, under the Hettman Platow.

The French had evacuated Paunsdorf, on the Saxons having gone over to the opposite army, but it was now again occupied by their infantry and artillery. General von Bülow, supported by a Russian and Prussian battery, attacked the village with his usual impetuosity, and carried it with the most distinguished bravery.

Towards three o'clock, Marshal Ney debouched with his whole force, out of the villages of Sellerhausen and Volkmansdorf. The Crown Prince of Sweden ordered the Russian brigade of cavalry to charge the enemy, which was executed with the greatest courage and effect, the French being driven back into the villages already mentioned, after a considerable loss of men, and four pieces of cannon. These progressive advantages enabled the Northern army to advance in several distinct columns, towards Leipsic. At this moment, the enemy showed heavy masses in the direction of Mölkau, and seemed to menace an attack on the flank and rear of the allied troops. It was Napoleon himself that attempted this manœuvre. As soon as the disaffection of the Saxon and other German troops was reported to him, he detached General Nansouty, with the whole of the Imperial horse-guards, and 20 pieces of cannon, to take the advancing columns of the Allies in flank, while he himself proceeded in all haste with a division of his guards, to Reudnitz, to oppose General Langeron. General Nansouty, on debouching by Mölkau, supported by the infantry already posted there, found General Count Bubna ready to arrest his progress, this experienced general, whose position was near the right wing of Bennigsen's corps, having caused his troops suddenly to change their front ; which manœuvre forced Nansouty to halt, and forego his intention. The Prince of Hessen-Homburg was in the mean time dispatched with his brigade to the same point. The Swedish artillery, by some unaccountable delay, not being up, the guns of the Saxon artillery that had come over to the Allies, were now turned against the enemy; they were supported by a battery of Congreve's rockets, and the French were repulsed on all sides, and Napoleon's designs completely defeated. General von Bülow had marched forwards from Paunsdorf, and, in spite of an obstinate defence, had dislodged the French from the villages of Stüntz and Sellerhausen.

Napoleon, from his post at Reudnitz, pushed forwards a division of his guards, to support Marshal Marmont, who now succeeded in forcing Count Langeron to retire from Schönfeld. But the Crown Prince, having caused the Swedish General Cardell to advance with twenty pieces of cannon, to maintain this threatened point, and at least to keep the enemy in check, General Count Langeron was enabled to retake the village towards the evening.

Our veteran Hero, whom we left on the 17th at his head-quarters near Lindenthal, promoted, by his dispositions on the 18th, the general good cause, and divided, by his well-directed operations, the forces and attention of the enemy. General von Sacken was directed to attack the suburbs of Leipsic, and the Rosenthal. General von York's corps formed on this day the reserve; but as General von Blücher observed that the enemy was sending off troops in his rear, on the road to Weissenfels, he, with his usual foresight and promptitude of action, detached General von York, with his whole corps, on the evening of the 18th, towards Halle, wisely considering, that on the left bank of the Saale, he might reach Merseberg and Weissenfels before the enemy.

Thus ended the third day's battle, and the confederate armies bivouacked for the night on the victorious plains of Leipsic *. The allied armies, after the most obstinate combats, and therefore the more glorious, had surmounted every obstacle before them, and by bearing in from all sides, at one and the same moment, had established their united forces within a few miles, nay, within sight of the gates of Leipsic. All efforts of resistance on the part of Napoleon had proved fruitless, or had spent their rage in vain. To maintain himself for a few hours in Probstheide, Napoleon had sacrificed an enormous number of men †, merely to

---

* During the heat of action on the 16th and 18th of October, there appeared in the afternoon of each day a most beautiful rainbow in the west, which, beaming in full splendour, spread its vivid arch over the field of battle. Could the pious observer of events, and the unprejudiced son of Christianity, be blamed in hailing the appearance, not only as a type and emblem of heavenly grace towards sinful man, but as a forerunner of victory in the good cause?

---

† During the battle on the 18th, a private French hussar, belonging to Napoleon's guard of honour, was carried through the gate of Leipsic on a bier, accompanied on foot by an officer of very high rank. The unfortunate youth was covered with seventeen wounds. The officer endeavoured to procure him admittance into one of the hospitals, but in vain—they were all full. After passing along some streets, exciting the pity and commiseration of the bystanders, unable to afford or to procure

undergo the degradation and shame of retiring discomfited and broken, under cover of the night, accompanied by no cheering prospects of ultimate success. It must, however, be admitted that he was not absolutely beaten out of the field; yet by awaiting the results of the next day, if the battle were renewed, he could hardly indulge the hope of making further resistance. Napoleon must now have been convinced, and convinced too late, of the necessity of a retreat, an opera-tion which might have been performed under much more auspicious circumstances on the 16th and 17th. He no longer delayed retiring by the only road left open. In the evening of the 18th, he returned to Leipsic, and with Murat took up his quarters at an inn. A retreat was determined upon, practicable in the direction of Weissen-fels alone; and consequently, during the night, the heavy baggage, a considerable part of his artillery and cavalry, and some of his guards, defiled by

---

relief, he arrived with his protegé, at the market-place, con-juring those near him, to show him to the house of a surgeon: the hussar, he said, was the only son of one of the richest and most ancient families in France, and he should have the cruel mortification to see him expire in his arms for want of surgical assistance: he offered 40 Napoleon d'ors, the whole contents of his purse, to any one that would either show him the way, or procure him a surgeon; but such was the state of distress and confusion all around, that no one was to be found to attempt the gaining so high a reward!

the road leading to that place; and the other corps followed as they came up in succession. The main body of Napoleon's guards remained in the vicinity of Leipsic, till the morning of the 19th *, when they filed off through that place.

On the 19th of October, in the morning, the victorious armies of the Confederates, headed by their gallant commanders, made every preparation to storm Napoleon in his last retreat; but the light troops soon reported, that the lines the enemy occupied the preceding night had been, for the most part, abandoned. No impediment obstructed the

---

* At a very early hour in the morning of the 19th, Napoleon's head-quarters were at the Dutch wind-mill, to the right of Stötteritz. Seeing himself surrounded on all sides by a powerful enemy, his corps driven from position to position, and a total defeat almost inevitable, he here made the last preparations, and issued the last orders to cover and regulate, in some degree, the flight of his discomfited army through Leipsic. An adjutant of Marshal Murat, from whom we have this anecdote, was very near him at this crisis, and had opportunity to observe his most minute actions. Rage and fury were but too visibly depicted on his countenance: he gave his orders in the most brief and hasty manner, and answered all questions with little more than monosyllables. After the audience to the numerous general officers, &c. had ended, Napoleon dismounted, and, to the surprise of every one present, threw himself, apparently in a fit of despair, on his face on the ground, and, with a convulsive motion of his hands and feet, seemed to strive to bury himself in the earth. A few moments elapsed, when, suddenly starting up, and again mounting his horse, he rode off at full speed towards Leipsic, to pay a visit to the King of Saxony.

march of the allied columns a moment, towards
Leipsic. To ensure his retreat, Napoleon had
confided the defence of the city to Marshal Macdonald and Prince Poniatowsky, whose troops
were posted for this purpose close to the walls, and
which, about nine o'clock, A. M. were the only
points they occupied.

The grand army of the Confederates approached
Leipsic : an assault was determined upon, and a
bombardment commenced. The Emperor of Russia and the King of Prussia had hardly joined the
army from Rötha, when a Saxon officer, with a
flag of truce, arrived, and, in the name of the
city, begged for mercy. The messenger was received by the Emperor Alexander in person, who
announced to him, that his request could not be
granted; and the preparations for the assault were
continued with alacrity, when a second flag of
truce appeared from Marmont, with an offer to
deliver up the rest of the Saxon troops, if the
French army might be permitted to retire unmolested, and the city spared a bombardment. Such
proposals being only made to gain time, were instantly rejected; especially as the allied troops
had already penetrated into the suburbs, and the
general attack had begun round the town.

General Baron von Sacken had advanced to the
north side of the city, and, after a severe action, had
taken the intrenchments in front of the Halle gate.
A galling fire of grape-shot somewhat retarded his

progress; but as soon as General Langeron, by order of General von Blücher, had filed off a body of troops for his support, through the meadows on the Partha, the enemy was forced to abandon the Halle gate, and the Russian soldiery entered as conquerors into the city.

Towards the east side of the place, the Northern army commenced its operations. The Crown Prince of Sweden commanded Lieutenant-general von Bülow to attack and occupy the city. The gates were defended with obstinacy, but nothing could withstand the Prussian bayonet: the French gave way, and, in defiance of all their attempts to rally in the streets and houses, the intrepid Prussians became masters of the town on this side*. The advanced-guard of General Ben-

---

* When the Prussians drove the French before them, in gallantly forcing their way, through the gates, into Leipsic, the inhabitants, in joyous exultation, threw bread and all kinds of refreshments out of their windows, to the hungry Prussians, who hardly stopped the impetuosity of their pursuit, to silence the calls of hunger, but devoured their morsels in the act of marching. One of these brave Prussians, with part of a loaf of bread in his hand, on which he was feeding with avidity, saw an unarmed Frenchman, crawling along before him, on whose countenance hunger and disease were frightfully depicted; he stepped towards him, and the poor object instantly fell on his knees, imploring quarter. The Prussian offered him his bread, saying: " There, take and eat; thou want'st it more than I do." In uttering these words, he marched forwards, and a few moments afterwards levelled his musket, and shot one of the flying French.

nigsen's army entered the city at nearly the same time, after a severe engagement in some of the avenues leading into the place. The immense quantity of baggage, artillery, and equipages of every description, that the French had relinquished on their tumultuous retreat, had choked up every street, gateway, and outlet; and the retreating troops were thus thrown into a chaos of confusion, while each sought his individual safety in flight.

Napoleon did not quit Leipsic till ten o'clock, A. M. only a few minutes previously to the entrance of the Allies. He escaped through the Peter's gate, and when he had passed the bridge at the extremity of the entrance, it blew up, and all the troops and materiel in the rear, were left to the discretion of the conquerors. The whole of the rear-guard under Macdonald and Poniatowsky, were either killed, wounded, or taken prisoners, by the Confederates. Towards noon, the French were driven from all points *, and tranquillity

---

* Some instances can be given of single acts of despair, that most forcibly mark the character of the French soldier.

During the irregular retreat of the French through Leipsic, on the 19th, a French soldier stood at the corner of a street, and, levelling his musket at a Swedish orderly dragoon, riding by at full gallop, fired, and missed him. The dragoon pulled up his horse, but in the act of cutting at the Frenchman with his sabre, the latter threw down his musket, dropped on his knees, and begged for quarter. The Swede was generous enough to give was once more restored to the inhabitants of Leipsic.

A moderate calculation from an official source states the number of killed on the part of the French at 13,000. More than 30,000 prisoners, all effective men, fell into the hands of the Confederates, besides the 23,000 sick and wounded, found in Leipsic. The military trophies consisted of 250 pieces of cannon, 900 tumbrils and baggage-waggons, and 40,000 firelocks.

The allied Monarchs, except the Emperor of Austria, who arrived somewhat later, proceeding from different quarters, at the head of their guards, made a solemn entry into the city about one o'clock, P. M. and met in the great square of Leipsic *, amid the joyous effusions of the deli-

---

him his life; he had, however, scarcely turned round his horse, when the wretch took up his musket, loaded it, and, as the dragoon was galloping off, fired again at him, but luckily without effect.

Enraged that his generosity should have been so ill requited, the Swede soon overtook the runaway, who again implored quarter: " No," said he, " we pardon soldiers, but no murderers: die thou must !" and, with a hissing stroke of his sabre, cut him down, never to rise more.

From an eye-witness.

---

* The Emperor of Austria, the Emperor of Russia, and the King of Prussia, were scarcely assembled in the market-place, when General von Blücher approached the three Monarchs to pay his respects. The Emperor of Russia, the moment he saw

vered citizens, and the lively and unfeigned acclamations of the victorious soldiers. It was
a moment of exultation that richly rewarded
those who had suffered so many years of misery.

The unanimity of the Confederates, combined
with an energy of co-operation that blended wisdom with promptitude, rendered the stupendous
battle of Leipsic such a brilliant exploit in arms
as may ever seek in vain for a parallel.

Never had any field of battle, in modern history, been so inundated with human gore. But
thus, and thus only, could the inordinate vain-
glory of Napoleon be for ever eclipsed, offering
a memento appalling to nature, but truly beneficial to mankind. It will show to posterity, that,
though daring enterprise may attain to vast dominion, it cannot be preserved at the expense of the
rights and feelings of the vanquished; and that
though the oppressor, in the day of his prosperity,
and in the haughty confidence of his might, may

---

our veteran, dismounted to embrace him with the heartiness of
the most intimate friendship, called him the deliverer of Germany, and presented him with a valuable gold-hilted sword,
set with brilliants. The Emperor of Austria was profuse in
his encomiums; and his grateful Monarch did but look at
him, but with a look that spoke the overflowings of his heart,
with more eloquence, than the well-turned periods of language
could have expressed. On the following day, the King promoted our Hero to the rank of General-Field-Marshal.

scorn the voice of the oppressed, yet power never can be supported by violence alone.

The results of this tremendous conflict of four successive days, in which the nations of Europe made so noble a struggle for their privileges as citizens, and their birth-rights as men, were equal to the interests that were to be decided. The tyrant and oppressor of the age could now with agony exclaim : " *That game is lost, for which I played, to gain the empire of the world.*" It was here firmly fixed, that the precepts of Christian morality should maintain their due influence over the civilization and improvement of the human race. Its effects restored religion to its wonted energies; and the wily serpent, whose pestiferous breath exhaled selfish atheism, and destruction to all moral order, had now cast his skin of infallibility, was sunk into hopeless bondage, and condemned to bite his chains, detested and abhorred.

CHAPTER X.

Field-marshal Blücher pursues Napoleon, after the Battle of Leipsic—Co-operation of Bavaria—General Count Wrede—Battle of Hanau—Blücher passes the Rhine—Progress of the Crown Prince of Sweden—Hamburgh.

THE immediate consequences of this stupendous and sanguinary battle of Leipsic, this splendid and immortal triumph, that avenged the injured cause of mankind in so singular a manner, were nothing less than Napoleon's retreat in all haste to the Rhine; a retreat that soon degenerated into a disorderly flight. The corps of General von York, as part of Field-marshal Blücher's Silesian army, that had been detached, on the 18th, to the Saale, reached Halle on the 19th; and the rest of the army, under Generals Sacken and Langeron, followed the same route, on the evening of that day. General von Blücher passed the Elster, in the rear of Skeuditz, and, pushing forward a column to Lützen, surprised a body of 2000 men of the enemy, and made the whole of them prisoners. The corps of Sacken and Langeron now took the road to Merseberg, while that of von York filed off in the direction of Mücheln. A bridge was soon thrown over the Saale, and the main body of

Blücher's army marched close on the heels of the flying French, towards the Unstrut. A part of Blücher's advanced-guard fell in with a convoy of Austrian, Prussian, and Russian prisoners, near Nebra, consisting of 200 officers and 4000 privates, dispersed their escorte, and released the whole of them. Our gallant indefatigable Hero overtook the confused multitude of retreating French, on the 21st, near Freiburg, when attempting to pass the bridge over the Unstrut: a bloody conflict ensued, in which the enemy sustained a severe loss of artillery and men. Towards three o'clock, P. M. the French troops gave way, and fled in the utmost disorder over the bridge. Blücher's artillery thundered upon their masses of all arms, and made a most dreadful slaughter. His numerous cavalry charged at every opening, and cut in pieces all that made resistance. The passage over the bridge was actually blocked up by the crowds of fugitives, that attempted to pass. The bridge broke down, and, horrible to relate, hundreds were precipitated at once into the flood beneath. It was a terrible sight. The number of men that here found their grave in the Unstrut was so great, that the current was obstructed, and the river overflowed its banks for a considerable distance.

Numerous bodies of Cossacks, under the Hetmann Platow, having joined the confederate army, their rapid marches, at this period, most essentially aided the operations of the Allies. They formed, under General Czernischef, strange as it may appear, the advanced-guard of Napoleon's retreating army. They surprised Gotha on the 24th, and made above a thousand prisoners. They occupied Eisenach soon after, at the time that Napoleon had only reached Gotha. Their services proved here of infinite value; and as light troops, to harass the enemy, intercept his supplies, beat up his quarters, scour the country, procure intelligence, and, above all, to prevent intelligence being obtained, no troops in modern warfare can be compared to them. Terrible, merciless towards the foe, mild and obliging in quarters, pious in their deportment, gentle and humane in their intercourse with strangers; who has ever passed at night-fall a Cossack bivouack, and unmolested stood listening to their evening hymns, that will not bear witness to the inoffensive character of this truly brave and honest tribe of untutored warriors? Their fame needs no eulogium*!

---

* In the tumult of the retreat through Leipsic, a Cossack, in turning the corner of a by-street, came suddenly upon a French foot-soldier, who, at the sight of the Cossack's pike, threw down his musket, and, falling upon his knees, begged for quarter. The Cossack dismounted, broke the Frenchman's firelock against the stones, and stripped him of his knapsack and bundle of moveables: it happened that a citizen of Leipsic saw the transaction from his house-door, and, to show his loyalty, brought out to the Cossack a bottle of brandy and a loaf of bread, just as he had finished his search about the person of his prisoner. The Cossack smiled at the sight of the bottle, took it,

Napoleon made rapid strides to reach **Erfurt**, where he paused a while, to organize and refresh his jaded troops. Blücher's army, in conjunction with Bennigsen's, followed close upon his rear, and caused him a daily loss of artillery, baggage, and prisoners. The road to Hanau was covered with the wrecks of his disorganized army. Near Gotha, Colonel Mensdorff, of Blücher's advanced-guard, had a warm affair with the enemy. Field-marshal Blücher, on reaching Eisenach, on the 26th, caused the place to be taken by assault, and occupied the road to Cassel. General von York encountered the enemy, when in full march through the Hörselthal, not far from Eisenach; he attacked him without delay, drove him from the ground, and carried the village of Eichrodt, by which operation he cut off the fourth French corps from the main body, and forced them into the Thuringian forest, whence they were obliged to reach Vach by a circuitous route. On the 27th of October, Field-marshal von Blücher's army

---

and made signs that he wished for another; it was brought him; but, to the astonishment of his benefactor, it now appeared that he wanted it empty. His request was complied with; and he instantly poured the half of his brandy into it, broke the loaf into two equal pieces, and shared them both with his prisoner, making signs for him to eat and drink, while he did the same; and then, with a nod of thanks to the donor, he mounted his horse, and drove his prisoner before him.—Where is there an adherent of Napoleon and his principles that would have so acted?

passed the defiles of Eisenach, and pursued and harassed the enemy in all directions. Here we have to lament the consequences of a foresight, however wise and laudable it might be thought, that formed a portal through which Napoleon actually reached the Rhine, with the shattered remains of his humbled followers and worthless Satraps. The Bavarian army, under General Count Wrede, was known to be in march on Ha-nau, to intercept the French army; and a very natural conclusion was drawn by Marshal Blücher, that Napoleon would, in all probability, direct the course of his columns on Coblentz, to cross the Rhine at that point, rather than throw himself, weak as he was, into the arms of Wrede. The supposition was an unfortunate one. If our Hero had followed up his march, Napoleon's total defeat and capture at Hanau could not, according to all human calculations, have been averted. But the Silesian army changed its line of operations; and Napoleon, somewhat relieved from his apprehensions of being placed between two fires, hurried on to Hanau, regardless of those he left behind; as, upon reaching that place, he could, by his superiority of numbers, with safety enter the lists with Wrede.

In the beginning of October, Bavaria declared herself as the ally of Austria, and, by this step, dis-membered for ever the Confederation of the Rhine.

General Count Wrede *, a most distinguished warrior, was appointed to the command of the Bavarian army in camp at Nymphenberg, to which a

---

* *Memoirs of General Count Wrede.*

This renowned General was born at Heidelburg, on the 29th
of April 1767. He was destined for the profession of the law,
and, after finishing his education at Heidelburg, was appointed
counsellor of the court of justice at Manheim; being at the
same time high bailiff of Heidelburg.

During the war of the French revolution, in 1794, he was
a commissary of war for the Rheinpfalz, with the character of
brevet-colonel in the Elector of Bavaria's service. The repeti-
tions of jurisprudence had had, it seems, no charms for our General; and he, at this period of his life, turned his attention
entirely to arms. His important occupations required his constant attendance at head-quarters, which he continued to follow
during the ensuing campaigns, until the year 1799, when he
received orders from the Elector to organize a battalion of his
own, for the purpose of protecting the Rheinpfalz. At the
head of this battalion, supported by cavalry and artillery, his
spirit of enterprise had several opportunities of showing itself,
by some fortunate expeditions against the French, by which he
acquired the public thanks of his Sovereign, and the esteem of
his brother-officers. On the 19th of August 1799, the Elector
of Bavaria appointed him a colonel of the general staff; and,
on the 11th of December following, his Serene Highness invested him with the honorary military badge, as a gracious
mark of his satisfaction for his distinguished services. In
March 1800, Count Wrede was promoted to the rank of Major-
general, and commanded a brigade of a body of troops, at that
time in the pay of Great Britain. He headed his brigade at
the battles of Möskirch, Neuburg, and in the unfortunate affair
of Hohenlinden, with determined bravery and prudence.

When peace was concluded, he was appointed commander of

corps of Austrians was added; and, on the 15th of October, he put himself at the head of this confederate army, which did not exceed 30,000

the brigade in Suabia, having his head-quarters at Ulm. In the year 1804, he commanded a corps of infantry, forming part of the Bavarian army encamped at Nymphenberg; and, before the camp broke up, was advanced to the rank of Lieutenant-general.

In the war with Austria, which commenced in 1805, he commanded a division of the Elector's army, protected the environs of München, and subsequently advanced into Moravia. Napoleon made him grand officer of the legion of honour, and his Sovereign, when peace was established, in 1806, invested him with the Grand Cross of the military order of Max. Joseph. The Bavarian army having returned to their several garrisons, after the peace of Presburg, Count Wrede was appointed commander-in-chief of the province of Suabia. The war against Prussia and Russia, which soon followed, afforded General Count Wrede many opportunities of distinguishing himself in a most signal manner, at the head of his division. The battles of Glogau, Breslaw, and Pultusk, bore witness to his intrepidity. On the return of peace, he again resumed his military command in Suabia. When the Congress was sitting at Erfurt, in 1808, he was intrusted with the command of the Bavarian army, then in camp near Augsburg, which soon broke up, as the threatened hostilities did not take place.

France, by her ambitious projects, having again, in 1809, lighted up the flames of war against Austria, our General commanded the second division of the Bavarian army, and fully justified, by his eminent services, that confidence which His Majesty the King of Bavaria and the nation had placed in him. At the battle of Wagram he received a dangerous wound. The excessive fatigues of this campaign, and the effects of his wound, induced our experienced General, at this period, to men, to commence his operations against the common enemy. By a series of forced marches, he reached Würtzburg on the 24th of October,

---

decline all public functions, and to retire to one of his estates, to re-establish his injured constitution. After a short interval of repose, His Majesty promoted him to the rank of General of the Cavalry, as a proof of the high esteem in which his great and meritorious services were held by his grateful Monarch.

About the middle of February 1812, when the Bavarian army took the field in the memorable campaign of Napoleon against Russia, the command of the second division was given to our General. At the bloody battle of Pollozk, the Bavarian Commander-in-chief, General Count von Deroy, being mortally wounded, General Count Wrede took upon him the command of the army. With the miserable wrecks of this fine corps of Bavarians, Wrede retreated over the Niemen and Vistula, and, under difficulties almost insurmountable, brought back the brave remains of his army, by his wise dispositions, in safety, to the frontiers, but breathing insatiable vengeance against the blood-thirsty author of all their calamities.

When the famous campaign of 1813 was opened, by the march of the confederate armies into Saxony, a Bavarian army of observation was assembled in a camp near Nymphenberg. It consisted of nearly 25,000 men, mostly volunteers from the national guards, that had offered to serve in the line. General Count Wrede took upon him the command of this army on the 15th of October, now strengthened by a corps of Austrians. The army immediately left the camp, and, by a series of forced marches, reached Uffenheim, a distance of more than two hundred miles, on the 23d, where head-quarters were fixed. Here General Count Wrede received intelligence of the victory of Leipsic; on its being made known to the army, it became a spark that kindled into flame a thousand fires, that had till now been glimmering under the ashes. An summoned the place to surrender, and, on refusal, commenced a heavy bombardment.   On the 26th, the place capitulated.   General Count Wrede, with-

---

enthusiastic love of civil liberty burst forth throughout the ranks, and the same enthusiasm for the good cause proclaimed itself unanimously, as in the north of Germany. The march was directed on Würtzburg, which capitulated on the 26th; and the head of the columns reached the vicinity of Hanau on the 28th. The advanced-guard of Napoleon's discomfited army, on its irregular retreat to the Rhine, showed itself on the road from Erfurt. Our General lost no time in making his dispositions, both prompt and vigorous, to stop the enemy's progress. Several bloody encounters ensued: in one of the latter, our brave General was again severely wounded. When recovering from his wound in Hanau, the Emperor of Austria sent him the commander's cross of the military order of Maria-Theresa, accompanied by the following letter, written by himself:

" My esteemed General of the Cavalry,

   Count Wrede,   *Fulda, November 2d*, 1813.

 " The gallant deeds that have covered you and the confederate army under your command, with glory, have induced me to give you a proof of my grateful sentiments, by sending you the grand cross of the military order of Maria-Theresa. Most sincerely do I wish your speedy recovery from your dangerous wound, hoping that Providence will preserve for his country and the cause of Germany, an officer at once so brave and prudent.   Francis."

 His Majesty the Emperor of all the Russias had sent our General, prior to this, the order of Alexander Newsky: on which occasion he received the following letter from the Russian cabinet minister, Count Nesselrode :

" General,   *Meinungen, October 30th*, 1813.

 " The Emperor has directed me, as a mark of his particular esteem, and proof of his satisfaction at the great services which

out delay, continued his march on Hanau, where
he arrived with his whole army on the 28th, in the
morning. The Austrian-Bavarian army took up

Your Excellency has so lately rendered the good cause, to send
you the insignia of the order of St. Alexander Newsky. The distinguished talents of Your Excellency will most powerfully promote the further success of the confederate army ; and His Majesty places the most unbounded confidence in your operations,
and in the sentiments by which you are animated. I esteem myself peculiarly happy in being the organ of those flattering opinions which the Emperor entertains towards you, and to offer
you the assurances of my high esteem.

                     " COUNT VON NESSELRODE."

In fine, all the confederate Princes were loud in their eulo-
giums on the conduct of Wrede. His energetic exertions to
reach the enemy, his personal bravery, and the wise circumspection of his plans, gave birth to an admiration at once well-
founded and general. Having happily recovered from his
wound, he crossed the Rhine at the head of his corps of gallant
Bavarians, and forming part of the grand confederate army
that entered France at the commencement of the year 1814,
shared the glory of the victory of Brienne, on the 3d of
February. On the 13th, General Count Wrede attacked, in
combination with Blücher, Marshal Victor, at Nogent, and,
after an obstinate conflict, forced him to retreat. A series of
partial affairs now followed, and, on the 16th, the Bavarian
corps directed its march to Sezanne, and, on the 17th, passed
the Seine, after having formed a junction with Wittgenstein.
Our gallant General and his corps, in sharing the fatigues of
those eventful days between the 27th of February and the 31st
of March, partook of the honour and glory, so dearly purchased, of entering Paris in triumph, as part of the grand
confederate army. His grateful Sovereign has since raised him
to the dignity of Prince of the realm.

a strong position near the place; and, as the van-
guard of Napoleon's retreating masses was in advance upon Hanau, General Count Wrede made the
necessary dispositions to obstruct its progress, and
delay its march. Some partial affairs only prepared the way to a most bloody and obstinate
combat. The head of the first French column
began to debouche on the 30th, about ten o'clock,
A. M. out of the Pupperwalde and Lamboy-wood *.

---

* On the 30th of October, three hussars belonging to the
imperial French guards, entered the village of Langendiesbach,
and ordered the bailiff of the place to follow them to the Emperor. The man refused, saying, that, in his absence, his
house and barns would be certainly plundered. Two of the
hussars then offered to remain on his premises, as a guard, if
he would venture to accompany the other to the Emperor's
quarters: to this proposal the bailiff agreed. On arriving
at Napoleon's bivouack, he found him seated on a bundle of
straw, near a watch-fire, and a number of maps before him.
Without any introduction, Napoleon asked the bailiff (through
an interpreter), whether he knew of any passable by-roads, by
which the high-road through Hanau might be avoided. He
answered in the affirmative. Horses were instantly ordered,
and the bailiff was obliged to ride with Napoleon into the
woods, and to point out every by-road and outlet in the neighbourhood. They were nearly five hours together. On his being dismissed, without any offer of a remuneration for his
trouble, he begged Napoleon to let him have a sauve-gard for
his village, in return for his local information; a gloomy scowl
followed, but no answer. He repeated his request, and Napoleon sullenly remarked: " *Lefebvre has the necessary orders.
He will take care of every thing.*"
The bailiff, somewhat elated at this assurance, hastened back

It was driven back with great loss. Napoleon made a second attempt, which met with the same fate, and the French were repeatedly repulsed till near three o'clock, P. M. The French horse-guards now presented themselves, drawn up in a solid body, and, in spite of a heavy cannonade, debouched, then formed with great rapidity in three lines, and charged the Bavarian and Austrian horse; they were met with intrepidity, and repulsed; but at this moment a battery of French twelve-pounders, that had been planted in ambush, in the rear of the imperial horse-guards, opened a destructive fire on the flank of the allied cavalry, and they were obliged at last to yield ground. Napoleon had now opened himself a passage, and the first column of his troops, consisting mostly of guards, filed off on the road to the north of Hanau. General Count Wrede, having received reinforcements on the 31st, took post to the south of Hanau, having evacuated the place early the same morning *: some brisk attacks followed, with va-

---

to his village. He found it (could any one expect otherwise?) completely sacked and pillaged. And the two hussars, left in his house, had been the first to set the example, by emptying it of every portable article of value. Such are the proofs of the gratitude and honour of Napoleon and his satellites.

---

* A deputation from the magistrates and inhabitants of Hanau was admitted to an audience of Napoleon, in Puppenwalde. He was seated in the front of a tent, surrounded by a crowd of officers. Upon their being introduced, by one of his adjutants,

rious success, and Hanau was stormed by the
Bavarians, towards three o'clock, p. m. with the
view of cutting off some part of Napoleon's troops.
General Count Wrede was wounded in gallantly
leading on his troops to the assault.   During the
night, the rest of the French columns took the road
to Francfort.   The loss, on both sides, was very
severe.   General Wrede, in his attempt to arrest
Napoleon's career to the Rhine, showed the most
invincible courage, in maintaining this very unequal contest.   The attempt was crowned with
glory, as he suffered no positive defeat, and yet

Napoleon addressed them in a singularly abrupt and unceremo-
nious manner :

" You are the deputation from Hanau?   It is the worst city
in Germany.   The citizens have received the Bavarians and
Austrians with every mark of exultation and joy.   I know I
cannot force them to love the French ; but, methinks, common
sense should have told them to show at least more attachment
to France, than to Russia.   The one is much nearer to afford
succour and help, when necessary.   But, however, as a punishment, I bombarded the town last night.   Has the fire
done much damage?"   On being answered in the affirmative,
he replied, " It was my intention to have burnt at least half the
city about your ears."   And then turning to Augereau, who
stood near him, demanded, " What he could say in favour of
Hanau?"   The Marshal, in his answer, gave some praise to
their former conduct.

" C'est bon," replied Napoleon ; "je sais que les magistrats
sont de brave gens, mais la bourgeoisie est de la canaille :—for
this time, let their present punishment suffice."   And they were
then dismissed.

kept Napoleon at bay for two days, disputing
with him every foot of ground; and only by the
overwhelming force of numbers, did the enemy
open his road to Francfort, and General Wrede
find himself unable to stop his further march to
the Rhine.   Napoleon halted not at Francfort, but
pursued his march to that river, in the direction
of Mentz, where he crossed it on the 7th of
November. It was the last battle which Napoleon
fought in Germany to save himself; and his influence and dominion over it were thus for ever
destroyed.   The dawning prospect of better times
seemed already to indemnify the Germans for so
many years of misery ; and the scum and filth of
the French nation, that had been raised to the top,
by the force of their vices, and by such talents as
they devoted exclusively to purposes of immoral
tendency, had received a chastisement, that, if it
did not promote repentance, at least humbled them
in the dust.

In now casting a retrospective glance over the
operations of the grand confederate army, subsequent to the battle of Leipsic, and preceding the
passage of the Rhine, we do but pursue the thread
of our narrative.

Napoleon, to secure his retreat from Leipsic,
had destroyed every bridge over the Elster, and
the numerous small arms of that river, and the
Luppe, between Leipsic and Lindenau, and was
thus able to remain in the latter place till near

three o'clock, p. m. of the 19th of October. The
extraordinary efforts of the allied army, during
the last six days, had produced, it cannot be
concealed, such a general state of exhaustion
throughout the troops, that not only the impediments thrown in their line of march by the enemy,
but the absolute necessity of some hours of repose
to the men and horses, obliged them to halt for a
while in Leipsic and its environs. Their light
troops alone continued, without intermission, to
harass and distress the flanks of Napoleon's disorganized masses, and prepare obstacles for their
future movements, which only a war like the present could render possible. Naumburg was occupied by a corps of Austrians, and a strong column
advanced by the way of Pegau, to press on the
left flank of the enemy, and to prevent their con-
centrating themselves behind the Saale. The
Northern army pursued Napoleon's right flank, in
the direction of Querfurt, Artern, and Sondershau-
sen, detaching strong corps towards the Weser.
The head-quarters of the grand Bohemian army
were at Weimar on the 24th, continuing its march
parallel with the left flank of Napoleon's forces,
whose advanced-guard, composed of his young
guards; his centre column, of the wrecks and remains of all his other corps; and his rear-guard,
that covered the retreat, of his old guards, were
incessantly exposed to the bold attacks of the
Cossacks on all sides. His retreat was of a de-

scription that almost exceeds the limits of possibility. Clouds of light cavalry were advanced before him, breaking up the roads, destroying the bridges, and removing every article of human sustenance. The route of his troops was marked with an hourly loss of men and warlike stores. He reached Hanau on the 29th, and the Rhine a few days afterwards.

General von Blücher had, for very cogent reasons, directed his line of march from the vicinity of Eisenach to Coblentz, on the 28th of October. The intelligence of Napoleon's retreat on Mentz soon reached him; he entered Francfort on the Maine, at the head of his gallant army, and, on the 30th of December, issued the following proclamation :

" Brave Warriors of the Silesian Army !

" Your gallant progress, from the Oder to the Rhine, has torn provinces out of the hands of the enemy which he had formerly subdued. You are now to pass the Rhine, to force the enemy to accept of peace, who can ill brook the having lost, in two campaigns, his conquests during nineteen years.

" Soldiers ! I need only point out the path of glory to the victors on the Katzbach, near Wartenberg, Möckern, and Leipsic, to be sure of the result. But it is here incumbent upon me to impose on you new duties. The inhabitants of the left bank of the Rhine are not inimical to our cause. I have promised them safety and protection of property; I have done it in *your* name. You must keep this promise sacred. Bravery confers honour on the soldier; but obedience and discipline form his brightest ornaments.

" BLÜCHER."

The Rhine seemed, as it were, to form a kind of barrier to the further operations of the victorious allied armies at the end of October and the beginning of November, particularly for the centre and left wing; and, during the whole of November, no serious preparations were made to pass this river with the main body. Mature deliberations, in the mean time, on the part of the august Allies, produced a well-digested plan of future operations, which, towards the middle of December, was put in execution, with a harmony and unanimity, blended with a general enthusiasm, that gave fair promise of the most brilliant results to the arms of the Confederates.

At the commencement of the new year, 1814, all the corps of the confederate army had passed the Rhine *. The grand army, under the com-

---

* An official statement of the strength of the allied armies and corps that took the field at the opening of the campaign into France may not be unacceptable to our readers.

Bavaria

mand of Prince Schwartzenberg, consisting of the
corps of Colloredo, Lichtenstein, Giulay, Crown

Countries.	Numbers.	Generals.	Armies.
Bavaria............	36,000	Wrede	Grand army.
Hanover..........	20,000		
Brunswick	6,000		
Oldenburg	1,500	Duke of Brunswick......	North army.
Hanse Towns.......	3,500		
Mecklenburg - Schwerin	1,000		
Saxony............	20,000		
Weimar...........	800		
Gotha.............	1,100	Duke of Weimar........	North army.
Schwarzburg	650		
Anhalt............	800		
Hesse-Cassel	12,000	Prince of Hesse........	Silesian army.
Berg..............	5,000		
Waldeck...........	400		
Lippe-Schaumburg...	650		
Nassau............	1,680		
Coburg............	400	Duke of Coburg	Silesian army.
Meinungen.. ,.....	300		
Hildburghausen.....	200		
Mecklenburg-Strelitz	600		
Würtzburg	2,000		
Darmstadt	4,000		
Francfort and Isenburg.............	2,800	Prince of Hesse-Homburg	Grand army.
Reusz	450		
Würtemberg	12,000		
Baden	10,000		
Hohenzollern.......	290	Prince of Würtemberg ...	Grand army.
Lichtenstein	40		
The Austrian armies in France and Italy	250,000	Field-marshal von Hiller..	Italian army.
		Prince of Schwartzenberg	Grand army.
The Russian armies..	250,000	General Barclay de Tolly	Grand army.
		General Wittgenstein	
		General Bennigsen	North army.
The Prussian armies..	200,000	Field-marshal Blücher....	Silesian army.
		General Kleist.........,	Grand army.
The Swedish army ...	30,000	Crown Prince of Sweden..	North army.
	874,160		

N. B. The English army, including Spaniards and Portuguese, under the Marquis of Wellington, the auxiliary corps of Danes, the Neapolitans, and the army of the Netherlands, are to be added to the above number.

Prince of Würtemberg, and Wrede, as likewise the whole of the Russian and Prussian reserves under General Barclay de Tolly, directed their march through the western part of Switzerland, passed the Rhine, and moved onwards into Alsace, towards Langres and Chaumont, after leaving behind them the necessary detachments to blockade and besiege the several fortresses which they had left in their rear.

Field-marshal von Blücher began to pass the Rhine, by Kaub, Bacharach, and Coblentz, with his Silesian army, on the 1st of January 1814. General von York's corps had the honour of leading the march, and was the first that crossed the Rhine. In the night of the 31st of December 200 men, of the regiment of Brandenburgh, landed on the left bank of the Rhine, and, after a trifling resistance, drove in some of the enemy's out-posts. About ten o'clock, A. M. nearly 4000 men, infantry, had crossed the river in barges. Bacharach and Oberwesel were taken. The bridge of pontoons at Kaub was ready the same day, and the corps of General Langeron, and the main body of the army, followed on the 2d of January. General Sacken crossed the Rhine, with his corps, at Manheim, and General St. Priest at Coblentz.

Marshal Blücher issued the following proclamation to the inhabitants of the left bank of the Rhine:

" I have led the Silesian army over the Rhine,

that the freedom and independence of nations may be established, and peace acquired.

" The Emperor Napoleon has incorporated Holland, a part of Germany, and Italy, with the French empire; he has declared that he would not give up a single village of these conquests, even if the enemy appeared on the heights of Paris.

" It is against this declaration—against these principles, that the armies of all the European powers are on their march. Will you defend these principles? Well, then, enter the files of Napoleon; try the chance of battle against that just cause which Providence so evidently protects. If not, you then find protection with us. I shall defend your property.

" Let every citizen, every peasant, remain tranquilly in his dwelling—every magistrate at his post, and continue, without interruption, the employments of his office. But from the moment the allied troops occupy a place, all connexion with the French empire must cease. Whoever acts against this ordinance commits treason towards the allied powers, will be brought before a court-martial, and be punished with death.

" VON BLÜCHER."

On the left bank of the Rhine,
  January 1, 1814.

It was now that France experienced all the disadvantages resulting from an unsettled, tyrannical government, and that all her power and all her strength had been employed merely for the purpose of acquiring conquests, that had neither secured her boundaries, nor rendered actual invasion impossible.

But before we proceed further, we think it necessary to call the attention of our readers to the minor operations of the extreme right wing of the confederate army after the battle of Leipsic.

The Crown Prince of Sweden*, at the head of

---

* *Memoirs of the Crown Prince of Sweden.*

Charles John Bernadotte was born on the 24th of June 1763, at Pau, near the foot of the Pyrenean mountains. His father had attained considerable eminence in the law, and gave his son a liberal education. On reaching manhood, he gave way to his favourite propensity, and chose the profession of arms; and his first campaign was made under Rochambeau, in America: he was there taken prisoner by the British forces. When the French revolution broke out, we find him, in his twenty-sixth year, in the regiment of royal marines. He became a staunch republican; and, having distinguished himself during the subjection of the Low Countries, he was made a General of Division. He gave singular proofs of his conduct and bravery at the battle of Fleurus, 1795, and at the crossing of the Rhine in 1796, being at that period attached to the army of General Jourdan. His division blockaded Mentz for some time; and had, afterwards, a considerable share in the success of the battle of Neuhoff. General Bernadotte was detached, with his division, to strengthen the army of Buonaparte in Italy, which circumstance gave rise to a very intimate acquaintance between these two personages. Napoleon ordered him to take Gradiska, which he accomplished. After the battle of Rivoli, Buonaparte sent General Bernadotte, with the colours taken from the enemy, accompanied by a strong recommendation to the Directory, in

the Swedish army, and two divisions of Russians
and Prussians, directed his march, from the victorious plains of Leipsic, towards the Weser, and arrived

---

favour of the General. He was received in Paris with distinguished and very flattering marks of respect; and was thereupon appointed commandant in Marseilles. Soon after the
peace of Campo-Formio he repaired to the Austrian capital as
ambassador from the French republic. The displaying of the
three-coloured flag before his hotel, caused a vehement popular
commotion in Vienna, and General Bernadotte was induced to
retire to Rastadt, to await the decision of the Directory. On
the breaking out of a new war, General Jourdan was appointed
to the command of the army intended to act against the Archduke Charles, and Bernadotte was intrusted with one of the
wings. This army was soon obliged to repass the Rhine. General Bernadotte was now placed at the head of the war depart-
ment. The Directory, a short time after, commanded him to
resign his place in favour of Mallet-Mureau, and to repair again
to the army. It appears that this abrupt conduct of the Directory gave considerable offence, as Bernadotte made immediate
application for his dismission, which was granted him, with a
pension ; and he retired from all public affairs to his estate in
the country. Ties of relationship attached him to the family of
Buonaparte, his lady being the sister of the wife of Joseph
Buonaparte, eldest brother of Napoleon. The army of the West
was intrusted to his command; and, at its head, he contributed to
the destruction of the faithful royalists at Quiberon Bay. The
peace of Luneville being ratified, he resigned his command to General Laborde ; and was on the point of proceeding to the United
States, as ambassador, when hostilities again broke out between
England and France. In the year 1804 the First Consul sent him
to Hanover, where he succeeded General Mortier in his command, and, by the mildness of his measures and suavity of his
manners, he made himself universally esteemed by the Hanove-

at Hanover on the 25th of October, pushing forwards his left wing towards the Ems. He halted with his army a few days, to refresh his troops, and to give Denmark an opportunity of making overtures. Meanwhile Marshal d'Avoust *, who

---

rians. The year following, the First Consul declared himself Emperor of the French, and invested Bernadotte with the dignity of Marshal of the Empire. He assisted at the battle of Austerlitz. During his stay in Germany, in 1806, Napoleon created the Marshal a Prince, as Prince of Ponte-Corvo, at the same time that Talleyrand was made Prince of Benevente. The Prince distinguished himself at the battle of Jena, and at the affair of Lübeck, against General von Blücher. From the year 1807 to 1809 he commanded the army of observation in the north of Germany. At the head of the Saxon troops, he took part in the battle of Deutsch-Wagram. When peace was signed, he retired, in 1810, to his estates, at Lagrange la Prevôte, near Melun ; from whence he was called to inherit the throne of Sweden, by the unanimous voice of the Swedish nation. As Crown Prince of Sweden he powerfully assisted in the deliverance of Germany, which must ever be remembered with gratitude by the nation.

---

* *Memoirs of d'Avoust.*

It is the part of the biographer to relate stubborn facts ; he is obliged, not only to detail the virtues, but the deceit and cruelty of individuals, their ambition and avarice, their meanness and violence. The task may be useful, but no one will have the hardihood to say, that it is, in the latter case, a grateful one ; for the man, whose duty it is to point out an individual, as an instance of unexampled moral turpitude, to the inquisitive world, must be conscious, not only of the utility, but of the feelings of abhorrence, arising from his exertions. Each sentence he pens presents to his view some horrid, monstrous, and diabo-

had been suffered to intrench himself up to the
ears in Hamburgh, had taken up a strong position
between the two Hanse towns of Lübeck and

---

lical trait of character—some feature, stamped with the appalling image of a black and callous soul: greatness, found
without generosity—valour, without mercy—and wisdom, without virtue. The subject of the present memoirs is such a portrait. The mass of authentic anecdote, dispersed throughout
this chapter, portrays, in striking colours, his prominent features.

D'Avoust has drawn down upon himself the eternal hatred of
all good Germans, in a much higher degree than any other of
Napoleon's Satraps. The origin of this deadly hate may
be traced to his persecutions of German authors *, his
avowed contempt of every thing relative to the Teutonic nation, his eager inclination to discover, in the most private connexions, imaginary conspiracies against France; and, above
all, the unnatural severity with which he at all times executed
Napoleon's decrees.

A few minute particulars concerning the life of this man,
will no doubt prove acceptable to our readers.

D'Avoust, Duke of Auerstädt and Prince of Eckmühl, was
born at Annou, in Burgundy, and is descended from a noble

---

* Mr. Becker, an admired German writer, and Councillor of the Court, at
Gotha, was arrested, conveyed to Magdeburg, and thrown into a dungeon,
in direct violation of the rights of nations. The Duke of Weimar endeavoured
to procure his release, and caused representations of his innocence to be made
to Marshal d'Avoust, to which he returned the following brutal and insolent
answer, in a letter still extant, in which, after a positive refusal of liberation,
he proceeds thus : " And, besides, the Germans are altogether a stubborn
people ; and they will hardly become tame and docile, until I have made some
striking examples, by hanging up, on one tree, a German prince, a man of
letters, and a merchant, as a warning to the rest !—"

Hamburgh. After the denunciation of the armistice, a corps under General Wallmoden, and a division of Swedes under General Vegesack, in the

---

family. His father had more than once exercised the functions
of an ambassador. He was killed, by accident, on a shooting-
party, leaving his son an orphan of tender years. At a suitable
age, young d'Avoust was placed in the military school at
Brienne, where he imbibed the first rudiments of his knowledge
of military tactics. It is singular that Napoleon was formed at
the same school.

At what period d'Avoust first entered the army, and obtained
a commission, we are unable to say; but we find him, in the
year 1785, as second Lieutenant in the royal Champagne regiment of cavalry.

When the revolution broke out in France, the greater part of
his brother-officers emigrated. D'Avoust's mind seemed, however, adapted for the scenes of the revolution ; and, although
exposed, as a royal officer, to some vexations, he declared
himself a staunch republican. In the year 1790, d'Avoust was
appointed commander of a battalion of volunteers of the Yonne,
was attached to the army of the north, and was present at all
the affairs of Dumourier's campaign. When Dumourier deserted
the cause of the republic, and came over to the Austrians, it
was d'Avoust that made the daring, but frustrated attempt to
prevent him, and take him prisoner as a traitor. He was made
a General in 1793, and served in the army of the Moselle. He
soon afterwards passed the Rhine under Pichegru ; was left to
defend Manheim, and taken prisoner in the place. Upon being
exchanged, he again passed the Rhine, with a division, in 1797.
Peace was made; and d'Avoust accompanied Napoleon into
Egypt as General of Brigade in the corps of Dessaix. After
the convention of El Arisch, he embarked, with Dessaix, for
France, and landed at Toulon. He was immediately called to
Paris by Napoleon, and received the command of the cavalry

whole about 20,000 men, had been left in Mecklenburg-Schwerin, to observe and keep d'Avoust
in check. The strength of d'Avoust's corps, including from 10 to 12,000 Danes, might be moderately estimated at 32,000 men. He had, therefore, a considerable superiority of numbers. In the
course of the month of August, d'Avoust penetrated to Schwerin *, the capital of the Dutchy,

---

attached to the army in Italy, and finished the campaign under
Brune. In the tenth year of the republic d'Avoust was appointed commander-in-chief of the grenadiers belonging to the Con-
sular guards. When Napoleon styled himself Emperor of
France, he was made a Marshal of the empire. He commanded
a corps d'armée at the battles of Austerlitz and Jena, and in
that of Deutsch-Wagram. Subsequent to the peace of Tilsit,
he commanded a body of troops in Germany, having his head-
quarters at Erfurt, from whence he took up his residence in
Hamburgh, on being appointed General Governor of the Hanseatic Departments. He commanded a corps under Napoleon
in the famous campaign into Russia, and returned to Hamburgh in May 1813, to become the instrument of Napoleon's
rancorous malice and vindictive thirst for revenge. We need
not enter into arguments to prove the true character of d'Avoust :
his inhuman acts cry aloud to the uttermost corners of the
earth, and leave an impression on the minds of every good
Christian, that is difficult to describe, but very sensibly to be
felt.

---

* When d'Avoust arrived at Schwerin, the capital of the
Dutchy of Mecklenburg-Schwerin, he expressed himself much
surprised to find that all the authorities and opulent inhabitants
had left the place. He sent for Mr. Röder, chamberlain of the
court, and gave him to understand what miseries awaited the

and bivouacked his army on strong ground near the lakes. Here he remained, for some time, in-

---

country when deserted by its magistrates, and bid him repair to the reigning Duke, and tell him, that if he did not immediately send the bailiffs of the crown baillages, and other members of the civil power, to perform the functions of government, he would make mayors of his hussars, and lord-lieutenants of his gensd'armes. "My first step," he added, "will be to order the conflagration and destruction of all the Duke's palaces, castles, and moveable property of every description." The Duke, however, very properly disdained returning any answer to such brutal threats, more worthy the commander of a body of Vandals, than a Prince of polished France. D'Avoust, on the whole, treated Mecklenburg with some lenity, and an outward show of moderation, but in doing so, he was actuated only by his own private and selfish views ; and these were, that Napoleon had actually promised him the Dukedom of Mecklenburg-Schwerin, with an increased extent of frontier.

At a conference which Mr. Bülow, Grand-marshal of the court of Mecklenburg, had with d'Avoust, during his present occupation of the Dutchy, the latter mentioned, in a haughty, supercilious manner, that the Emperor of France had already, at a conference, on the 27th of April, with the Duke of Weimar, at Erfurt, previous to the battle of Lützen, fixed the fate of Mecklenburg's Duke, by speaking of him in these terms : "He has ceased to be reigning Duke: I shall give his territories to another more worthy of my confidence. He was the first German Prince to desert the Confederacy of the Rhine. I shall trust him no more."

It was remarked, as rather extraordinary, that, regardless of the above-mentioned threats, the Duke's residences, castles, domains, gardens, &c. were particularly spared, and carefully kept up, by d'Avoust during his stay in the Dutchy. He made very detailed inquiries concerning their number, their value, active*. A division under General Loison was advanced to Wismar. General Wallmoden and General Vegesack occupied Neustadt and Rostock, near which latter place some partial advantages were obtained over the enemy. The intelligence of the complete defeat of Marshal Oudinot at Gross-Beeren, reached d'Avoust about the latter

---

and the revenues of the Duke's private property and estates; the peasantry of which latter were less pillaged than the others. To obtain the necessary information he did not scruple employing the vilest vagabonds—people who, under the government of the Duke, had been guilty of embezzlements of the worst description. A man, in particular, of the name of Susemihl, a name branded with every attribute belonging to the character of a traitor, became one of his most intimate counsellors.

Related to the editor by Baron von K—n.

---

* In the month of August 1813, the head-quarters of d'Avoust were at a favourite hunting-seat of the Duke's, called Frederick's-Thal, near Schwerin. Many petty dilapidations and robberies were committed by his suite, to mention which, would be doing them too much honour; but that the public may know the man, we will here relate one of those numerous acts of pitiful peculation and rapine of this satellite of Napoleon, as being done under his own immediate eye and direction.

In the banquetting saloon hung those four well-known English caricature prints, by Rowlandson, of the Fox-chase and the Fox-hunting Dinner. They seemed to strike d'Avoust's fancy mightily, and he gave express directions to one of his adjutants to have them taken out of their frames, carefully rolled up, and sent to Hamburgh: these orders were immediately put in execution.

Related to the editor by Baron von K—n.

end of the month, and he forthwith made a retrograde movement with his army in the night of the
3d of September, and, by a forced march, reached
the line of the Stecknitz, near Ratzeburg. His
retreat did not escape the circumspection of General Wallmoden, whose light troops, consisting
of the volunteers of Mecklenburg, the Hanseatic
cavalry, the Hanoverian sharp-shooters, and the
free corps of Reiche and Lützow, pressed hard
upon d'Avoust's rear-guard, and took from it above
a thousand prisoners, besides a considerable quantity of baggage and stores. General Wallmoden
pursued the enemy, and took position at Boitzenburg. D'Avoust threw a corps of about 9000
men, under General Pecheux, over the Elbe, with
the view of making a diversion on the side of
Magdeburg. General Wallmoden having received
early intelligence of this intended movement, passed the Elbe at Dömitz, with a part of his army,
and, after a warm affair at Görde, on the 16th of
September, completely beat Pecheux, taking from
him 1800 prisoners, 8 pieces of cannon, 12 tumbrils, and much baggage. The shattered remains
of this corps afterwards found their way back to
Hamburgh, by the route of Lünenburgh. D'Avoust,
with a singular obstinacy, still remained immoveable in his position on the Stecknitz till the month
of November.

The hopes of the Crown Prince of Sweden, in
regard to the politics of Denmark, were not rea-

lized; and, consequently, towards the middle of November, his advanced-guard of 6000 men put itself in march from Hanover, to join General Wallmoden at Boitzenburg, and his Highness crossed the Elbe, with the main body of his army, near the same place, on the 30th of November. After forming a junction with General Wallmoden, his Highness made the necessary dispositions to assault the almost impregnable position of d'Avoust behind the Stecknitz; and a corps was ordered, as a diversion, to cross the Elbe at Geesthacht, and thus to threaten d'Avoust's direct communication with Hamburgh. This detested adherent of Napoleon found himself in jeopardy, and in all haste evacuated the line of the Stecknitz, retreating behind the Bille, or, more properly speaking, throwing himself and his army into the devoted city of Hamburgh.

The Crown Prince pursued him till under the walls of Hamburgh, and, leaving a corps of observation before the place, directed his march on Lübeck, which place opened its gates to him on the 6th of December. The auxiliary corps of Danes, attached to d'Avoust's army, filed off from the Stecknitz towards Segeberg and Rendsburg. The Crown Prince detached a corps to observe their operations, which marched by the way of Neumünster. Some well-contested affairs took place, and the Danes made good their retreat to Rendsburg on the 15th of December, after a very

severe and bloody action, in which much bravery
was shown on both sides. The Prince of Hesse,
who commanded the Danes, now offered terms
for a cessation of arms; they were agreed upon;
and an armistice, till the 29th of December, was
concluded. Meanwhile General von Bennigsen
had arrived before Hamburgh with his army of
Russians and Poles, and the Crown Prince being
relieved, retraced his steps towards the Weser and
the Rhine. Hamburgh was now strictly blockaded on all sides*; and the brutal d'Avoust had

---

* 1°. When the Russian army was on the point of investing
Hamburgh, d'Avoust issued an order, commanding all owners
of horses of every description to provide themselves with forage
for six months. As soon as this was complied with, at an enormous expense, another mandate appeared, ordering that all
horses, not belonging to the garrison, should have their throats
cut, which was immediately put in execution; and the forage
collected by the citizens, was then seized upon by d'Avoust,
under the pretence of its now being useless.

2°. The inhabitants were commanded by d'Avoust, upon
pain of expulsion, to provide themselves with six months provisions, with an assurance, publicly announced, that private
property would, in every event, be respected. Hardly had
eight days expired, before a new regulation, in two separate
ordinances, appeared, by which *each* member of a family was
bound, under penalty of exile, to deliver fourteen pounds
weight of provisions into the French magazines!

3°. A very eminent physician of Hamburgh, on venturing to
make remonstrances to d'Avoust, concerning the converting his
house into an hospital, at half an hour's notice, stating that it
was the only relic of his property still left untouched; that his

free scope to exercise his monstrous passion for devastation, and the sight of human misery in all its gradations. The fate of Hamburgh will form, for ever, an epoch in the history of French principles, when describing their effects, and the actions of their propagators, well calculated to incite every well-wisher of his native country to hold them in utter detestation. D'Avoust was General-governor and Commander-in-chief*. His

---

books, his physical apparatus, his anatomical collection, &c. could not be moved in so short a space of time, and would inevitably be destroyed by the lawless soldiery; d'Avoust answered, in his usual brutal manner: "How, Sir! your property? Where can you have property? (And then, laying hold of a button of his coat, added,) Not even this button can be called your property; it belongs to the Emperor. You must turn out of your house within half an hour. Begone!"

---

* I°. At a conference which d'Avoust had with one of the Senators of Hamburgh, soon after his reoccupation of the place, he casually remarked, that he should only punish the criminal.

"Who may they be?" inquired the Senator.

"The rich," he rejoined, scoffingly.

2°. The General of d'Avoust's Etat-major observed, in the course of a conversation with the Editor, "that the city had shown a furious enthusiasm at the sight of the Russians, for which the inhabitants would, in return, have the pleasure of seeing their pockets turned inside out." To this the General added a remark, which at that time had much point: "As to the English," he said, "they had accustomed themselves to travel too much on the Continent; they would, in future, have less liberty and opportunity."

preparations for defence were upon a large scale,
and he appeared determined to defend himself to
the very last extremity.   His acts of oppression
exceed all human conception *.   Nothing seemed

---

* The rigorous measures adopted by d'Avoust against the
personal interests of the citizens of Hamburgh, can with difficulty be defended by any kind of sophistry; and the state
of men's minds in the north of Germany could not but
serve to render every action of this satellite of Napoleon detested. D'Avoust, in his subsequent defence, seems to lay
much stress on his asserting that " he defies any one to prove
his having done an action unbecoming an officer and a man of
honour;" or, in other words, confesses he was only a subordi-
nate instrument in more powerful hands. But can mercy and
forbearance be less necessary to an officer in obeying the orders
of his sovereign, than to a private citizen? No sovereign ever
issued mandates to make war upon private individuals. We will
allow d'Avoust every advantage to be derived from the basis
on which he founds his innocence and exculpation—we will
not even dispute his right to seize his means of defence where-
ever they were to be found, either in the bank, in the houses
of the citizens, or in their lives and property. The honour or
dishonour of executing cruel mandates to their utmost extent,
instead of modifying them by the laws of humanity, we will
leave to be determined by that diversity of opinion which must
necessarily exist, and only from plain, unvarnished, and authentic facts, venture to mark his character with those blots of
atrocity and inhumanity, which, when once fixed, it is not, nor
ever can be, in his power to efface.

His master's orders were to defend the place, and to complete
its fortifications. A glacis of sufficient extent from the out-
works was a main object, the obtaining of which must have appeared necessary from the first moment of his re-entering the
city. A good engineer knows the space required accord-

sacred to him. The private property of the citi-zens, placed in the bank *, was greedily seized

---

ing to the nature of the ground; consequently the suburbs, villages, and houses lying in the way of forming such a glacis could be ascertained on the first survey of the out-works by the General of Engineers, and reported accordingly to the Com-mander-in-chief: that such reports were made, are facts that cannot be controverted; but it would ill have suited the thirst for vengeance that rankled in the heart of this cat's-paw of despotism, towards the inhabitants of a corner of Germany so recently in a state of the highest enthusiasm at the transient recovery of their freedom, to have shown them any marks of mercy and forbearance. Instead of a general warning to the inhabitants of all the suburbs and villages, that the site of their houses, grounds, and gardens would, or must, form the glacis on this or that side of Hamburgh, they were deceived and ca-joled into a belief of safety, that their property might become an easier prey to Napoleon's plundering hordes; and d'Avoust could glut his malicious animosity at the sight of individual dis-tress, and the elegant retreats of the brave citizens of Hamburgh a prey to the flames. The French re-entered the city on the 30th of May 1813; and it was only in December following, in the middle of winter, that the orders for burning and destroying were issued, with a specious notice of forty-eight hours' time to quit, but which was never in any instance observed. We will here relate the events at Hamm, a large village, full of coun-try-seats, and beginning close to the out-works on the east side of Hamburgh, as a counterpart to what passed on the north and west sides, and leave the question to be decided by our readers, whether d'Avoust did act the becoming part of an officer and a man of honour towards the citizens of Hamburgh and its vicinity. In the second week of December an adjutant from General Gengoult brought the mayor of Hamm an order, that

* See page 303,

upon. Thousands of industrious families were reduced to absolute beggary and starvation. He con-

---

it was Marshal d'Avoust's will to have every house in the village
of Hamm, to the number of forty, as far as the church, burnt
and levelled to the ground ; but that the inhabitants were to be
favoured with forty-eight hours' time to remove their property :
several of these houses were then full of fugitives and property
saved from dwellings burnt prior to this, it being the fourth
time, within the last fortnight, that the mayor had to announce
such heart-rending tidings to the parish ; and, dreadful to relate, hardly thirty hours were elapsed of this prescribed time,
before a swarm of pioneers, with their firebrands, burst, before
break of day, into the houses like furies, and, turning a deaf
ear to all the mayor's remonstrances, devoted to the flames, or
pillaged, the beds, clothing, and property of many a widow and
helpless family. The church and churchyard became their
asylum. The monstrous barbarity of setting fire to houses before the expiration of the forty-eight hours so solemnly granted, and before the inhabitants had left them, induced the
mayor to write a letter to d'Avoust, of which the following is
an extract :

" Monseigneur, *Hamm, Dec.* 13, 1813.

" The officer who brought the order for burning all the
houses as far as the church, assured me, that you had graciously
been pleased to grant to the poor sufferers a respite of forty-
eight hours, to enable them to remove their property. It is a
painful task for me to announce to you that the respite has not
been attended to, the pioneers having, by break of day this
morning, set every dwelling on fire, although the respite granted expires not before three o'clock to-morrow morning. The remaining inhabitants of Hamm beseech you, in the most pressing
manner, to inform them how far the burning of their houses

verted an opulent, populous city into a desert, and
smiled, with horrid joy, when viewing the ruin he

---

may yet extend, as they only demand time and notice to remove their effects. I entreat to be favoured with a word of
consolation on this head, that I may communicate it to the dis-
tressed parishioners.   B—, Mayor."

General Gengoult undertook to deliver the letter; but, instead of an answer, he next day showed the mayor a letter
from General Loison, containing very pointed praises for his
having merited the thanks of Marshal d'Avoust, for the punc-
tuality and celerity with which his orders had been executed.
The mayor received no answer whatever to his letter. But, on
the 23d of December, General Gengoult gave him a verbal
assurance in the name of Marshal d'Avoust (thus we save our
honour; we let others act the hangman's part—we are innocent), that he was authorized to announce to the inhabitants
still occupying houses in Hamm, it was his (the Marshal's) intention not to devote any more of them to the flames. Two
days afterwards, however, came the order to cut down all the
trees within two hundred and fifty yards of the present line of
posts ; and, on the 15th of January 1814, d'Avoust sent an
order that every remaining house in Hamm should be burnt the
same evening ; so that only two houses were left standing
in this beautiful and romantic village, once studded with
the tasteful edifices and gardens of Hamburgh's opulent mer-
chants, and extending, in a straight line, nearly two miles and
a half in length from the out-works of Hamburgh. The coun-
try-seats, houses, barns, and stables last set on fire were full
of fugitives, with effects and property of every description that
had been saved from earlier conflagrations ; there was, however,
no time, no means to save an article, the whole was consigned
to the flames, and, like a troop of parish paupers, the population of Hamm were turned out into the high road, in the midst

had caused. The inhabitants that remained in the place, were exposed, every hour, to acts of diaboli-

---

of a very severe winter, to seek a shelter—to seek a morsel of bread; and we may say, driven to speechless despair at the sight of many a household relic, treasured up for years in a family, feeding the flames of the watch-fires of their infuriate persecutors. It may be advanced in extenuation, that d'Avoust's means of defence required these barbarous measures, or were strengthened by them; but the sequel proves the falsity of such assertions, and places the act in a more glaring light of atrociousness and malignant personal revenge. On the 26th of January 1814, at an early hour in the morning, the Russians attacked, with three columns, the French line of posts in Hamm, drove them in with a trifling loss, and the whole of the French in Hamm, who had retreated to the church, consisting of nine officers and three hundred men, were taken prisoners; a very natural consequence, by the first attack, as, according to military tactics, the position of Hamm, with regard to the outworks of Hamburgh, is only a defile to be defended by sharpshooters; for, when the enemy is in possession of Wandsbeck, it affords no offensive position, because it can always be assaulted from the commanding grounds on the left flank.

---

* (*Referred to in p.* 300.)—After the bank had been completely gutted by d'Avoust, of silver coin and bars, to the value of nearly £700,000 sterling, he refused paying the salaries in arrears (not exceeding a few hundreds) due to the clerks and bookkeepers, many of whom, with their families, were thus reduced to a state of actual want. Mr. Pehmöller, one of the worthy bank-directors, commiserating their forlorn situation, was induced, on the 19th of April, to obtain an audience of d'Avoust, to make representations of their distresses. This unfeeling Marshal answered Mr. Pehmöller's very pathetic description of their misery in

cal tyranny. A look was sufficient to cause any one
to be thrown into prison—spies swarmed in almost
every house—women were forced to dig in the
trenches—the innocent were shot without mercy,
for the most trifling offence. To conclude: d'Avoust,
it will be seen, laughed to scorn all religious institutions, all moral precepts*.

---

the following terms : " He had but one object in view, to which
all others must become subservient : his peculiar situation demanded this of him, and that was, to defend the place to the
last extremity.—Economy was requisite in making use of the
funds he had taken.   Nothing but a general peace could induce
him to leave the city ; the enemy would never force him to evacuate it.   In this state of things, the persons belonging to the
bank had done much better to have quitted the town. He should
give no order for their being paid their arrears."   And then,
waving his hand, the conversation ended.   Mr. Pehmöller had
no other consolation to soften the pain caused by such diabolical apathy, than the conscious feeling of having done his duty.
One of these families was afterwards found in a state of absolute starvation !

---

   * Every one must be seized with horror on reading the tales
of woe caused by d Avoust's inhuman orders to clear, in a few
hours, the public hospital for the insane and infirm, near Hamburgh.   The sacred rights of humanity were thereby most bar-
barously violated with bitter scorn and derision.   If any thing
were wanting to fill up the measure of d'Avoust's crimes, here
nothing that is devilish, accursed, and horrid, could be added.
The shrines of Christianity had been beastly insulted by drunken
soldiery ; infants murdered at the mother's breast ; but here the
poor insane wretch—the squalid idiot—the melancholy maiden—
the raging madman—the blind, and bed-ridden—were tumbled

indiscriminately together, into the open fields, in the midst
of winter, and left exposed to hunger, cold, and a miserable
death, the sport of bantering gens-d'armes, the object of every
species of ill-treatment; and their fits of convulsive laughter,
weeping, cursing, and praying, were alike permitted to be
the soldiers' scoff and mockery! Most of them, near five hundred in number, of both sexes, passed the night in a field covered with deep snow, without the least shelter; and more
than thirty were found dead the next morning!

CHAPTER XI.

The March of the Silesian Army into France—
Battles of Brienne and La Rothière—Progress
of the allied Armies.

THE corps of Russians, under General Count von
Wittgenstein, reinforced by the troops of the
Grand Duke of Baden, had passed the Rhine at
Fort Louis, and, after blockading the fortresses of
Strasburg, Landau, and Schlettstadt, continued
their march, by the way of Zabern, towards Join-
ville.

General Count St. Priest ordered General Bistram, with his brigade, to attack the intrenchments which the enemy had thrown up opposite
the Lahn, and, after a slight resistance, they were
carried. Upon this, General Bistram advanced
towards Coblentz, took it by assault; and 7 pieces
of cannon and 500 prisoners fell into his hands.
General von Hünerbein drove the French out of
Rheinbellen and Waldalgesheim, and marched
into Kreutznach on the 2d of January, in the evening: General von York now followed with the
whole of his infantry.

A division of the enemy, under General Riccard,
which occupied the banks of the Rhine, from

Mentz to Coblentz, endeavoured to make a stand at Zimmern, on the Hundsrück. General Count von Henkel marched in that direction, burst open the gates in the night, stormed the place, and made above 200 prisoners in the several affairs.

General Count von Sacken concentrated his troops near Manheim. The French had erected a strong pallisaded work, mounted with four guns and two howitzers, on the other side of the Rhine, opposite the influx of the Neckar into that river. General Sass was sent over with a detachment, in boats, and carried the works by storm. The commandant, 7 officers, 300 privates, and the artillery, remained in the hands of the victors. General Count von Sacken now directed the march of his corps to Frankenthal and Worms, detaching General Prince von Curland, with his brigade, in the direction of Alzei, to open a communication with the corps of von York and Count Langeron. He found a small body of the French posted at Alzei, which he dispersed, making a Lieutenant-colonel, 5 officers, and 120 men prisoners. In the mean time, Major-general Karpoff had charged eight squadrons of the enemy's cavalry at Mutterstadt, and dispersed them on all sides. Three Lieutenant-colonels, 22 officers, and 198 dragoons, were on this occasion taken prisoners. General Count von Langeron occupied Bingen, on the 3d of January, and drove the enemy into

Mentz. During these three days, 13 pieces of cannon and 1500 men were taken from the enemy.

The Silesian army spread itself over the terrain between the Moselle and Manheim, and pushed forwards in the direction of Metz and Nancy. The greater part of Langeron's corps remained to blockade and besiege Mentz; and several other detachments of the Silesian army undertook to observe the fortresses of Luxemburg, Thionville, Metz, Verdun, and Longwy. The army was in consequence much weakened; but on the other hand, it was considerably reinforced by the junction of the Prussian corps under General von Kleist.

The following corps were at this period placed under the immediate command of Field-marshal Blücher:

1. The 1st Prussian corps under General von York, and the Generals of Division, Charles von Mecklenburg, von Horn, and von Hünerbein:

2. The 2d Prussian corps, under General von Kleist, and the Generals of Division von Klüx, Prince Augustus Ferdinand of Prussia, and von Pirch:

3. The Russian corps, under General Count Langeron, von Sacken, and Tscherbatoff:

4. The Saxon corps, under the Duke of Weimar and General von Thielman.

The two following corps joined soon afterwards:

5. The 4th corps of German troops, consisting
of Hessians, under the Prince of Hesse:

6. The 5th corps of German troops, consisting
of detachments from Berg, Waldeck, Lippe,
Nassau, Coburg, Meinungen, Hildburghausen,
and Mecklenburg-Strelitz.

Forming, in the whole, an effective army of
150,000 men, well provided with every appendage
to take the field.

Marshal Blücher issued the following proclamations; the one to his soldiers, the other to the
French, on entering their territory:

Field-marshal von Blücher to the 2d Prussian
    Corps, and the 4th and 5th German Corps.

" The allied Monarchs are satisfied with the Silesian army: they have proved this, by doubling
its strength, in adding to its files the brave soldiers of the 2d Prussian corps, who fought under
the eyes of the august Monarchs at Culm, and in
the bloody conflict of Leipsic: and you, honest
Hessians! who never denied your German character, nor failed in being faithful to the Princes
born in your country; and you, warriors of the
fifth German corps, who never lost sight of your
name, even in the ranks of the enemy, although
composed of several tribes, yet are you firmly
united by the same sentiments, the same abhorrence of foreign dominion, that has so long oppressed and degraded you,

" Soldiers ! I feel myself most highly honoured
in being your commander. The Silesian army of
1813 receives you as brethren—as worthy members, with whom they will joyfully share every
thing. The Silesian army of 1814 will continue
to pursue the path of honour. And you, Germans ! led by your hereditary princes, be assured
that it will become my first care, my highest
pride, to let the arrogant enemy feel the force of
your arms, that he may confess—whatever success
wily craft may have formerly had—that the ancient
Teutonic bravery still lives in us, and that by your
heroic deeds a lasting peace may be secured."

To the inhabitants of France the Field-marshal
issued as follows :

" Frenchmen ! do not let yourselves be deceived
by scandalous reports, spread abroad by the evil-
minded. See in the hosts of the confederate Sovereigns, the friends of humanity, whose only
enemies are the enemies of peace.

" Your relations, your friends, your brothers,
your children, prisoners in a foreign land, unite
their wishes with ours, for the attainment of a
peace, whose first benefit will be for them to return to the bosoms of their families.

" VON BLÜCHER."

In the cities of Worms and Speier, General von
Sacken's corps found hospitals of the enemy, and

a quantity of military effects. On the 3d of January, General Lukofkin had a brilliant affair of cavalry near Neustadt.

Marshal Marmont was posted on the 5th, with his corps, near Kaiserslautern, and passed the Saar, near Saarbrück, on the following day, after being joined by the corps of Generals Durutte and Riccard, who had retreated from Hundsrück, in the direction of St. Wendel.

The enemy broke down the bridges over the Saar, and occupied all the passes. They were briskly pursued by von Sacken's corps towards Saargemünd; a number of prisoners were taken, and another military hospital fell into their hands at Zweibrücken. General von York's corps advanced upon Saarlouis and Merzig, by the way of St. Wendel. Colonel Count Henkel entered Triers on the 6th, and more than a thousand sick and wounded, and a quantity of muskets, fell into his hands. The enemy were pursued to Luxemburg. It seemed his intention to hold a firm position on the Saar, so as to gain time to provision his fortresses, and reorganize his new levies. A part of Langeron's corps marched as reserve towards Saarbrück. Marshal Blücher fixed his head-quarters, on the 9th of January, at St. Wendel. In the course of the day, Major-general Karpoff pushed over a detachment of Cossacks to the other side of the Saar near Saargemünd, obliged the enemy to evacuate the place, and began to re-establish the bridge. In the mean while, General von York had caused another bridge to be thrown over the Saar, near Becking, and on the 10th, passed it at the head of his cavalry ; but the enemy had deserted all his positions, and retreated to St. Avold. Towards noon, the bridges at Saarbrück and Saargemünd were ready, and the light troops of both corps penetrated as far as Forsbach. On the 11th, the enemy's advanced-guard were still at St. Avold, but on the appearance of a battalion of Prussians, they precipitately fled towards Metz. General von York pursued them on this road, leaving a brigade to blockade Saarlouis, and detaching another to Thionville and Luxemburg.

The retreating enemy were overtaken, and driven, sword in hand, to the gates of Metz. Sacken's corps now advanced to Nancy and Pont-à-Mousson. The cavalry of the advanced-guard reached the latter place on the 13th of January. The enemy, however, made no stand at any point; he evacuated the line of the Moselle on the 14th, retiring to Toul, and Major-general Prince von Curland presented the keys of the city of Nancy to General Count von Sacken. The rapid march of the Silesian army, after the passage of the Rhine, was but little expected by the enemy. Our veteran Field-marshal paused not a moment, but pursued his course with a numerous and well-appointed cavalry without intermission towards the Meuse.

The Field-marshal removed his head-quarters on the 16th from St. Avold to Nancy.

The grand Austro-Russian army advanced into France from the south towards the north-west, and Blücher's army from the north-east towards the south; and the two armies formed a junction on the 15th of January, between Langres in Champaigne and Nancy. The head-quarters of Marshal Blücher were still at Nancy on the 17th, and those of General Count Wrede at Charmes. The enemy had withdrawn himself over the Meuse, but still occupied Toul with infantry and artillery. General von Sacken advanced by the way of Pont-Vincent. Field-marshal Prince von Schwartzenberg having reported to our veteran Hero that Langres was taken, and the enemy driven at all points over the Meuse, he ordered Toul to be stormed from the side of Woid. The dispositions were made: the enemy did not, however, wait the attack, but surrendered at discretion to General von Lieven. General von Sacken's corps marched in advance, to clear the Meuse of the enemy, and General Langeron occupied Toul, as reserve. General von York's cavalry were posted before Verdun. The corps of General von Kleist marched upon Metz. Two of General von Sacken's columns filed off in the direction of Ligny and Joinville. In the afternoon the enemy debouched out of Ligny, with a force of about 2500 horse, and, after cannonading the cavalry under General Wasiltschikoff, retired, on seeing that not a foot of ground was yielded to him. Ligny was stormed and carried on the 23d, by order of our veteran Marshal, by the division of Prince Tscherbatoff; and on the 25th, the French were driven out of St. Dizier, and pursued on the road to Vitry, by the same general, who continued his march to Brienne on the 26th, to form a junction with the other part of Sacken's corps. St. Dizier was kept occupied by General Lanskoy, with 800 dragoons, to await General von York's corps coming up from St. Mihiel.

During these unimportant marches and advances, Napoleon had left Paris for the army on the 25th, and arrived at Chalons on the 26th, in the evening. He here commenced an attempt to act on the offensive with an army of 80,000 men, by proceeding to Vitry. Being, no doubt, informed, that Prince Tscherbatoff had filed off from St. Dizier, he seized the opportunity of attacking General Lanskoy at that place with a force of 25,000 men, who was, in consequence of such numbers, obliged to make a retrograde movement to Joinville. But no sooner was this event reported to our veteran Hero, than he made his dispositions with his usual foresight and vigorous promptitude. Having removed his head-quarters from Nancy to Toul on the 28th, he drew in General Lanskoy's detachment, concentrated the corps of General von Sacken, and a division of

Langeron's corps, under General Olsufieff, near Brienne, pushed detachments of cavalry in advance towards Arcis and Troyes, which the enemy had occupied with infantry; and in this position awaited the developement of Napoleon's further operations.

The 4th corps, under the Prince of Würtemberg, and the 3d, under General Count Giulay, were in position near Bar-sur-Aube; the former spread itself towards Thil and Doulevent, to form a junction with the 5th corps, under General Wrede, which corps, as well as that under General Count Wittgenstein, were ordered to arrive at Joinville on the 29th. General Giulay extended his corps in the direction of Vandamon, and General von Kleist's corps. was to pass the Meuse by St. Mihiel on the 2d of February, to support the corps of General von York. The remaining corps of the grand army were on the march to Bar-sur-Aube, but which they could not reach before the 1st of February.

In this state of affairs Marshal Blücher saw himself, at the moment, under the necessity of depending solely upon his own strength and the good countenance of his troops.

Napoleon's intentions were very obvious, being no other than to attempt cutting off Blücher from the main army, or to push him, by manœuvring, so far aside, as to have it afterwards left to his own individual choice which army to attack singly to the greatest advantage. But here, again, the military talents of our Hero shone forth in all their native splendour. To effect a march upon Nancy was every thing to Napoleon, and none but those movements which our veteran so coolly and intrepidly performed, could have placed so great a barrier in Napoleon's way. They secured Blücher's communication and junction with the grand army, and the enemy was unable to follow up his first plan of operations. General von York in the mean time remained standing with his corps between Nancy and the Marne, to observe Metz, and the occurrences that might take place in that quarter. Thus situated, Napoleon was compelled to follow the movements of the Silesian army. With the main body of his troops, consisting of the corps of Marshals Victor and Marmont, the major part of his guards, and the brigades of cavalry under Generals Milhaud, Grouchy, and Colbert, he moved on to Vassy on the 28th, and pushed forwards, by the way of Montierender, towards Brienne on the 29th of January. It was impossible for the Field-marshal to judge what the real intentions of Napoleon were; whether to attack, to manœuvre, or only to make demonstrations. At all events, however, he continued to concentrate his forces round Brienne. General von Sacken's corps, which had marched to Lesmont, now returned, and General Count Pahlen, who had joined, at this juncture, the Silesian army, with the advanced-guard of Count

Wittgenstein's corps, covered this movement of Sacken's, in the morning of the 29th of January, and at the same time observed the deploying of the enemy's forces. Some important dispatches of the enemy happened to fall into the hands of Blücher, on this day. They contained orders for Marshal Mortier, who was still in position at Troyes, with a part of the guards, to leave this place, and the Aube, and to post himself on the right wing of the French grand army. It was therefore clear, that Napoleon intended to unite the whole of his forces. This induced Blücher to attempt approaching the confederate army still nearer, as a complete junction could not take place at Bar-sur-Aube before the 1st of February, and a secure position at Trannes, which extended to Maisons, where the Prince of Würtemberg was preparing to post himself on strong ground, offered him many peculiar advantages. Our Hero was upon the point of making this movement, when the enemy advanced with numerous strong columns upon Brienne. This event instantly changed his plan of operations, and as it was near three o'clock, P. M. he determined to accept battle, although he well knew the numbers of the enemy were much superior to his own.

Brienne le Chateau is quite an open place, with no walls, composed of wooden houses, and lying at the foot of a hill, on which the castle or manor-house stands; a rising ground stretches itself from

thence towards Lesmont; but, on the side towards Montierender and Trannes, the face of the
country forms an extensive plain.

The corps of General Olsufieff still occupied
Brienne, and that of Sacken was drawn up in columns, on the road from Brienne to La Rothière.

A considerable body of the enemy's cavalry began
to debouch in front of General Count von Pahlen,
and made it necessary for him to retreat on Brienne,
in order not to entangle himself with such superior
numbers. The enemy pushed on the right wing
of his mass of cavalry to the foot of the heights,
with the view of out-flanking him, to prevent
which, General Count von Pahlen marched, with
his division, through the town, and joined General
von Sacken. In the mean time, Napoleon proceeded to attack Brienne, with columns of infantry, supported by a numerous artillery; he commenced a brisk cannonade, and set the town on
fire in several places. These movements were
made from Napoleon's right wing, the cavalry of
which, after Count Pahlen's retreat, remained
inactive. On his left wing few cavalry were
posted.

The gallant General Olsufieff succeeded in repulsing all the furious simultaneous attacks of the
enemy. His Russians fought with their wonted
intrepidity, and every attempt of the enemy to
lodge himself in the place proved of no avail.

Napoleon, who was in the field, here committed

a fatal and unpardonable error, in the disposition
of his troops. General Count von Pahlen having
retreated, and Napoleon's mass of cavalry, on his
right wing, becoming, of course, useless, it was
highly incumbent on him, as a good general, to
have filed them off to his left wing, where alone
they could prove of service, and be disposable.
But this he did not do; and this egregious error
did not escape the vigilant eye of Blücher, who
instantaneously gave orders to execute one of
these bold, decisive, and grand movements, by
which doubtful contests are decided. Our Hero
commanded the cavalry of General von Sacken's
corps, and the cavalry brigade under Count Pahlen, to act in concert, and to throw themselves
upon the enemy's left wing. His commands were
obeyed with precision and alacrity. The close of
evening favoured the secrecy of their approach;
the Russian dragoons rushed to the attack, charged, and overthrew whole columns, cut in pieces
all that made resistance, and pursued the fugitives
towards the town, sword in hand. The whole of
the enemy's left wing was broken and dispersed,
and twelve pieces of cannon taken from them. A
noble emulation seemed to fire the Russian cavalry, and, if possible, they surpassed themselves.

The enemy, however, from the points of his
right wing, continued to renew his attacks on the
place, with fresh troops; but they were again repulsed. During the night, the French found

means, from the side of the castle, through an
unoccupied pass, to get possession of a part of
the town.   But the corps of General von Sacken
advanced, and stormed the place at eleven o'clock
at night: the whole of the town fell a prey to the
flames, the Russians kept possession of it, and
only a few French riflemen occupied the castle.
The troops fought with that ferocious animosity
which generally accompanies night attacks, and
the loss of the French was immense.

Marshal von Blücher postponed his intended
march upon Trannes till the following day, and
kept Brienne occupied with a detachment of cavalry.

On the 31st of January, the enemy advanced
his reinstated left wing, and, towards noon, pushed on his columns of infantry to Brienne, and
commenced a heavy cannonade upon the Russian
cavalry, posted behind the place; upon which the
latter drew back slowly into the position of
Trannes.

Napoleon now followed with his whole army,
which he drew up in two lines, his right wing
leaning on Dienville, his centre on La Rothière,
and his left wing on La Gibrie.

General von York had, on the same day, advanced upon St. Dizier, attacked and carried it,
forming, at the same time, a junction with General Count von Wittgenstein's corps.

The enemy deployed a great body of his cavalry

in front of the position of Trannes, in the morning of the 31st of January, with the intention, most probably, of ascertaining the exact strength of the confederate forces. He occupied the wood of Beaulieu, being the only point from which the allied position could be attacked to advantage. The strong ground at Maisons was taken up by the corps of the Prince of Würtemberg, in the course of the day, by which occupation he formed the right wing of Field-marshal Blücher's army. General Count Giulay posted his corps, as a support, between Bossancourt and Arsonval. General Barclay de Tolly collected the Russian and Prussian guards in reserve, between Colombe and Bar-sur-Aube, to be able to support any threatened point. The corps of General Count Wrede having been concentrated between Joinville and Mussec, on the 30th, was, in conjunction with General Count Wittgenstein, to have attacked Vassy on the 31st; the dispositions were already made, and the Bavarian-Austrian army was in march, beyond Joinville, on the morning of the 31st of January, when the report was made that Count Wittgenstein had carried it in the night. This circumstance, added to the advance of Napoleon to Brienne, determined General Count Wrede to direct his march to Soulaines, where the enemy had posted from 5 to 6000 men; but they did not wait the result of an attack, the place being evacuated at midnight.

It was resolved to make a general attack upon the whole line of the enemy, on the 1st of February. Prince Schwartzenberg placed, for this purpose, the corps of Count Giulay, the Prince of Würtemberg, and the reserves of Russian grenadiers, under the immediate command of Marshal Blücher, independently of his own army. With these gallant and tried troops our Hero was to commence the onset, the dispositions being entirely left to his judgment.

Marshal Blücher determined to make the attack at noon, in three columns. The Prince of Würtemberg had orders to break up from Maisons, and to arrive at Eclance at twelve o'clock, to attack Chaumenil from this point. General Baron von Sacken was to attack La Rothière, and Count Giulay, Dienville. The Russian grenadiers were drawn up as reserves.

The battle commenced by the Prince of Würtemberg attacking, with his corps, the wood in front of Eclance, while La Rothière was assaulted in a grand style, by General von Sacken's infantry. The cavalry of this corps charged that of the enemy, though superior in number, but were at last obliged to fall back on their infantry. Having been reinforced, they renewed the charge with undaunted bravery; a severe conflict ensued, which lasted some time with sanguinary obstinacy; the French were driven from one rallying point to the other, and finally broken and dispersed,

with a terrible loss; their infantry were put into
disorder, some batteries charged sword in hand,
the field of battle was cleared of the enemy entirely, and thirty-two pieces of cannon formed
part of the trophies so dearly earned, by the firmness, discipline, and courage of the Russian cavalry in particular. It may be said, that from this
moment the battle was won, although Napoleon
still occupied Dienville, La Rothière, and Chaumenil.

A brigade of Russian grenadiers was sent, by
Marshal Blücher, to reinforce the Prince of Würtemberg; and General Barclay de Tolly moved
in advance to La Rothière, with the reserves of
guards under his command.

At this period of the battle, our Hero put himself at the head of the columns that were intended
to force La Rothière. He led them personally
into fire, with the animation and energy so
conspicuous in his actions, when the hour of
emergency and danger calls them forth. A Cossack was shot dead, close to him. But the place
was carried, and the enemy dislodged out of it, at
the approach of night. Nature seemed to have
aided in rendering this combat most grievously
painful. A dreadful fall of snow hid, at intervals, the columns from each other, and the wind
drove it in the faces of the troops with such violence, that it was utterly impossible for them, at
times, to fire in steady platoons.

Our Hero was present every where; he executed his dispositions himself, fearlessly exposing his person. His chivalrous example electrified his troops to an uncommon degree, and great was the increase of his fame on this glorious day. How admirable was the coolness he displayed, in leading, arranging, and heading the grand assault upon La Rothière and Chaumenil, which he, with so much foresight and penetration, had deemed the most important points to be gained; although the enemy, by way of a demonstration, pretended to threaten the flank of the confederate army; yet no artifice could mislead the judgment of our experienced Captain and Commander. The instant the enemy began to fly from La Rothière, the Prince of Würtemberg pushed on his troops from Petit Megnil, fell upon their right flank, and took five guns. The French still obstinately occupied the houses in La Rothière, and defended each like so many forts. Napoleon, at the head of his guards, stormed the town three times successively; but all his attempts were in vain. Russian grenadiers maintained the place, and the fame of their ancient glory *.

---

* We have had opportunities of remarking, that the Russian possesses, in an eminent degree, nearly all those qualities that are accounted necessary to form a good soldier. Obedience, devotion, patience, courage, bodily strength, and a good constitution, are in no nation of Europe so generally to be found as in the Russian. They may be reproached with the want of clean-

In animating his troops, Napoleon several times exposed his person; he strained every nerve, and fought like an exasperated tiger, to boast of having gained the first victory over the Confederates on the·French soil, and to restore the lost confidence in the fortune and omnipotence of his arms.

During these important events, General Count Wrede had advanced, with the 5th corps, from Soulaines to Brienne.   His advanced-guard, under

---

liness, by the superficial observer, because, when in the field, the niceties of their dress form their least care; yet, whenever a clear spring presents itself, they never neglect to bathe themselves, even in the severest weather.   But in no situation incident to a soldier's life, is the Russian so much superior to the Frenchman, as in an hospital.   An hospital full of sick and wounded Frenchmen is a den, where despair, melancholy, and base dejection brood in gloomy silence.   That of Russians, on the contrary, is a scene of cheerfulness and merriment.   A Russian is resigned, but it is a resignation intermixed with a grateful sense of God's mercies, while a Frenchman's resignation degenerates but too easily into selfish despair.   A total neglect of every measure of cleanliness is always evident amongst the French in such a state, while the Russians occupy themselves with nothing else.   The latter have a custom in their hospitals which may not be unworthy of imitation, as being preferable, in many instances, to wetting the floors, when cleaning them, which is this: fresh sand is regularly spread over the floors, half a foot thick, every morning, and a large quantity of pine or fir branches, chopped small, is then strewed over the surface, which affords a fragrant and refreshing effluvium, that overpowers, in some measure, those unpleasant smells that arise, and seems to clear and rarefy the foul air engendered from the steam of perspirations so general in crowded hospitals, and which so often prove contagious.

General Hardegg, made such an impetuous attack on the enemy, that their junction with the corps at Chaumenil was completely prevented. General Count Wrede, with the view of co-operating with the corps of the Prince of Würtemberg, stormed the village of Chaumenil, without loss of time, at the point of the bayonet, and carried it. Napoleon soon perceived that he had thereby lost an important point of his line of operations; and, by ordering up the artillery of his guards, endeavoured, by a heavy and murderous cannonade, to dislodge the Bavarians out of the place. But his sanguinary efforts proved fruitless, when coming in contact with Bavarian intrepidity. They bravely stood their ground. The Bavarian Colonel Diez, with a brigade of cavalry and a regiment of Austrian dragoons, seized a favourable moment, and throwing himself on all sides at once, on the enemy's square masses of infantry, that covered their batteries, succeeded in breaking them, and hotly pursued the flying foe till night was far advanced. A battery of sixteen pieces of cannon was taken, sword in hand.

The right wing of Napoleon's army still kept its ground at Dienville. Count Giulay here exhibited much gallantry and resolution; he advanced at the head of his troops to the assault six several times. Repulses and rallies trod close on the heels of each other, but the well-known steady coolness of Austrian bravery overcame every obstacle; and, by the sixth assault, near twelve at night, the place was carried with a dreadful carnage. It was about this time that Napoleon made the last, but fruitless, attack upon La Rothière; and the trumpet of victory was now sounded at all points, in honour of the allied arms.

Grand and glorious were the trophies that graced the martial deeds of the gallant Confederates on this day*. Our Hero had to boast of having taken from Napoleon, in the field, 73 pieces of cannon and 12,000 prisoners, including two generals and a proportionate number of officers.

The Emperor of Russia and the King of Prussia had placed themselves in the centre of the

---

* The next morning, by break of day, the intrepid Field-marshal, on finding the enemy had relinquished the field of battle, rode down the front of the Russian columns, at the head of his numerous staff, and paid due honours to these illustrious corps, who had behaved in so distinguished a manner, and omitted nothing to show that he knew what it was, to be well served, by acknowledging their merit in the strongest terms. As he approached the several divisions, he addressed the troops and officers in the most emphatical manner, in nearly the following words:

" Brave comrades in arms! I shall thank your Emperor for having done me the honour to command such excellent soldiers! This honour, and this pleasure, will accompany me to the grave!"

The commanding officer explained these words in the Russian language to the troops, and shouts of transport rent the air. The trumpets sounded victory, and every eye glistened with joy and rapturous delight. It was an ecstatic scene.

confederate army, between Trannes and La Rothière, and animated the troops by their presence.

Napoleon was several times in danger of being
taken prisoner by the Cossacks. His troops
fought desperately, and their obstinate defence,
under Marmont, Mortier, Victor, Colbert, and
Grouchy, fully proves what exertions Napoleon
made to step forth as victor from the combat.
But he was beaten. Blücher*, the gallant and
the brave, the Marshal *Forwards* of the day, beat
Napoleon, and forced the stubborn tyrant to fall
back discomfited, with the main body of his army,
from Lesmont to Troyes.

Napoleon made good his retreat by two routes.

---

* During the battles of Brienne and La Rothière, the army
had to struggle with many privations. Its veteran Chief shared
them with evident cheerfulness. For several days nothing was
served at his table but boiled potatoes, of which he partook in
a manner that endeared him to his troops.

Firm and intrepid, and at all times affable, jocose, and in
high spirits, whether in a shower of balls or in a shower of rain,
whether sleeping on straw or on the bare ground, whether in a
storm or in sunshine, no man certainly ever showed a greater
equality of temper, steadiness of character, ardour, and zeal,
than Blücher did at this period.

Silent and attentive, sitting before a watch-fire, smoking his
pipe, he would listen to the counsel and opinions of his staff
officers, and at last give his judgment for and against, with his
own peculiar energy and decision. Over-scrupulous considerations never had any weight with him, and what he had once
determined upon, he executed, at the head of the advance,
fighting and commanding sword in hand.

With the main body, he took the road by the way
of Lesmont towards the Seine, along which river
Schwartzenberg's corps, on the other side, endeavoured to fall on his rear. The reserves, under
Marmont, posted on the heights of Brienne, to
cover his retreat, were ordered to march on Vitry.
Every day, at this period, was marked by an affair
of out-posts, at once bloody and disadvantageous
to Napoleon.

That our readers may be the better enabled to
comprehend the subsequent occurrences, and operations of the several conflicting armies, we previously lay before them the following observations.

The line of those operations which were carried on by the belligerents, might be compared to
a triangular figure, of which Paris formed the
point, and a line drawn from Cologne to Geneva,
the basis; the north side, from Cologne to Paris,
found protection from the emancipated Low
Countries, assisted by Great Britain; and the
south side, from Geneva to Chambery, should
have been protected by Switzerland, but this
country did nothing whatever for the furtherance
of the good cause. It was therefore necessary that
the Confederates should divide their strength, that
they might cut off the south of France from Italy,
and make threatening movements in the rear of
the Viceroy, but at the same time to advance upon
Lyons, to obstruct a concentration of Napoleon's
forces on the Seine.

The Silesian army, under Blücher, and the grand army, under Schwartzenberg, were to come in contact with each other on the Marne. The one drew his reinforcements from Brussels and Liege, and the other by the way of Basle.

The Crown Prince of Sweden formed, with his Northern army, the last link to the chain. He had, however, exclusively of his Swedes, a considerable body of troops, under Generals Bülow, Winzingerode, and Czernischeff, which he had marched, in November, towards Holland, and that now, in conjunction with the Dutch army, and the Saxons, under the Duke of Weimar, joined the right wing of the Silesian army, and took part in the principal combat.

It must here be obvious to every one, that the line from Geneva and Basle to Paris was the weakest and the longest, in the rear, and in the wings of the grand army; that is, it was the most distant from its supports. The corps of Bubna and Simbschen were evidently too weak. The line from Düsseldorf or Cologne, to Paris, acquired, by Holland and the sea, a much greater degree of safety. The support was nearer. The number of fortresses did, to be sure, in some measure render communications and advances somewhat difficult; yet the enemy, under Carnot and Maison, could only act on the defensive.

On the other hand, Augereau, in the south of France, having at his disposal all the forces of the country, could act on the offensive; in which case, the fortresses were of infinite service to the success and continuation of his operations.

Consequently, if the forces of Austria should be broken through, between Basle and Paris, much might be lost. It is this very circumstance, maturely weighed, which fully explains the slow advances of Prince Schwartzenberg.

Marshal Blücher was compelled to advance with all possible celerity. If he were beaten (and this could only be possible in front, or on his right wing, near which the grand army stood), he could fall back without difficulty on the Northern army, recover his losses, and recruit his strength.

But Schwartzenberg was so peculiarly situated, that he could be beaten in front, on his left wing, and in his rear; and if the enemy should succeed in throwing back Blücher's army more to the north, he was actually surrounded on all sides. After the bloody combats in February, he was therefore cautious of not advancing too rashly. He kept his eye upon Lyons, upon Mentz, and upon Basle; and could, by so doing, under the pressure of unfavourable events, be prepared for acting.

This was the reasoning, and these were the reflections of the Commander-in-chief. There is just as little foundation for blame, in the measures adopted by Prince Schwartzenbeg, as in the more active conduct of our veteran Hero. Blücher must march forwards—he must advance—he must bid open defiance to the enemy.

CHAPTER XII.

Blücher marches his Army on Paris—Retreat to Chalons—The Field-marshal out-manœuvres Napoleon—Forms a Junction with the Corps of Bü-low, Woronzow, and Winzingerode.

It is certain that Napoleon laid down the plan of his operations, upon the basis of the review drawn up at the end of the last chapter. It was his intention to break off the right point or corner of the Confederates' triangle of operations, in his desperate attacks upon Blücher's army forming that point, and then to destroy the left point under Schwartzenberg and Bubna. But three times was he forced to recoil, from Blücher's gallant resistance; twice did Schwartzenberg humiliate him; and, from Lyons to Geneva, Napoleon failed entirely. The course of the events will afford a copious theme for explanation. Marshal Blücher, after his signal victory at La Rothière, proceeded onwards, in conjunction with General von York's corps, to Paris. On the 3d of February General von York conducted his attack on the united corps of Macdonald and Arrighi, and the divisions of cavalry under Sebastiani and Excelmans, with so much address, that he drove them back on Chalons-sur-Marne, and summoned the town to surrender. This being refused, he storm-ed the suburbs of the place, on the side of Vitry, and set the town on fire, in four places, by a shower of shells which he threw into it. A de-putation from the inhabitants came out of Cha-lons, with the permission of Marshal Macdonald, and entreated that hostilities might cease. It was afterwards arranged with the Marshal, that all the stores and magazines were to remain in the place, and neither be moved to the rear, nor in advance, and that the town should be delivered up in its present state. The victorious Prussians marched into it on the 6th of February. But the Mar-shal, after consenting to these conditions, did not scruple immediately to violate them, by causing the stone bridge over the Marne to be blown up, notwithstanding the representations of the inhabitants. General von York, however, in spite of this breach of faith, passed the river, and followed up his pursuit of Macdonald to-wards Paris. The gallant conduct of General von York, on these two days, was very conspi-cuous, and afforded his troops an opportunity of distinguishing themselves in the several attacks. Meanwhile Prince Schwartzenberg, with the grand army, kept in a line, and in the same direc-tion with the Silesian army, along the banks of the Seine.

The two armies were separated, most probably,

to procure themselves easy means of subsistence; but they were near enough to each other to act conjunctly if necessary.

Napoleon having received reinforcements out of Spain, succeeded in throwing himself between the two armies, with a force of at least 100,000 men, and in such a position, that he had it in his power to press hard upon the right and left of the confederate armies, as best suited his views.

The army of Blücher, on its march to Paris on the 10th of February, occupied a line which extended from Vertus, where Blücher and Langeron had their head-quarters, by the way of Champaubert and Chateau Thierry, to La Ferté-sous-Jouarre, on a plain of nearly sixty miles in extent. It was this circumstance that rendered Napoleon's attempt to break through it but too successful. General Alsufieff was posted at Champaubert with 4000 men of Blücher's army, where he was assailed by Napoleon on the 10th, and obliged to relinquish the position he had assumed, with severe loss. He himself was taken prisoner. Generals von York and von Sacken formed a rapid junction in this precarious situation; but, with all their heroic exertions on the 11th, they could not force their way from Montmirail to join Blücher, on the shortest route, and from whom they were in a manner cut off. They, in consequence, withdrew over the Marne on the 12th, near Chateau Thierry, and marched upon Chalons. Marshal

Mortier followed hard upon them, **and** crossed the
Marne on the 13th February. In the mean time
our veteran Hero, with the corps of Kleist and
Langeron, had, with the most strenuous efforts,
repulsed Marshal Marmont from Etoges on Montmirail. Napoleon, having received notice of this
bold and unexpected advance, that favoured the
operations of Generals von York and Sacken,
hastened back by a forced march in the night of
the 13th, with his guards, and divisions of cavalry,
from Chateau Thierry, whither he had followed
Mortier, and formed a junction with Marmont.
His great superiority of cavalry enabled Napoleon,
after an obstinate and bloody conflict, to surround
Blücher's army; which event he vainly regarded
at the time, as productive of the total defeat of
the Field-marshal. But, instead of this, our Hero,
with the greatest energy, foresight, and presence
of mind, formed the main body of his army into
square phalanxes, braved with dauntless valour the
gathering storm, and fought his way, at the head
of his invincible Prussians, in the direction of
Vertus to Chalons, under a constant fire of musketry and charges of cavalry.

A retreat of this kind was accompanied with
considerable difficulty, as the contest was with
superior numbers, and every thing was to be effected by the good countenance of the troops
alone. The following minute particulars of this
unexampled retreat may not prove unacceptable

to the reader. The scene in which our Hero happened to be principally occupied, was equal to the scope of his abilities, and it may be also said, that it was worthy of his talents.

Marshal Marmont, in pursuance of his orders, made a retrograde movement, on the 14th, out of the village of Fromentières. Our veteran Commander, who had bivouacked during the previous night, near Champaubert, determined on following him. The enemy retreated as far as the village of Joinvilliers, at which place a considerable mass of the enemy's cavalry was observed to have been posted. In the heat of pursuit, six pieces of Prussian artillery, that were too far advanced, fell into the hands of the French. But the Prussian cavalry, under General Ziethen and Colonel von Blücher, a son of the Field-marshal, charged instantly, with furious impetuosity, the enemy's horse, that were endeavouring to secure their booty, repulsed them with loss, and retook the guns. From the intelligence obtained from the prisoners, it was ascertained that Napoleon had just arrived on the field with his guards and a considerable body of cavalry, having made a fatiguing forced march during the night from Chateau Thierry. Meanwhile Blücher's infantry kept advancing upon the village, in columns and battalions, on the open grounds from both sides of the high road that led through the place. The enemy's horse, strengthened by reinforce-

ments, soon returned to the charge, penetrated
the weak advanced-guard of Blücher's army,
and fell upon the infantry drawn up in columns
on the plain. This movement and manœuvre
of Napoleon was, however, foreseen by our Hero.
The columns having been previously formed into
square phalanxes, they received the tumultuous
charges of the enemy's horse with unparalleled
firmness, stood their ground as if rooted to the
spot on which they were posted, and kept up an
unremitting and destructive fire of musketry from
all sides on the advancing enemy. To the right
of the village six of the Prussian squares were
attacked at one and the same instant, and were
all equally successful in driving back the daring
adversary. Blücher's cavalry having again rallied
under the protection of the infantry, the French,
instead of being the assailants, now found themselves attacked in their turn; the murderous fire
of the Prussian infantry had thrown them into
disorder, and the charges of the Prussian horse
were attended with the most brilliant success. Napoleon, however, still continued to bring fresh
troops into action, and large bodies were observed
in motion on both flanks. Two battalions of Blücher's advanced-guard, that had already penetrated
into the village, had scarcely time to form into
squares; and a large portion of them were either
killed or wounded. The cavalry of the Field-
marshal's army did not exceed 1100 effective men,

while the enemy showed at least from 5 to 6000 horse in the field : no acts of bravery could counterbalance so great a disproportion of numbers, in an arm so very essential in the open country wherein our Hero was now posted. To prevent the serious consequences that might eventually result from further resistance, the Field-marshal resolved to withdraw himself from a position exposed to such an unequal combat, and gave orders that the infantry should put itself in march, formed in alternate squares and columns, with the artillery placed between the open spaces that separated each column. Numerous bodies of sharpshooters, with divisions of cavalry, covered the flanks and rear : and in this order the retreat began. The country round the line of operations was without inclosures of any kind, and only intersected here and there with spots of underwood, which caused the movements of the enemy's cavalry to be less exposed to the observation of the Allies. To render success more certain, the infantry carefully avoided throwing themselves under cover, and, by proceeding along the high road in firm columns, could keep the enemy more effectually in check, and ensure their own safety from being endangered by the numerous bodies of cavalry that now hovered around them. A continual succession of attacks and repulses followed each other, at short intervals, from the village of Joinvilliers to half way between Champaubert and

Etoges, being a distance of nearly twelve miles. Every column and every square was charged or attacked in turn, and exposed to the enemy's galling fire. The Prussians, nobly supported by their allies the Russians, were not backward in returning their fire with steady precision. Marching, loading, and firing alternately, and yet preserving the most perfect order, the most exact discipline—no hurry—no confusion—their retreat more resembled the evolutions of a review, than the strenuous efforts of a handful of brave men, headed by an adored Chief, to extricate themselves, by dint of personal courage and resolution, from the toils which a wily enemy had spread for their destruction. The French cavalry, in the heat of charging, often precipitated themselves between the Prussian columns, and their disorderly retreat soon attested the success of the Confederates' bayonets. Several heavy and regular charges were attempted by Napoleon, whenever the terrain offered a favourable opportunity, all of which were ultimately repulsed with heavy loss.

Towards sunset it was observed that the enemy had succeeded in turning the flanks by a bye-road, and throwing himself across the high-way, in front of Blücher's advanced-guard, between Champaubert and Etoges. It was Napoleon's obvious intention to block up the Field-marshal's line of march entirely. The masses of cavalry were numerous, and not only occupied the road itself, but the open country on both sides of it.

It is not to be denied, that the emergency of the moment was great, and big with event.

Our veteran Hero saw himself actually surrounded on all sides. To the sudden, but vigorous resolves of the gallant Blücher, the troops were indebted for their safety, their honour, and their glory; and these were no other than to force his way, at the point of the bayonet, through every impediment, without loss of time. It was evident that nothing but delay could prove vitally dangerous to the Field-marshal. After ordering up his artillery in advance, that began a heavy cannonade upon the enemy's horse, the columns of infantry continued their march, although incessantly galled on all sides by the French rifle-men; and, when within musket-shot, opened a regular fire in platoons upon the cavalry that opposed their progress.

The enemy's cavalry could not withstand such undaunted resolution, assisted by an enthusiasm that rendered the most desperate enterprise easy to such warriors. They were obliged, after a severe loss, to relinquish the high road to Blücher's army, and to content themselves with partial attacks on the flanks and rear of the Prussians. The columns and squares, posted advantageously on the flanks and rear, were attacked, but none of them were either broken, put into disorder, or obliged to yield ground to the enemy, sooner than their line of march demanded it.

As night approached, the cavalry in advance was attacked again by infantry; but the march of the army continued without interruption towards Etoges. The troops, on entering the village, were fired upon by the enemy, posted in the houses and gardens. In driving the French out of the place, the divisions under General von Kleist and General von Kapzcewitz particularly distinguished themselves; they cleared the village of the enemy, opened a passage for themselves and the remainder of the army, and, covered with glory, bivouacked for the night on the heights of Bergères.

Marshal Blücher's loss, on this memorable retreat, may be computed at 3500 men killed, wounded, and taken prisoners. Napoleon's object was to crush the whole corps: his means of offence were more than double to those of Blücher; of cavalry he had three times the number; and yet, with this decisive superiority, he achieved but little. Nor ought it to be omitted, that the effects of the enterprise, instead of proving disastrous to the general cause, were, on the contrary, calculated to abate the energy of the French troops, and destroy all confidence in themselves.

Blücher's artillery was more numerous, and much better served, than that of the enemy; and the dreadful chasms it at times produced in the hostile cavalry, by a well-directed cross-fire, must have occasioned an enormous sacrifice of men on the part of the French.

The glory of the Prussian and Russian arms was not only supported by the able, gallant, and meritorious conduct of the troops engaged, but they acquired fresh splendour at this important and critical æra, by their intrepid resistance against a powerful and adventurous enemy.

The happy union and perfect harmony which was preserved between the Prussian and Russian forces, and the wonderful exertions of wisdom and policy in their heroic Commander, must be reflected upon with singular satisfaction, by every well-wisher to the good cause.

Victory might be said, although retreating, to follow their standards, and to carry along with her a series of successes through an extended variety of attacks of difficulty and danger.

The excellent dispositions of General von Gneisenau, who directed the movements on the high road, and the conduct of General von Ziethen, and Prince Augustus of Prussia, did not a little contribute to the success of the retreat. Their regular co-operation proved of the most signal service.

These operations having been happily effected, Marshal Blücher determined upon taking up the position at Chalons; while this movement presented a singular advantage, by ensuring his junction with the other corps of his army. Generals von

York and Sacken had, according to intelligence received, occupied Rheims, and General Winzingerode was only two or three marches from that city; these corps formed, in consequence, a junction, to their mutual gratification; and, on the 17th of February, the whole Silesian army was again in line in the vicinity of Chalons *. The Commander-in-chief permittted his brave companions in arms to enjoy a day's repose on the 18th of February; but, on the next day, again put his army in motion, advanced on the 21st to Mery, and joined the corps of General Count Wittgenstein, posted in that neighbourhood. The enemy assaulted Mery on the 22d. Every necessary disposition was made to defend the town, and the bridge over the Seine. But a variety of unforeseen impediments

---

* At this time, when the Field-marshal had made good his retreat to Chalons, to form a junction with the corps of General von York, Sacken, and Winzingerode, and the Confederates, by the affair at Montereau, were thrown into a temporary consternation, our Veteran wrote the following very laconic, but cheering words to the Emperor of Russia:

" Let not anxiety, for a moment, plant a wrinkle on your Majesty's brow; for I shall catch him (meaning Napoleon) at last.   BLÜCHER."

(THE ORIGINAL GERMAN.)

" *Eure Majestät mögen Sich kein graues Haar wachsen lassen, ich werde ihn doch schon am Ende fangen.*   BLÜCHER."

Imparted to the editor by Baron von K—n.

occurred ; a terrible fire broke out in the high
street, the artillery was obliged to be withdrawn,
and the town evacuated. It was re-attacked by
the Allies on the 23d, the French driven out of it
after a desperate resistance, and the place maintained.

In the mean time Napoleon had seen himself
forced to direct the whole strength of his army on
the Seine, in order to check the progress of the
Confederates under Prince von Schwartzenberg.
Marshal Victor and General Oudinot, although
reinforced considerably by detachments from Spain,
found themselves too weak to act on the offensive against the grand army of the Allies under
Schwartzenberg. The latter had left Troyes on
the 10th of February, stormed Nogent and Sens
on the 11th, and driven the enemy over to the left
bank of the Seine on the 14th. General Count
Wrede, at the instigation of Blücher, forced the
passage of the Seine in the night of the 12th, at
Nogent, towards Provins; and the Prince of Würtemberg, Generals Bianchi and Giulay, near Bray
and Montereau. General Count Wrede and General Count Wittgenstein forming, with their
corps, the extreme advance of the grand army,
were posted near Nangis, on the 15th of February,
not being more than forty leagues from Paris; the
detachments of Platow and Hardegg occupying
Fontainbleau on the 17th. General Count Wrede
was on the point of executing the orders of the

Prince von Schwartzenberg, to advance upon Sezanne, in the rear of Napoleon's line of operations,
when he was obliged to halt.   It seems Napoleon
had hastened back again, by another forced march,
in the direction of La Ferté sous Jouarre, and,
falling suddenly, with an overwhelming superiority
of numbers, on General Count Wittgenstein's
corps, had compelled him to pass over to the left
bank of the Seine.   During his pursuit, Napoleon
fell in with the Prince of Würtemberg's corps
near Montereau, whose detachments had already
occupied Melun.   The Prince defended himself
with signal bravery and obstinacy for several
hours, but, after a great effusion of blood, was
obliged to fall back.   Napoleon marched onwards
by the way of Nogent, and took possession of
Troyes, which, by virtue of a convention, had
been previously evacuated by the Allies.

Before farther progress could be made, the energetic conduct of our intrepid Veteran prevented
any fatal consequences ensuing from Napoleon's
ephemeral successes.   Blücher's movements were
rapid and well digested ; and his support rescued
the Confederates from an unpleasant situation, the
consequence of some mischances, for which no one
can in the least degree be censured.   Blücher's affair
with the enemy, by Mery, on the Seine, on the 21st,
in which he maintained his position, materially prevented General Count Wittgenstein's corps from
suffering a severe check, and covered, in a great

degree, the retrograde movement of the Prince of Schwartzenberg, which he was making along the Aube, as far as Columbey, to the north west of Chaumont, where he arrived on the 25th of February *. The Field-marshal had acted in direct

---

* The manly and independent spirit of Marshal Blücher could ill brook silence when military operations were about to take place, which did not exactly coincide with his own judgment. The retrograde movement of the grand army to Columbey was not made with his concurrence; and in his lively zeal for the good cause, he presented the following forcible remarks, drawn up with his own hand, both to the Emperor of Russia and King of Prussia:

" It has been reported to me by Colonel von Grollman, that the grand army is to make a retrograde movement. I think it my duty to lay before your Majesty the unavoidable, disastrous consequences that must ensue from such a step.

" 1º. The whole French nation will be under arms, and that part which has declared itself for the good cause, will be ruined.

" 2º. Our victorious army, flushed with success, will become dispirited.

" 3º. Our retrograde movements must be made through a country, where our troops, urged by want, will deprive the inhabitants of their last morsel, and drive them to despair.

" 4º. Napoleon will thereby recover from the shock which our rapid movements have caused him, and regain the opinion of the nation in his favour.

" That your Imperial Majesty has permitted me to act again on the offensive, claims my most unfeigned thanks. I can promise to myself the most brilliant success, if your Majesty would be graciously pleased to issue positive orders that the corps of General von Winzingerode and General von Bülow conjunction with the grand confederate army but a few hours, when he ordered his to move forwards, and after repulsing Marmont, who endeavoured to stop his progress, or to interrupt his plan of operations, he crossed the Aube, directing his march to La Ferté Gauchery, and consequently towards Paris. His principal object was to unite his forces with those of Generals Bülow, Woronzow, and Winzingerode, formerly attached to the army of the Crown Prince of Sweden, but who were now pressing forward with alacrity into the scene of glorious action, towards Rheims and Soissons. The Field-marshal's army would then be strengthened to 100,000 men. And with this army, animated with enthusiasm, and intoxicated with victory, he proposed to undertake the bold and decisive march—direct on Paris, from the north side; by which manœuvre Napoleon would be rendered unable to face and make head against both Schwartzenberg and Blücher, with the whole of his army, without leaving the one or the other an open field of action, on which he

---

may obey my directions. In co-operation with these Generals I shall march forwards to Paris, and shall be as little afraid to meet Napoleon as any of his Marshals, if they should oppose my advancing.

" Permit me to express to your Imperial Majesty the satisfaction I shall feel in fulfilling your Majesty's commands and wishes at the head of the army intrusted to my care.

" *Mery, Feb.* 22, 1814. BLÜCHER."

could carry on those operations that must ultimately
prove fatal to Buonaparte. This movement of the
Field-marshal's upon Meaux, which would cut off
the enemy's communication with Paris, and which
caused great apprehensions in that capital, forced
Marshals Mortier and Marmont to evacuate La
Ferté sous Jouarre; and the Commander-in-chief
passed the Marne, without any obstruction, on
the 28th of February.

The reports of this march had scarcely reached
Napoleon, before he broke up with the flower of
his army from Troyes, on the 27th of February,
in hopes of striking a deadly blow against the plans
and views of the Allies. He left behind him a
trifling force of 30,000 men, to observe the Prince
of Schwartzenberg, whose army might be estimated at this period at 80,000.

Napoleon crossed the Marne on the 1st of
March; but, to his great vexation, General von
Bülow was already in possession of Soissons; by
which circumstance all the single corps that were
to form Blücher's army, and come under his command, could be united in this central and very
important position.

Soissons was a point of singular importance;
and the junction of the several corps was formed
in the following manner:

On the 26th of February General von Bülow
undertook an expedition from Laon against La
Fere. The covering of his right wing, and the

security of his supplies, rendered the occupation of this fortress of great moment, and, consequently, General von Thümen was detached with his brigade against La Fere, and a necessary number of howitzers to bombard the town. The brigade advanced upon the place, and this highly valuable and meritorious officer displayed his usual zeal. After throwing shells into the body of the town for a few hours, and then summoning it to surrender, the commandant capitulated, and General von Thümen marched in, at the head of his troops. The possession of the place was, in every point of view, of great importance; but, under the present circumstances, it proved a most severe loss to the enemy, as it contained a grand arsenal for the artillery in all its branches: more than a hundred pieces of brass cannon were found within it, as well as immense stores of every article appertaining to an artillery-train.

The certain intelligence of Field-marshal Blücher's intended advance upon Paris having reached General von Bülow, he again put his corps in motion on the 1st of March towards Soissons, after leaving a small detachment in La Fere; and, at the same time, General Winzingerode moved from Rheims by the way of Fismes.

General von Bülow arrived before Soissons on the 2d of March. This town is surrounded with ditches filled with water; and a high stone wall, flanked by towers, renders the place secure against a coup de main. The garrison consisted of from 12 to 1400 men, mostly Poles, the best troops which Napoleon had at this time in the field, and they were well provided with artillery. The opening of a communication with Blücher rendered the possession of the place absolutely necessary; but the attempt to take it by main force might have cost the Allies several thousand men. In consequence of this consideration, after the town had been briskly cannonaded, articles of capitulation, very honourable to the garrison, were proposed by Generals Winzingerode and Bülow: they were accepted by the commandant, upon Captain von Martins, who was intrusted with the negotiation, making some successful representations concerning the hopelessness of relief; and he was permitted to march out, at the head of the garrison, with the honours of war.

The necessity of occupying this town was even more pressing than the possession of La Fere. The weak corps of General von Kleist was already thrown back on the road from Soissons, on the 2d of March; and on the 3d, the day after its occupation, the main body of the Silesian army arrived in its vicinity to assume a position.

CHAPTER XIII.

Blücher concentrates his Army near Soissons—Victory of Laon—Progress of the allied Armies—Triumphal Entry of the confederate Monarchs into Paris.

In this march of the Field-marshal, from Mery to the heights of Soissons, of such a novel and critical nature, the gallant Hero displayed his accustomed foresight and judgment, and conducted it in a most able and judicious manner. Notwithstanding the celerity of the movement, the utmost regularity was preserved, and no one untoward circumstance took place.

It was towards the evening of the 4th of March that the complete union of all the corps was formed, composing an enterprising army of 100,000 warriors. Blücher immediately directed Soissons to be occupied with 10,000 men, belonging to General von Langeron's corps; and the main body of the army assumed a position behind the Aisne. Meanwhile Napoleon had marched, in all haste, upon Fismes, made a booty of some baggage left in the rear, and occupied Rheims; by which operation he cut off all communication between the corps of General St. Priest, the grand army under the Prince of Schwartzenberg, and that of Blücher.

But the Field-marshal had penetrated the probable manœuvres of his adversary with precision and ability. He had sacrificed willingly all his communications, and, in case of necessity, meant to trust to the strength of the Netherlands. It was not the developement of Napoleon's plans that urged him to act, but the execution of his own deep-laid operations. To establish a footing on a new line of offence, presents a spectacle of a movement of an army, never surpassed in the military annals of the world, and is a circumstance of glory that, in itself, would immortalize the name of Blücher.

During the 5th of March, Soissons was kept occupied by two Russian corps, and the Field-marshal appointed Lieutenant-general Rudczewicz to be governor of the place. The army still bivouacked behind the Aisne.

The operations of the enemy commenced on the 6th. He endeavoured to obtain possession of the suburbs of Soissons by a heavy cannonade. His attacks were repulsed by the bravery of the troops and the able dispositions of the governor, and, although they were continued till night, yet the French gained not a foot of ground.

On the afternoon of the same day Napoleon had succeeded in getting possession of the ferries at Berri-au-Bac, and pushed forward his troops to

Corbeny. General von Winzingerode sent a division to Crannes to oppose his progress; and the army was drawn up on the heights between L'Angegardien and Crannes, so as to make front against the enemy, and to act upon the offensive by the way of Crannes, if necessary.

Towards noon, on the 6th of March, the enemy's columns began to deploy from Berri, and to advance more to the right. The Field-marshal von Blücher immediately ordered his army to advance upon the high ground running in a straight line from Crannes, to be able to debouch into the plain from that place. But Napoleon had already occupied Crannes with his guards, and had filled the woods and defiles with sharp-shooters, so that some considerable difficulties presented themselves in debouching the army. The glacis was also too confined for a body of 80,000 men to act upon with effect; and, it being reported that an enemy's column was on its march, by the way of Corbeny, towards Laon, the Field-marshal determined, at seven o'clock in the evening, to detach General Winzingerode, with 11,000 men, mostly cavalry, and a due proportion of horse-artillery, with orders to march off to the left, to intercept the enemy in the direction of Corbeny, on the road to Laon, and to act immediately on the offensive.

General von Bülow was likewise detached to occupy the position of Laon, and thereby to ensure his communications with the Low Countries.

When it was reported to the Commander-in-chief that General von Bülow occupied Laon, he directed the Generals von York, von Kleist, and von Langeron, to move towards Fethieux, to serve as supports to General Winzingerode. The corps of General Winzingerode still remained drawn up on the glacis near Crannes. General Sacken's corps formed his reserve. The Field-marshal had calculated that the detached cavalry under General von Winzingerode could arrive near Fethieux before break of day, and that the infantry would reach the same point in time for his support. But, unhappily, the whole of these complicated movements could not be executed with that precision so necessary for their taking effect. Some difficulties occurred to General von Winzingerode in crossing the river Cette, which detained him and the corps that followed. General von Kleist fortunately surmounted every obstacle; and, although he was detached ten hours later, yet he arrived before General von Winzingerode in the position at Fethieux. Meanwhile Napoleon impetuously attacked the corps of General Winzingerode with the whole of his forces. According to previous instructions, General von Sacken, who commanded the right wing, retired slowly, and in the finest order, from height to height, keeping up a brisk and well-directed cannonade upon the enemy. The exertions of the French were particularly directed to turn, if possible, General von Sacken's position, and to press him hard by their superiority of cavalry. In this action, a favourable result was deemed of such importance by Napoleon, that several of his Marshals performed the duties of Generals of Brigade and Division, and Victor and Grouchy were wounded. This obstinate combat ended with the day, without Napoleon having succeeded in breaking through, or making any impression on the line of the Allies, whose troops made a most noble stand against a superior force, without losing a single piece of cannon or a prisoner. Indeed, it is barely possible to do justice to the gallantry and steadiness of the Russian artillery and cavalry on this day, which will thereby be ever conspicuously memorable in the annals of this war.

In the course of the night, General von Sacken also withdrew into the position of Laon, in which the Field-marshal had determined battle should be given. Under these circumstances, as Soissons was destitute of every article of sustenance, it was in consequence evacuated by General Rudczwicz.

The whole of Blücher's army was concentrated behind Laon on the 8th of March. The corps of General Bülow occupied the town and the glacis. The corps of Langeron, Sacken, and Winzingerode stood to the right, and those of von York and von Kleist to the left.

Two battalions of infantry, belonging to York's corps, kept possession of the village of Athies;

The 2d and 8th brigades, under Prince William of Prussia, stood in the first line; the 1st and 7th brigades in reserve.

Towards evening the enemy advanced upon the road from Soissons, and forced the advanced-guard of the Field-marshal's army upon Chiny. Early in the morning of the 9th, under cover of a very heavy fog, a body of the enemy's infantry drove in the out-posts, and carried the villages of Semilly and Ardon. But about eleven o'clock, A. M. as the fog began to clear away, the Field-marshal directed the corps of General von Winzingerode to act on the offensive. The two villages were retaken, and Winzingerode's right wing repulsed the enemy to Lasnicourt.

About three o'clock, P. M. it was reported to the Commander-in-chief that the enemy were in advance, in strong columns of all arms, supported by a numerous artillery, from the side of Rheims. As the combat on Blücher's right wing had happily taken a favourable turn, and no important operation was to be expected from this side, our veteran Hero was naturally led to expect that Napoleon intended his principal attack should be made on his left. The safety of Blücher's left wing was indeed of the utmost importance. The cavalry in reserve was intrusted to the command of General von Ziethen; he passed the brook near Athies, and took up a flanking position towards the cavalry of the enemy, which threatened to

turn the left wing on the first favourable opening.
On the right wing the corps of General von Bülow acted entirely on the defensive.

Marshal Blücher now ordered the corps of von
Sacken and Langeron to advance to the left as reserves to the corps of von York and Kleist, directing General von York, as soon as these reserves were come up, to assail the enemy by a
sudden and general movement forwards. It had
begun to grow dark as the reserves arrived. Generals von York and Kleist, prompt in the execution of orders, redoubled their pace in advancing upon the columns of the enemy's infantry.
The first attack fell to the lot of Prince William
of Prussia, leaving the burning village of Athies
a little to the right. The attack of Prince William was supported on this side of the village by
General von Horn with his usual gallantry ; he
stormed, at the head of his troops, an enemy's
battery with such rapidity, that only one round
was fired before the whole of it fell into his hands.
Meanwhile General von Ziethen executed so
admirably those manœuvres with which he was
intrusted, when he had turned the right flank of
the enemy, that the defeat of Napoleon was thus
rendered complete. General von Kleist commenced his attack along the low bushes lying in
his front, so as to concentrate its effects with that
of the other corps on the high road from Rheims.
These operations were happily effected, notwith-

standing a variety of impediments occurred, both from the nature of the ground, and the desperate resistance made by the enemy. The commanders, however, performed the service committed to their care with much precision, ability, and courage.

The enemy was on the point of occupying Athies with several heavy columns, when he had to meet the attack of Prince William. All firing was strictly prohibited, and the bayonet only was to be used. The troops pressed forwards with unloaded arms, rushed upon the enemy, and charged with fixed bayonets; the effect produced by such gallant conduct was such as might have been expected; they forced the French to retire in confusion, and the allied battalions still moved onwards, regardless of a most terrible and continued discharge of grape. But a short time, however, elapsed, and General von Kleist had completely repulsed, and thrown into disorder, the whole of the masses of the enemy's right wing, as likewise the corps of Marmont and Arrighi. In the mean time, General von Ziethen had charged the rear of the enemy, sword in hand, and put them entirely to the rout; and a conflict the most severe, was terminated most gloriously for the Allies, leaving in the hands of the victors forty-six pieces of cannon.

The bold and well-directed manner in which Prince William forced the enemy to fly from the high woody grounds near Athies, paved the way to victory. The heavy fire of musketry poured down upon them from the heights, could not for a moment arrest the progress of his troops, who undauntedly stormed the eminence, eager to close with the foe.

The good fortune and bravery of the Prussians prevailed in this memorable night-attack, notwithstanding the multitude of obstacles opposed to their success. The defeat of the enemy soon became general, and he fled in the greatest disorder and confusion. General von Ziethen, at the head of his cavalry, and supported by four battalions of infantry from the corps of Prince William and General Horn, pursued the French, and occupied the defile from Fethieux to Maison-rouge.

General von York continued, after surprising Marmont's corps *, to follow up his advantages.

---

* Marshal Marmont's corps was here completely taken by surprise. They were in bivouack, and busily employed in preparing their suppers. The Prussian cavalry approached through bye-roads, silent as death, followed by a battery. The infantry, covered by a wood, got close upon them. The Frenchmen could be very plainly seen lying round their watch-fires. A terrible cannonade and vollies of musketry now suddenly opened upon them. The bugle-horns of the Prussians were heard from all sides. The terror, confusion, and flight of the French baffle all attempts at description. It proved a bloodless hunting-party for the gallant Prussians. Every thing was left behind: the whole of their artillery, baggage, horses, and waggons, fell into the hands of the Confederates. Marmont was driven.

till late in the evening, taking a great number of prisoners.

In the mean time, Napoleon still stood in his admirable position before Laon. He attempted on the 10th to repeat his attacks upon the centre and the right wing, under Bülow and Winzingerode. But the Field-marshal anticipated the enemy's intentions, by issuing orders to General von Winzingerode to fall on the enemy's left wing, while General Langeron was to watch his movements; Napoleon's offensive operation proved, therefore, unsuccessful. The ground afforded every advantage to Napoleon, and by keeping up a severe cannonade and fire of grapeshot, he held the front of Blücher's line in check, till the close of the evening, when he again renewed a general attack. He caused the suburb Semilly, on the road to Soissons, lying at the foot of the hill on which Laon stands, to be assailed by some battalions of infantry. This suburb was occupied by Bülow's corps, and he defended it with unexampled spirit and coolness: he resisted the impetuosity of the French infantry, repulsed every repeated attack, and the enemy were at last compelled to retreat at all points. It is

---

with the shattered remains of his cavalry, to the Marne; and General von York returned from the pursuit, to fall again into line with the Field-marshal's army, now threatened with another attack at Laon from Napoleon, very probable, that the attack was only a feint on the side of Napoleon, to prevent, if possible, the total destruction of Marmont's corps.

This twofold victory, which the veteran Field-marshal gained over Napoleon on the 9th and 10th of March, near Laon, cost the allied army but an inconsiderable number of men, while the loss of the French may be moderately estimated at 18,000, in killed, wounded, and prisoners.

Napoleon's retreat was made in the most disorderly manner, and was the only step he could take, to prevent his complete discomfiture. He left all his wounded men behind him, in his flight towards the Aisne: the light troops of Blücher's army pressed hard upon his rear, and caused him a great loss in men and materiel.

This was the second grand battle, in which victory was wrested by our veteran Hero from the iron grasp of Napoleon on the French territory.

The great and unremitting exertions which the army had made during the last four days, and the unusual fatigues they had undergone, rendered it absolutely necessary that it should now have some repose, and, consequently, all the advantages that might have been derived from briskly following up the pursuit of Napoleon, the Allies were, at the moment, obliged reluctantly to forego. A pause, therefore, ensued in the operations of Blücher's army, which lasted nearly eight days.

The Field-marshal's conduct and continued activity during this memorable battle gained him the admiration of the whole army, exalted in an eminent degree the honour of his country, and gave pledges of his being ranked amongst the most illustrious officers of the age. His merit can scarcely be equalled; his exertions, personal courage, and ability contributed much to the success of the combat, and to enhance that character of military fame, to which his former services had so justly entitled him.

The only affair of importance which took place immediately after the battle of Laon, was the occupation of Rheims. On the 12th of March, General Count St. Priest attacked that city, carried it, and took about 1000 men prisoners. The enemy, with superior force, appeared before the place on the 13th. General Count St. Priest supported the unequal contest with great bravery, but was at last obliged to give way, with such a disparity of numbers under his command : he himself was wounded. A part of his corps withdrew to Chalons, and another in the direction of Berry-au-Bac, to join the Silesian army.

We will now draw the attention of our readers to the operations of the confederate armies.

The Crown Prince of Sweden, having been relieved in Holstein, and in the blockade of d'Avoust in Hamburg, by GeneralBennigsen, put his army in march towards the Rhine, on which he arrived on the 10th of February. The Crown Prince's army advanced from Cologne towards the Low Countries, and reached Liege on the 26th of February, where the Prince fixed his head-quarters. His advanced-guard under Generals Woronzow and Stroganoff, were detached to join Blücher. But an inactivity now showed itself in the further operations of the Swedish army, the cause of which is enveloped in a veil of mystery, even to this day. The Swedish army was cantoned on the Meuse: the head-quarters remained in Liege, and, by some unaccountable fatality, it was bereaved of sharing the honour of those glorious days that so soon followed each other in quick succession.

After the affair at Bar-sur-Aube, between the French and confederate armies, the former retired towards Troyes on the 25th of February, and took up a position in front of the town, between the Aube and the Seine. Generals von Wittgenstein and von Wrede briskly attacked the enemy in their strong position on the 3d of March, took the villages in the centre by assault, and drove the French in great disorder into Troyes. A number of cannon and prisoners fell into the hands of the gallant Confederates : Troyes was assailed and carried on the 4th, for the second time, and the General-in-chief, Prince Schwartzenberg, fixed his head-quarters in the place on the 6th of March.

A column was pushed forwards in pursuit of

the enemy, who retreated on the road to Nogent. Meanwhile the Prince of Schwartzenberg took up strong ground with his army in the direction of Sens.

The Prince of Würtemberg was on the 8th again in occupation of Montereau, that had once cost him such a number of brave men.

The Hettman Platow, at the head of a very numerous body of Cossacks, scoured the country in all directions between the Seine and the Marne, kept up the most advantageous series of intelligence concerning the different corps of the Confederates, and harassed the enemy at all points, depriving him of his convoys of provisions, and isolating him even in the midst of his own provinces.

Napoleon was now reduced to play a desperate game. After the unfortunate battle at Laon, he threw himself, as if in despair, on the confederate army, now standing on the Aube, only leaving a moderate corps to observe the Marne. He found his opponent drawn up ready to receive him, between Plancis and Arcis, his forces concentrated, and on strong ground. He crossed the Aube on the 20th of March, and, in the afternoon, passed through Arcis, at the head of 40,000 men; here he was instantly attacked by the Prince von Schwartzenberg, who repulsed him with heavy loss, taking from him 11 guns, and 400 men of his imperial guard. The Congress at Chatillon was dis-

solved the same day. The Prince of Schwartzenberg, not satisfied with the partial advantages of
the 20th, continued his attack on the 21st, and
drove him through the town of Arcis. To cover
his retreat, Napoleon occupied the place with a
large body of troops till the morning of the 23d,
when, having come out of the defile which had
served to protect him the day before, he was
briskly attacked in the plain by a division of Russian guards, defeated, and had twenty-three pieces
of artillery taken from him.

Napoleon found himself repulsed and driven
back by the Prince of Schwartzenberg; but still
obstinately bent on executing his plan, of keeping
this army and that of Blücher separated, he seemed
to think no sacrifice, no hazard too great, to obtain his purpose: and he now hastened towards the Upper Marne, to take firm footing on
the Meuse.

Prince Schwartzenberg, however, was not to
be deceived by this manœuvring march of Napoleon, but proceeded to detach a corps to strengthen
the communications on the Saone and Rhone, towards the south. Another corps, under Wittgenstein, of about 10,000 men, mostly cavalry, followed Napoleon, step by step, to observe him,
and, with the main body, the Commander-in-
chief marched straight across the country, towards
the Marne, to join Blücher, who was advancing

from that river, and, by this daring manœuvre, to cut off Napoleon at once from Paris.

During these operations, Field-marshal Blücher, after his army had enjoyed that repose so vitally necessary, commenced acting again on the offensive.

The corps of Generals von York and von Kleist were directed to advance upon Fismes. General Winzingerode occupied Rheims. General von Sacken's corps marched towards Vally, and that of General von Bülow in front of Soissons. The main body of Blücher's army passed the Aisne on the 19th of March, at Berry-au-Bac and Pont-avaire.

On the 22d, the corps of von York and von Kleist pursued their route upon Chateau Thierry.

The corps of Langeron, Sacken, and Winzingerode concentrated themselves at Rheims during the 23d ; and General von Bülow kept Soissons blockaded.

The grand confederate army stood near Vitry on the 24th, at the moment that Field-marshal Blücher had arrived with his army in Chalons and Rheims.

The two allied armies now formed a complete junction in the very rear of Napoleon's position ; a combination, to frustrate which, Napoleon had in vain exerted all his talents and all his physical endeavours. His grand manœuvre accordingly proved abortive, and was for him only the forerunner of great disasters, while it was preparing fresh triumphs for the gallant Confederates.

It was now determined that the two armies should make a combined forced march upon Paris, give up all communication with the Rhine, and, by this energetic but judicious measure, produce the most brilliant effects for the good cause.

The march of Prince Schwartzenberg's army on Vitry contributed to mask the intentions of the Allies, of turning to the right about and proceeding to Paris, when joined by Blücher.

General Wittgenstein's cavalry kept the rear of Napoleon's army upon the alert, and served to prevent the corps of Marshals Marmont and Mortier from joining him.

In the interim, Napoleon, after the affair at Arcis, had retired on Vitry. Fearful of fighting a pitched battle with Schwartzenberg, who seemed too much prepared for him at all points, Napoleon hoped, by this sudden flank march on Vitry, to cause the Confederates some apprehensions concerning their communications in the rear, and by their dispositions, in consequence, to keep them open, enable him to draw them still farther from Paris. On the 22d, his own head-quarters were at Obcomte, between Vitry and St. Dizier, spreading his army in the direction of Joinville, Ligny, Bar-le-Duc, Chaumont, and Langres; in which position he remained till the 24th of March.

According to all the rules of military tactics, after the grand union of the two armies, no other measure was to be expected than the giving Napoleon battle : it was, indeed, what he had prepared himself for, during the last two or three days ; but instead of this, the confederate forces no sooner came in contact, and shook hands upon their happy meeting, than they instantly began their steady, daring march upon Paris.

The corps of Marmont, Mortier, and Arrighi, had followed the army of Field-marshal Blücher, with the intention of keeping him on the Aisne ; and when Napoleon made his retrograde movement on Arcis, they were on march between Vitry and La Fère Champenoise, to join him. Marmont pushed forward a corps, in the night of the 24th of March, upon Vitry, without knowing that it was still occupied by the Confederates, having supposed that they had followed the movement of Napoleon.

The Prince of Würtemberg and General Rajewsky, with their several corps, the Russian reserve cavalry of the guard, and a part of Blücher's cavalry, fell in with Marmont's corps, charged and broke it, the remains retreating to La Ferté Gaucher, on the road to Paris. A very large and complete artillery-park fell, on this occasion, into the hands of the Allies. The two divisions of Pactod and Amey were surrounded, and, after a warm affair, the whole of them were taken pri-

soners near La Fère Champenoise. The Emperor
Alexander and the King of Prussia happened to
be present at this engagement.

There is not, perhaps, in the history of modern
campaigns, a stratocratic manœuvre upon a grander
scale to be found, than that which the Confederates had now put in practice, by interposing
themselves between Buonaparte and Paris. The
boldness of this memorable operation of the Allies, evidently unnerved Napoleon's whole system,
overturned the basis of his plans, and placed him
in the state of a mariner endeavouring to steer
his vessel without a compass. He faced about, it
is true, making a feint of marching, by the way
of Bar-sur-Aube, direct to Paris; but, as if stunned
and confounded, instead of proceeding on the line
of the Marne, to throw himself on the rear of the
Allies, and to offer battle, whatever it might cost
him, he made a flank march from the Marne to
the Aube, and from thence behind the Seine, and
by this short-sighted and bewildered measure
hastened in a superlative degree his own downfall
and destruction.

Field-marshal von Blücher, at the head of
his Silesian army, entered Etoges on the 25th of
March, and pressed forwards by the way of Montmirail towards Meaux.

Marshals Marmont and Mortier drew back to
Sezanne. Generals York and Kleist, having arrived the same day at Montmirail, detached a body

of their cavalry on the road to Sezanne, and
broke up by break of day on the 26th, to cut off
the enemy in the direction of La Ferté Gaucher.
They found La Ferté occupied, soon dislodged
the enemy, and established themselves in the place.
The French fled towards Coulomiers, closely pursued by the Prussian cavalry and a brigade of infantry; they were overtaken near that town, charged,
and dispersed; and 300 prisoners, together with
a number of tumbrils, were taken from them.
The Silesian army reached Meaux on the 27th,
in the most perfect order and regularity. In the
afternoon the rest of Marmont's and Mortier's
corps appeared on their march from Sezanne to
Coulomiers. The powerful and well-directed artillery of York's and Kleist's corps, which opened
their fire upon the French columns, as they marched in advance down the road, forced them to file
off from the high-way, and to throw themselves
into the bye-roads towards the Seine. If the allied
cavalry had happened to have been on the spot,
the remainder of these two French corps would
have fallen into their hands, or have been cut in
pieces.

Between La Ferté Jouarre and Meaux, an attempt
was made by a body of 10,000 national guards
to impede the march of Blücher's army. They
put on a good countenance, and seemed determined
to dispute the further advance of the Allies; but the
brave General von Horn being detached to charge

them at the head of his brigade of cavalry, executed his orders with such celerity, courage, and
firmness, that one of their masses of infantry
was entirely broken up and cut in pieces, the rest
put to the rout, and the French general who commanded them taken prisoner by General von Horn
himself.

The corps of Marmont and Mortier, being now
completely deranged, retired at all points, on
the 28th of March. When making good their retreat through Meaux, they blew up an immense
magazine of gunpowder, without any previous
notice to the inhabitants, and then pursued their retrograde march to Claye. The corps of York and
Kleist came up with the enemy at this latter place,
and after a desperate conflict, which lasted till
late at night, they succeeded in dislodging the
French, and occupied Ville-parisis and Montsaigle.

During these operations, the Silesian army defiled over the bridges of the Marne, near Triport,
which had been re-established, notwithstanding
the enemy's cannonade.

It was on the 29th of March that the grand
confederate army began likewise to defile over the
bridges near Triport and Meaux. The preconcerted union of Schwartzenberg's and Blücher's army
was now fully accomplished, in order of battle.
The confederate army pursued the high road to
Paris, while the Silesian army filed off on the road
from Mery to that capital.

Marshals Marmont and Mortier had advanced, by forced marches, with the shattered remains of their corps, by the way of Melun towards Paris, and had taken position in front of the wood near Landy; they were attacked by the advanced-guard, and driven back upon Pantin. The grand head-quarters were at Bondy on the 29th: in the mean time Blücher pushed forwards two principal corps to the right, in the direction of Mory, Drancy, and St. Denys, to reach Montmartre.

The French had taken position in front of the heights of Montmartre, under cover of some hasty intrenchments they had thrown up, and lined with 150 pieces of artillery; their line extended to the villages of Pantin, Romainville, and Belleville. The enemy's force consisted of about 8000 regular troops, and 30,000 national guards. The canal, and the nature of the ground altogether, rendered his position a strong one, particularly as the allied cavalry had no extent of terrain to make a charge. In the interim, Napoleon had issued orders to defend the capital to the last extremity, being himself, as he announced, on his march to relieve it.

Field-marshal Blücher's conduct, under the difficult circumstances in which he undertook this memorable march on Paris, may be accounted a master-piece of discretion and firmness. The bold measures of the Field-marshal, the splendid feats he performed, his well-chosen commanding positions, his energy of action, and the efficiency of his dispositions on the field of battle, all alike point him out as a military hero, not only worthy of the wonder and admiration of the age in which he lives, but of future generations.

Preparations for a general attack on the enemy's position at Montmartre were vigorously carried on, during the 30th of March. It was the plan of the Allies, that the grand confederate army, under the Prince of Schwartzenberg, should assault the heights of Romainville and Belleville, while the Silesian army was ordered to carry those of Montmartre.

Marshal Blücher made the following arrangements with the several corps of which his army was composed. General Count Langeron's corps formed his right wing, and those of von York and Kleist his left. The corps under the command of General Winzingerode remained in reserve, and that under General von Sacken was still in position near Meaux. General von Bülow covered Soissons. Our veteran General directed Count Langeron to take Audervilliers, to blockade St. Denys, if it would not submit, and to advance with his main body towards Clichy, for the purpose of attacking Montmartre from this side. Generals von York and Kleist were ordered to assault Montmartre from the routes of La Villette and La Chapelle.

The confederate grand army began their attack

upon the enemy's lines at Pantin, at five o'clock,
A. M.; that of the Silesian army did not commence till near eleven, A. M. at which time Romainville and Pantin had been already carried by
the allied army. The enemy still occupied Ferme
le Rouvroy with infantry, supported by a battery
of eighteen pieces of cannon, very advantageously
planted. The advanced-guard, under Major-general Katzeler, carried the place itself, but could not
debouch out of it, until the enemy's battery was
first silenced. The artillery necessary for this
operation did not arrive on the ground till near
three o'clock, P. M. along with Winzingerode's
corps, whose operations were favoured by the corps
of York and Kleist filing off to attack in conjunction with Count Langeron. The reserve of grenadiers, and a brigade of guards appertaining to the
grand army, and supported by six battalions,
under Prince William of Prussia, had just made
an attack from Pantin towards Paris, forcing the
enemy's battery near Villette to draw back its
right wing, as the reserves and the artillery of
von York's and Kleist's corps came into action,
and thereby enfiladed the whole of the French
battery. The enemy retreated instantly into Villette; but again faced about, and, although hard
pressed, endeavoured to charge with a large body
of cavalry, supported by infantry and artillery. It
happened that the cavalry of York's and Kleist's
corps had begun to form at Ferme le Rouvroy,

and two regiments of Prussian hussars boldly met the enemy's charge, repulsed them with heavy loss, threw themselves upon their infantry, and put the whole to rout, taking their guns sword in hand.

Four battalions belonging to General Woronzow's corps, taking advantage of the favourable moment, stormed La Villette at the same time, and the enemy fled in the greatest confusion, leaving their artillery and materiel in the hands of the victors: they were briskly pursued to the very barriers of Paris. On the road from Pantin, the guards had likewise penetrated to the barriers, from that side. The whole of the enemy's positions were, in this manner, either turned or stormed, about half past three o'clock, p. m. when the firing ceased on both sides.

Flags of truce now appeared, to entreat a suspension of hostilities, as the city of Paris would submit. They were conducted to the august Sovereigns, who had arrived near the barriers, and an armistice was granted for four hours, to afford time for the French forces to defile into Paris.

Imagination can scarcely form an idea of two situations more opposite to each other, than that of one army, flushed with a series of continued victories, and another, depressed with the mortifying reflection of unvaried discomfiture. The one rushes on with the cheerful confidence of certain conquest; the other proceeds with a reluctant diffidence, resulting from a humiliating retrospection of experienced defeats.

During these events, the corps of General Langeron had continued its movement, those of York and Kleist kept up a brisk cannonade, and advanced upon Montmartre. The village of La Chapelle was already carried, and the assault upon Montmartre upon the point of being attempted, as the intelligence of the armistice reached them. But Count Langeron being at a greater distance, his infantry had already stormed the heights of Montmartre, on that side, and taken twenty pieces of cannon, before the report arrived.

Prince Schwartzenberg and the veteran Marshal Blücher were now at the head of their respective armies, in positions, from which they could cannonade at their pleasure the city of Paris. The whole of the barriers were delivered up to the Confederates in the course of the evening, and on the following morning, the 31st of March, the capital of the French empire was in the hands and at the mercy of the confederate Monarchs. At seven o'clock in the morning, the whole of the French regular troops, under Marshal Marmont, evacuated Paris, in virtue of a convention entered into for that purpose.

The glorious trophies of the 31st of March consisted of 70 pieces of artillery, 3 standards, and 500 prisoners.

Scarcely were the issue of the battle at La Fère Champenoise and its consequences known to Napoleon, when, on the 27th of March, after pushing aside the two corps of Winzingerode and Czernischeff, he hastened from Bar-sur-Aube to Troyes, and, on observing that Paris was lost to him, he proceeded in the direction of Sens to Fontainbleau; where, on the 4th of April, he issued his last order of the day. Thus ended the plans he had formed for the welfare of Europe, the subjection of Russia, and to remain master of both Germany and Italy. But it must not be forgotten, that Providence achieved the work, which it took entirely upon itself, that its hand might be visible to all. The German nation has in particular to hail the hour of its deliverance, with unceasing sentiments of pious gratitude. It has recalled it from a state of bondage to the bright certainty of future honour and happiness, and prevented the diffusion of those principles which directly tended to destroy all property, subvert the laws and religion of a country, and to introduce the wild and ruffian system of rapine, falsehood, espionage*, base tyranny, and impiety.

---

* The following anecdote, which we have from an authentic source, is here introduced, that our readers may form some faint conception of the extent to which espionage was carried, under the reign of Napoleon.

Their Majesties the Emperor Alexander and the King of Prussia put themselves at the head of their victorious guards, and made their glorious

It happened that Fouché † and the Prince of Benevento, and that too in the presence of Napoleon, fell into a dispute concerning a transaction, of which each of them could have acquired a knowledge only by their several spies. They grew warm upon the subject; Fouché maintained that his intelligence of the affair was alone authentic, adding:

" I am so well served by my spies, that I can tell you, Prince, the name of every person that has entered your house, and whom you have seen, both to-day and yesterday, where you saw them, and how long you stayed with them."

" If," replied Talleyrand, " there be any merit in such kind of espionage, I value myself upon being your superior in that

---

† Fouché was formerly a professor at Nantes, and was a master at the excellent institution of the Oratorion, so useful to education. At the time Napoleon Buonaparte returned from Egypt we find Fouché minister of the police under the Directory. He took an active part in the revolution of Brumaire, and betrayed the Directory. He was dismissed in 1802, but having been the principal instigator of Georges's conspiracy, he once more came into favour, and returned to the ministry. It was Fouché who urged and goaded Buonaparte on to the murder of the Duke d'Enghien, that Buonaparte might also stain his hands with the blood of the Bourbons, as himself had already done, in voting for the death of Louis the Sixteenth. In the year 1810, he sent a confidential person, Mr. Ouvrand, to London, for some private purposes. Ouvrand returned to France, was thrown into the prison at Vincennes, and Fouché was again in disgrace. Being appointed governor of Rome, by Napoleon, he received, on the road to that city, an order from his master to retire to Aix, in Provence, as into a kind of exile, for having steadily refused to deliver up to him the whole of his secret correspondence as minister of the police. When Napoleon was unfortunate, he was recalled; but Cambacères, who is his sworn enemy, and Savary, who was afraid of losing his place, having caused fresh suspicions of his fidelity to arise, he was sent into Italy with an honourable mission, but which was nothing less than another exile. He returned to Paris when Napoleon Buonaparte abdicated the throne for the first time.

triumphal entry into Paris, between ten and eleven o'clock, A. M. of the 31st of March. It was one of those grand spectacles that occur but seldom during the course of many centuries. They were escorted and surrounded by all their distinguished generals, and endless files of heroes formed their train. The gazing multitude saluted them as they passed with reiterated acclamations of

" *Vive l'Empereur Alexandre !*"

" *Vive le Roi de Prusse!*"

" *Vive Louis XVIII. !*"

" *A bas Napoleon! La paix! La paix !*"

The allied Monarchs proceeded through the suburb St. Martin, across the Boulevards to the Place of Louis the Fifteenth, and from thence to the Champs Elisées, where their respective troops defiled in the most perfect order before them.

St. Denys capitulated on the 31st of March. All the military trophies which had been previously taken from the Allies, were found in Paris, or in the Dome des Invalides, from which latter

---

point ; for I not only know what has passed in your house, but what is to take place to-morrow. I know every dish you have had upon your table for this week past, and what has been ordered for the ensuing : even your tête-à-têtes are not——"

Here Napoleon's patience seemed to be exhausted, for he interrupted all further reply, in his usual abrupt manner :

" Hold your tongues, both of you! You are a couple of *polissons* ; but I alone can determine which is the greatest!"

place they were taken away by detachments of Russian and Prussian guards, on the 1st of April.

Napoleon had, in the mean time, halted at Fontainbleau. His Marshals and Princes renounced their obedience to him, and appeared in Paris, to await their fate from the decisions of the august allied Monarchs. Upon this important occasion it was seen, that the Marshals, who had hitherto acted as an united and formidable body, for the meretricious glory and unjust aggrandizement of France, not only took part with the Confederates, but almost immediately accepted posts under Louis the Eighteenth. Many were pleased to observe, " that the matter in issue was, in fact, whether a good, just, and liberal constitution was or was not to be maintained in France; whether the wild ideas of universal conquest, and of theory, were to overwhelm the wholesome maxims of established practice and well-founded experience; and whether those laws, under which Europe had flourished for such a series of years, were to be rendered null and subverted by a tyrant, unsanctioned by the people, at the head of a hated stratocracy, and the dread and abhorrence of neighbouring nations."

As Frenchmen, nearly and deeply interested in the real welfare of France, the Marshals seemed to hasten to convince the world, that the happiness of the French people was their sole object. They were eager to announce, that they held the principles and the system of their former Sultan as treasons towards France, and incompatible with the peace of Europe. On this great, this solid basis, the august Allies listened to their arguments of secession, and believed and trusted their promises and protestations. It was a critical period. To have done less, would have cast an odium on the noble and generous conduct of the Allies; and to have done more, would have implied a want of wisdom and sound policy.

The Silesian army combated for the freedom and independence of Germany, during a campaign of seven months and a half, in which it fought six pitched battles, three single-handed, and three in conjunction with the grand allied army; was concerned in eight bloody engagements and numberless skirmishes, took 48,000 prisoners from the enemy, and could reckon amongst its glorious, unexampled, and immortal trophies, 421 pieces of cannon, with a proportionate number of tumbrils, &c. &c.

It was composed of the best strength of the Prussian nation; and the veteran Blücher led into the field a host of heroes, worthy of the great Frederick, the names of their fathers, and heirs of their glory. Nor was this faithful people less backward in making voluntary sacrifices at the shrine of loyalty; the mother offered her son and her jewels; the father his horse, his sword, and wealth; the youth his life; and the infirm their blessings!

Field-marshal Prince Blücher, as forming part of the suite of his august Monarch, arrived at Dover on the 6th of June 1814, on his way to London, which he reached the day following.

His Royal Highness the Prince Regent honoured our Veteran with a valuable mark of his esteem, by presenting him, in public, with his miniature, set in diamonds, to be worn round his neck, suspended by a blue riband.

During his popular and interesting stay in England, which filled the whole country with conversation, and attracted the curiosity of the public, in a manner that was seldom or never witnessed, all ranks were eager to show their admiration of Blücher's heroic deeds, to signify their pleasure at the sight of the gallant veteran, and to express their satisfaction at being honoured with the visit of so famed a General.

He may be considered as one of the brightest members of that profession which has humbled the vain-glory of a feverish enthusiastic people, and taught the doubting world, that deeds in arms, aided by honour and justice, mercy and loyalty, will and must eventually be crowned with success, when taking up the gauntlet of defiance, thrown down by the hand of imperious tyranny and base perfidy.

CHAPTER XIV.

The allied Monarchs in Paris—The King of Prussia returns to his Dominions—Marshal Prince Blücher arrives at Magdeburgh—The Congress at Vienna.

THE 31st of March 1814 was a proud day for the allied Monarchs, as it exhibited a gallant army of faithful confederates defiling in splendid triumph through the gates of Paris: a triumph which has not only given an additional lustre to the patriotism and loyalty of their brave subjects, but conferred an everlasting honour on the countries over which they preside.

The banners of Prussia, Russia, and Austria, attended by victory, waved in the haughty city of Paris; which, for nearly four centuries, had not seen a foreign enemy before its walls.

Dire revenge might now be taken for the burning of Moscow; heavy contributions imposed for the pillage of Vienna and Berlin; and Paris stripped of those choice works of art and science, which had been her boast and ornaments.

But the generous conquerors, full of noble sentiments, here displayed those virtues and traits which always distinguish their characters, never, in any relations, to be perverted by the foul example of the chief of a system that aimed at the overthrow of all moral principle.

It may be said that Napoleon's greatness was at its zenith in Moscow, and that the goal of all his glory was at Paris. The man, who for so many years together had brought down upon the world unutterable miseries, was banished the continent *. Legitimate governments were restored,

---

* The life of Napoleon Buonaparte has displayed a variety of extraordinary incidents. His career of empire has been short, but it is nevertheless wonderful and astonishing.

It is but the other day, that this singular man was only a lieutenant in a company of artillery, and, after overturning thrones, and founding a stratocratic empire, upon bases formed of perfidy and impiety, we have lived to witness him an exile from the continent of Europe. Under the influence of his dazzling system, the French nation have displayed a gigantic strength, and made conquests that baffled all calculation. But the hostilities of Europe took a very different form to those of ancient times; they did not, as then, aim at the possession of some trifling slip of territory, or the obtaining of some petty right or privilege; but were openly avowed by Napoleon Buonaparte, as the main springs of action, to obtain universal dominion, and, upon the ruins of his conquests, to erect an empire governed by laws that held revealed religion and social order in utter scorn and contempt, and that merged all power, all influence over the human mind, into that of the sword alone.

On closely examining results, we are not much inclined to admit that Napoleon Buonaparte showed, upon all occasions, in the various turns of fortune he has experienced, and the critical relations between himself and the belligerent powers of Europe, those stupendous talents which have so long afforded a theme for wonder and for praise. He attempted to force the

the thrones of ancient dynasties secured from perfidious attacks, and the suffering world tranquillized with the consoling prospect of a durable and general peace.

The confederate Sovereigns, in testimony of their very honourable motives, during a period of warfare which had acquired an energy unknown in modern times, naturally contemplated the giving peace to the world, and to France, not by humiliating the nation itself, and making it suffer for the bloody deeds of the odious tyrant, but by hurling him for ever from his usurped seat on the throne of the Bourbons. These generous intentions were universally known and acknowledged in France, and particularly in Paris, whose inhabitants greeted the illustrious personages with every mark of enthusiasm and gratitude. " Alexander the deliverer!"—" Frederick the harbinger of peace!" was shouted from all sides.

---

suggestions of reason and sound policy to bend to his own imaginary infallible will. An unrelenting stubbornness marks the course of all his actions, which led him to commit the most absurd errors. He is a fellow of no principle, and the whole of his conduct and career exhibits a most flagrant and sinistrous aspect. Can a man make a proper use of his talents without moral principles to curb the ebullitions of his passions, when tending to crime? Impossible! The smiles of fortune seduce him, his passions gain the ascendancy, and such a man proves the most accursed scourge to humanity, when power to do evil is thrown into the scale of unusual and splendid abilities.

The taking of Paris gave peace to Europe.

Napoleon Buonaparte signed, on the 11th of April 1814, in the most formal manner, an act of abdication; adding, that, " there was no sacrifice which he was not ready to make, even that of his life, for the welfare of France :" and he arrived at the island of Elba on the 4th of May.

This singular personage thus closed a career which, since 1797, had excited the wonder and astonishment of the world, filled every one with fear and doubt, and been the cause that millions of the bravest warriors of Europe were sacrificed, and the treasures of France squandered in Spain and Russia. He had overturned several thrones, and erected others; but, by the downfall of his own usurped dominion, an end was put to the ephemeral existence of those to which he alone had given stability. There was a time, when, in every corner of Europe, the words that dropped from his mouth were held of importance, and esteemed as oracles; and now he owed his life to the consideration of one of his Marshals, and the noble generosity of those whose thrones he had once shaken to their very foundations. Instead, like a man of sound wisdom, of fixing the happiness of France upon the firmest basis, when he had destroyed the hydra of anarchy, he imposed upon her the more intolerable chains of tyranny and despotism. This man was, in a man-

ner, worshipped till the year 1813; but, from this
period, he became the scorn and abhorrence of
the world. The charm of his infallibility had
been broken; and the triumph of revealed religion
over gloomy atheism, moral rectitude over the iron
hand of power, and virtue over vice, was complete. The utter worthlessness of all Napoleon's
satellites, the monstrous progeny of the revolution, was now open to the comprehension of every
individual in every station. Napoleon Buonaparte
did not realize the summit of his ambition. His
mortification was, however, commensurate with
his former hopes, when he found himself exiled to
the island of Elba.

In military affairs Napoleon had no doubt enjoyed a spring-tide of fame, and first appeared on
the theatre of war replete with fair promise of future greatness. Various causes aided his attainment of glory; but let it be remembered,
that none could ever make him the tyrant he
was: the qualities of that monster amongst ci-
vilized nations were inherent in the man, and
they gradually expanded themselves as he rose in
power and authority. No one can deny that
Buonaparte possesses a decision of character
and energy of mind, combined with a pre-emi-
nent genius for military command, that place
him on a footing with the first generals of the
present and former ages. It does not, however,
follow, that he was faultless, or incapable of

error. The events of this campaign, as well as of former ones, present numerous instances of his stubbornness of character, of his committing great mistakes in military calculations, accompanied by an unpardonable temerity, that seemed to defy both fate, possibility, and the elements.

In his former campaigns he had led on to victory files of revolutionary enthusiasts, and had to contend with the automatons of military discipline. His last campaign was singularly marked by the contrary; the mantling spirit of the evolution had evaporated; he had to combat with troops inspired with loyalty and a just sense of national honour—and Paris was occupied by the Allies.

England was the only state in Europe that had uniformly refused to acknowledge the dynasty of Napoleon Buonaparte.

The congress at Chatillon was dissolved on the 20th of March, and the Senate of France solemnly called Louis Stanislaus Xavier, the brother of Louis XVI. to the throne of that kingdom, and drew up a constitution, which he was to swear to observe before he was to be proclaimed. His Majesty made his public entry into Paris on the 3d of May.

Towards the middle of May the confederate armies broke up from their cantonments to leave the soil of France, and to repass the Rhine on their return to their several countries.

Peace was signed between France, Austria, Russia, Great Britain, and Prussia, on the 30th of May.

The frontiers of France were nearly those of 1792. Swisserland remained an independent state; Austria received back her territories in Upper Italy; England kept possession of Malta; and to France were restored the whole of her colonies, except Tobago, St. Lucia, and the Isle of France. All claims were given up respecting the heavy contributions formerly imposed by France, on other countries.

The victors returned not evil for evil, but left France, though conquered, both great and powerful. Germany, if unanimous, could have nothing to fear from France; and of all the potentates that returned home, crowned with the laurels of victory and clemency, none could be more gratified than the Sovereign of Prussia.

Deeply sensible of the debt of gratitude this Monarch owed to his faithful subjects, he issued the following proclamation to his people on the 3d of June 1813, previous to his leaving Paris for England :

" That combat is now ended for which my people and myself sprung to arms; and most happily so, by the help of God, the faithful assistance of our allies, and the energy, courage, perseverance, and privations, which every one who calls himself a Prussian has conspicuously shown and endured in this severe struggle. Accept, for it, my thanks. Your efforts and your sacrifices have been great; I know and acknowledge them; and God, who watches over us, has likewise acknowledged them. We have acquired what we fought for. Prussia now stands before the present age crowned with glory, and independent by her own energies, existing both in success and in misfortune. All as one, one for all, you hastened to arms, only one sentiment pervading my people throughout! And such was the combat!—Such sentiments, I then exclaimed, God alone can reward. He will now reward them by the peace which he has given us. Better times will return through this peace. The industrious farmer will no longer sow for strangers, but will reap for himself. Commerce, trade, and the arts, will once more flourish; opulence throughout all ranks will again take root; and under a new order of things, those wounds will be healed which your long sufferings have inflicted.

" FREDERICK."

Paris, June 3, 1814.

The Prussian monarchy regained its influence on the continent, as one of the first powers of Europe, not merely by increase of territory, but by the heroic efforts of her army, and by a pure national spirit, which has shown itself on many memorable occasions.

His Majesty the King of Prussia now hastened to reward his brave Generals and Commanders in the field.   Our veteran Hero was raised to the dignity of Prince; General von York was created Count York of Wartenberg; General von Kleist, Count Kleist of Nollendorf; General von Bülow, Count Bülow of Dennewitz; General Tauenzien, Count Tauenzien of Wittenberg; and the Quarter-master-general von Gneisenau, Count Gneisenau.   The Monarch accompanied these marks of his gratitude with presents of domains equal to the elevated rank of his intrepid and skilful commanders, and honourable to the munificence of Frederick the Beloved.

General Count Kleist was appointed to the command of the troops stationed on the Lower Rhine.   General Count York was made Governor of Liege.   Colonel von Kraussenbeck was stationed in Mentz, as Commandant.   Between the Moselle and the Meuse, a Prussian army went into cantonments.

The King of Prussia returned to Paris from his visit to England on the 29th of June 1814, and arrived at Berlin on the 4th of August.

Prince Blücher of Wahlstatt, accompanied by the Crown Prince of Prussia and Prince William, His Majesty's nephew, reached Magdeburgh on their return to Berlin, from the most glorious and bloody campaign recorded in history, on the 24th of July 1814. And the flower of the Prussian army, 66,000 men strong, under the command of Count Tauenzien-Wittenberg, made their triumphal entry into Magdeburgh on the 4th of July.

In the interim, a Prussian corps under General Count Kleist of Nollendorf, was stationed on the Middle Rhine; another, under Count Bülow of Dennewitz, near Coblentz; and on the banks of the Meuse stood the troops under the command of General Thielman. The head-quarters of all these corps were at Aix-la-Chapelle, General von Müffling being appointed Quarter-master-gene.al.

An army of British, Hanoverian, Dutch, and Belgic troops, was cantoned in Belgium, from Namur to Nieuport, and from the Meuse to the North Sea.

We must now call the attention of our readers towards the Congress at Vienna, which, according to the Convention of Paris of the 30th of May 1814, was to deliberate upon the future welfare of Europe, and on the issue of whose consultations the peace and happiness of so many millions of human beings were to depend. This illustrious assemblage of European princes and experienced statesmen seeks in vain for a parallel in history. Their avowed principle, into which all others merged more or less, of fixing the balance of power in Europe upon the firmest basis human foresight was capable of forming, caused this grand council of state to become the most dignified in regard to its object, and the most splendid in respect to its members; and, no doubt, it will prove for a long period, the most glorious memorial of unanimity and wisdom the Christian world may have to offer. The deliberations of this august assembly commenced on the 1st of November 1814.

Whatever the opinions of politicians might be, or the hopes that were entertained, throughout the states of Europe, yet no one was found hardy enough to oppose that system with which the happiness of all was so closely interwoven. The object was not to serve *one*, but to serve *all*. Virtue and morality, long since banished from one corner of Europe, were to be reintroduced under the auspices of a legitimate Sovereign, and the pleasure-yielding paths of honour and esteem were again opened to those that had been led astray.

This dream of future happiness kept up its delusive powers but a few short months. The sittings of Congress were not even ended, when Buonaparte, the scourge of mankind, banishing truth as well as virtue from his conduct, and leaguing with duplicity and cunning, set at nought his oath and his declaration to all the Kings he had warred with, again stepped forth on the theatre of carnage, equally perfidious, equally unjust and faithless to his engagements as ever he had been heretofore.

CHAPTER XV.

*Napoleon Buonaparte's Escape from Elba—Renewal
of Hostilities—Battles of Ligny, Les Quatre
Bras, and Waterloo—Our veteran Prince Blücher enters Paris a second Time.*

In detailing the particulars of Napoleon Buonaparte's escape from the island of Elba, we present
a picture of perfidy and perjury on the part of this
usurper, of a most striking and impressive nature.

On the 26th of February 1814, Napoleon seized some vessels in the harbour of Porto-Ferrajo,
and embarked with about 400 infantry and 100
Polish lancers of his guard. He landed with his
troops on the 1st of March in the gulf of Juan, in
France. On the 7th he reached Grenoble, and
entered Lyons on the 10th. He slept at Fontainbleau on the 19th, and made his public entry
into Paris on the 20th of March 1814.

Thus terminated this momentous enterprise. It
caused, in the interval of its execution, no blood
to be shed, proving, however, but a deceitful
calm, as a prelude to the avenging storm that was
to burst over the abettors of this base act of
treason and impious arrogance. A most profound
emotion and sentiment of depression were felt by

every one at seeing France once again fallen under
the yoke of a military despot, supported by a perjured army. The constitution which the generosity of the allied Monarchs had permitted France
to form and to swear to support, was here at one
blow subverted.

Prince Talleyrand communicated to the allied
Sovereigns at Vienna, in the name of the King of
France, the landing of Buonaparte in France, adding, that the kingdom was threatened with a civil
war. The Sovereigns having assembled, gave on this
occasion a new mark of that magnanimity, of that
chivalrous spirit which animates them.   They
unanimously resolved not to separate till Europe
should be restored to a state of tranquillity, and,
weary of the agitations and misfortunes which
had so long oppressed their people, would not
lay down their arms till order should be every
where restored. Measures dictated by prudence
were immediately resorted to with energy. Several Prussian corps on the Oder, in Silesia, and
on the Elbe, received orders to march to the Lower
Rhine. The Russian army, under General Bennigsen, left Posen, their head-quarters, for Germany; and the Austrian and Bavarian troops put
themselves in motion towards the Upper Rhine.
The Prussian army under General Count Kleist
proceeded from their cantonments on the Rhine
to the French frontiers, and the British army in

the Netherlands received considerable reinforcements.

Those criminals who for twenty years have
been employed in daily crimes, and their chief,
who had acted as if there were nothing sacred upon
earth, but what he pleased to term his will, hastened, by their perfidious acts, to receive that
ample punishment for which their treasons and
their treachery so loudly called, but from which the
noble generosity of the allied Monarchs had hitherto suffered them to escape.

The nations of Europe were driven to arms by
the fearful apprehension of again seeing despotism
and the sword extinguishing the rights of humanity.   Their princes and their leaders had felt the
direful consequences of the want of unanimity
amongst themselves in former times; and with an
unexampled coalescence of interests they once more
took the field against the common enemy of mankind.   Their efforts have been crowned with victory, and the ruthless subverter of peace and tranquillity, of civic independence and religion, has
been stripped of all his meretricious military fame,
and expelled society.

His Majesty the King of Prussia adopted the
most prompt measures to bring an active and efficient army into the field, accompanied by the following proclamation to his people, which was received with enthusiasm.   In fact, the people of
Prussia, always distinguished for their patriotism,

never gave more striking proofs of it than at this moment. Citizens of all ranks and ages crowded to enrol themselves, and more eager to depart.

" Vienna, April 7, 1815.

" When, in the time of danger, I called my people to arms, to combat for the freedom and independence of the country, the whole mass of the youth, glowing with emulation, thronged round the standards, to bear with joyful self-denial unusual hardships, and resolved to brave death itself. Then the best strength of the people intrepidly joined the ranks of my brave soldiers, and my generals led with me into battle a host of heroes, who have shown themselves worthy of the name of Prussians. Thus we and our Allies, attended by victory, conquered the capital of our enemy. Napoleon abdicated his authority : liberty was restored to Germany, security to thrones, and to the world the hope of a durable peace.

"This hope is vanished. We must again march to the combat ! A perfidious conspiracy has brought back to France the man who, for ten years together, has filled the world with sorrow. The people, confounded, have not been able to oppose his armed adherents. Though he himself, while still at the head of a considerable military force, declared his abdication to be a voluntary sacrifice to the happiness and repose of France, he now regards this, like every other convention, as nothing.

He is at the head of perjured soldiers, who desire
to render war eternal ; Europe again is threatened :
it cannot suffer the man to remain on the throne
of France, who loudly proclaimed universal empire to be the object of his continually renewed
wars ; who confounded all moral principle, by his
repeated breach of faith, and who can, therefore,
give the world no security for his peaceful intentions.

" Again, therefore, arise to the combat ! France
itself wants our aid, and all Europe is allied with
us.   United with your ancient companions in victory, reinforced by the accession of new brethren
in arms, you, brave Prussians, go to a just war
with me, with the Princes of my family, with the
Generals who have led you to conquest.   The justice of the cause we defend will ensure us
victory.

" Thus united, with all Europe in arms, we again
enter the lists against Napoleon Buonaparte and
his adherents.   Arise then, with God for your
support, for the repose of the world, for order, for
morality, for your King and country.

" FREDERICK WILLIAM."

The King of Prussia gave Prince Blücher the
command-in-chief over the Prussian armies.   General Count Gneisenau was at the same time appointed Quarter-master-general to the army of the
Lower Rhine, the staff of which was composed of

General von Müffling, Colonels Pfühl, Grollmann, &c. &c. &c.

The Prussian army that was now preparing to take the field, amounted to about 230,000 men. It was divided into seven corps.

The 1st corps, under the command of Lieutenant-general von Ziethen; the 2d corps, under the command of Lieutenant-general Count Bülow von Dennewitz; the 3d corps, under the command of Lieutenant-general von Borstel; the 4th corps, under the command of Lieutenant-general von Thielman; composed the army of the Lower Rhine, under Marshal Prince Blücher, having its head-quarters at Liege. Never did a finer and more enthusiastic army form under the banners of a more distinguished leader, and never had an army a more righteous cause to maintain.

Our illustrious veteran Blücher took leave of his Sovereign, and departed from Berlin for the Prussian army in the Netherlands, on the 10th of April 1815. On his arrival at Liege, he addressed the following proclamation to his army :

" Comrades! His Majesty the King has been pleased to confide to me the chief command of the army. I receive this favour with most lively gratitude. I am rejoiced to see you again—to find you on the field of honour, prepared for a new contest, full of new hopes. It is given to us again to combat for the great cause—for general peace! I congratulate you upon it. The course of glory is again opened to you. An opportunity offers to increase, by new deeds, the military renown which you have already acquired! Placed at your head, I doubt not of certain and glorious success! Show me, in this new struggle, the confidence you have placed in me during the last, and I am convinced that you will gloriously extend the fame of your brilliant deeds in arms.

" BLÜCHER."

A declaration of the allied powers, dated from Vienna, pronounced in a solemn and decisive manner, " That there is no peace with Buonaparte." This great sentence loudly proclaimed the desire of the belligerent Sovereigns to procure themselves a sure and durable peace, and that they will never recognise a military despotism with the means of incessantly threatening its neighbours, and which would force other powers continually to make efforts and new sacrifices.

The Duke of Wellington arrived at Brussels on the 4th of April, as Commander-in-chief of the grand allied army of British, Dutch, and Hanoverians, collecting in the Netherlands, and had several interviews with General Count Kleist of Nollendorf, then commanding the Prussian forces, concerning the intended operations.

Field-marshal Prince Blücher was at Brussels on

the 28th of April, to be present at a grand review of the British cavalry, and had a long conference with England's hero.

The Prussian army was cantoned in the neighbourhood of Liege, Namur, and Hannut; General von Ziethen's head-quarters were at Jemappe, General von Borstel's at Binch, and General von Bülow's at Hannut.

Hostilities first commenced between the Prussians and the French on the 25th of April, near Falmignoul, two leagues from Givet, the French out-posts being driven back, with some loss, upon the latter place.

It was for the common interests of Europe that this grand assemblage of gallant warriors, under Blücher and Wellington, was formed, mutually inclined to respect and regard each other. United by one sentiment, as well as by the general danger, standing in need of reciprocal aid, and breathing alike the same lofty spirit of honour and independence, the two armies never ceased to cultivate those ties that bound them closer together, and thus promoted an uninterrupted harmony in the councils of their illustrious chiefs.

Proudly conscious of the glory they had acquired in the last struggle, and full of confidence in themselves, the two armies awaited with manifest impatience the orders for marching beyond the frontiers of France to meet their enemy in the field.

The other confederate powers were, meanwhile,

not less intent upon completing their armies, and preparing them for an eventful campaign, and hostile entry into France, from the most vulnerable points.

The necessity of waiting till the whole of these mighty preparations were fully completed, caused at this period the armies of the Allies in the Netherlands to remain inactive.

Napoleon Buonaparte, at the head of the military power of France, adopted in the interim every coercive measure within his grasp, to reorganize his army, and to increase and consolidate his means of aggression. The time that now elapsed in a state of suspense, presented an awful interval full of hope, doubt, and fear to men's minds. It agitated the whole of Europe, set the theories of politicians at nought, and left little to console the heart of man but confidence and trust in Divine Providence. It seemed to be the miserable fate reserved for mankind, that a state of society in which all are soldiers—in which a military code was to predominate over civil institutions, and a new situation affecting the political relations of every power and the private condition of every individual, was going to be once more realized. The month of May passed without any event taking place worthy of record. It was the interest of the Confederates to gain time, and to permit Buonaparte to be the first aggressor. They were not to risk the danger of exciting the popular feeling of France herself against their honourable views. It was the man, and not the nation, they warred with ; and a material point was gained, if the nation remained convinced that Buonaparte and his adherents alone were to be chastised, on the Allies again entering their country as victors. England, Prussia, Russia, and Austria, therefore, avowed and declared their sole object to be the destruction and subjection of a nest of thieves, that preferred a life of rapine and plunder to the peaceful occupations of husbandry and civic independence.

Nothing that sprung from moral rectitude had been able to control the perfidious despot; and it was resolved, that the fetters of penal restraint should now bind him fast, and disable him from all commission of further evil.

The flower of the British, Prussian, Dutch, and Hanoverian armies, concentrated themselves in the Netherlands; reinforcements daily joined, offering a pledge for a proportionate increase of energy to their exertions, when the campaign should open.

The French army now assembled on the frontiers towards the Netherlands, might be computed at little short of 140,000 men. Every nerve had been exerted, and all physical powers stretched to their extreme tension, to bring it to a state of high organization, and to improve its discipline. In the stupendous attempt of Buonaparte, both daring and important, of again rendering his seat firm on his usurped throne, it is to be supposed that he would not leave a single soldier in his rear, as reserve, that was fit to take the field; and consequently the whole efficient military strength of France might be considered as concentrated at this point.

In the early part of June 1815, Napoleon Buonaparte left Paris, and put himse'f at the head of five corps of the French army, exclusive of the imperial guards and cavalry, taking up a position between Maubeuge and Beaumont. He commenced hostilities on the 15th of June, by driving in the Prussian videttes and out-posts, and advancing on the right and left bank of the Sambre, by Thuin, against Charleroi, which, after a trifling affair, was occupied by the French. The points of concentration of the Prussian army of the Lower Rhine, under our veteran Prince Blücher, were at Fleurus and Namur. General von Ziethen had collected his corps near the former place, and after a very warm action with the enemy, on the 15th, maintained himself there in his position. The terrain of Sombref, about a league and a half from Fleurus, being chosen by Field-marshal Blücher, on which to meet the enemy, the three other corps of the Prussian army were consequently directed upon that place, where the 2d and 3d corps were to arrive on the 15th, and the 4th corps on the 16th. In the morning of the

BATTLES of WATERLOO and LIGNY,
fought 16th & 18th June 1815.

A. Battle of Ligny fought June 16th
B. Battle of Waterloo fought June 18th 1815
C. Battle of Lesquatre Bras
D. Retreat of Blücher to Wavre.
E. 1. Position of the French army on the 17th

E. 2 Blücher's position on the 18th
F. (Blücher's & Bülow's attack on the right flank) of Napoleon's army on the 18th
G. Disorderly flight of the French army

British ━━━ Prussians ━━━ French ━━━ Roads ══ Rivers ━━━

Neele sc. Strand

16th, the Prussian army was posted on the heights
between Bry and Sombref (see *Plan of the Battles
of Waterloo and Ligny*), and beyond the latter
place, and occupied, with a large force, the villages of St. Amand and Ligny, situated in a ra-
vine, on its front.   Meantime only three corps of
the army had joined; the fourth, under General
Count Bülow, was stationed between Liege and
Hannut, had been delayed in its march by several
circumstances, and was not yet come up.

The French army occupied the following positions: the left wing, under Marshal Ney, was
posted at Frasne; the right wing, under Marshal
Grouchy, in the rear of Fleurus.   But, on Napoleon having reconnoitred the strength and positions of Marshal Blücher's army, he, about noon,
changed front, and marched his left wing upon
Les Quatre Bras, and his right and centre upon
St. Amand and Ligny.

In the mean time the Duke of Wellington had
collected his troops near Soignies and Brendleçon;
and, on the 16th, Prince William of Orange, by
order of the Duke, took post with his corps at
Les Quatre Bras, to be nearer the Prussian army;
and, by dividing the attention and forces of Napoleon, prevent his pressing with too great a superiority of numbers on Marshal Blücher's line of
operations.   The Prince of Orange was supported
by the Duke of Brunswick's division, and a division of British troops, under Lieutenant-general

Sir Thomas Picton; his left wing leaning on Sart à Maveline, and his right on the former place. The Duke of Wellington directed the whole English army to march upon Les Quatre Bras. Marshal Ney, with the 1st and 2d corps, and the 2d of cavalry, commenced the attack at about three o'clock, P. M. A wood, to the right of Les Quatre Bras, was several times taken and retaken; and the village of Pierremont, on the left, was carried at the point of the bayonet. And, after a sanguinary conflict, the army of the Allies maintained its position, and completely defeated and repulsed every attempt against it, though repeatedly assaulted by large bodies of infantry and cavalry, supported by a numerous and powerful artillery.

Our veteran Prince Blücher still resolved to give battle in his position at Sombref, although his 4th corps was not yet in line, and his army, in point of numbers, was much inferior to that of the French; but, notwithstanding, every foot of ground was obstinately contested, and the position maintained with unparalleled bravery and resolution. At about three o'clock, P. M. great masses of the enemy, under Marshal Grouchy, attacked the village of St. Amand; it was defended with intrepidity, and its transient occupation cost the French an enormous number of men; the Prussians rallied, and it was again carried after a sanguinary conflict; again lost; then stormed, for a third time, by a gallant battalion with our vete-

ran Hero at its head, and the heights of La Haye
and Little St. Amand were at last regained, and
occupied by the Prussian army.   It was near five
o'clock, P. M. and the enemy now directed his efforts against Ligny : this is a large village, solidly
built, situated on a rivulet of the same name.   It
was here that a contest began, which may be
considered as the most sanguinary in history.
The terrain of action was confined to a very narrow space, fresh troops were, on both sides, continually brought into fire, and the combat was
maintained about Ligny with unexampled fury.
By regaining the height of La Haye, affairs seemed to take a favourable turn for the Prussian arms.
The issue, however, seemed to depend on the arrival of the English troops, or on that of the 4th
corps of the Prussian army.   In fact, the co-operation of this last division would have afforded the
Field-marshal the means of making immediately,
with the right wing, an attack, from which great
success might be expected; but news was brought
that the English division, destined to support Prince
Blücher, was violently attacked by the French
army, under Marshal Ney, and it was with great
difficulty it had maintained itself in its position at
Les Quatre Bras.   The 4th corps of the army did
not appear; so that our veteran Marshal was forced
to maintain alone the contest with an enemy greatly
superior in numbers.   For four hours the combat
about Ligny continued with the same fury, and

the same equality of success; the danger became
every hour more and more urgent; our dauntless
Hero, sword in hand, repeatedly led his divisions
into fire; the arrival of the succours so necessary was in vain invoked, and there was not
any corps in reserve to support the prodigious
efforts of the troops, and the personal bravery and
example of our intrepid Blücher. It proved,
however, a drawn battle, as no ground was lost
or won on either side. Towards nine in the evening, Napoleon attempted, with his masses of cavalry, to attain his object of interrupting the
communication between the armies of Marshal
Prince Blücher and the Duke of Wellington. The
attacks of the French cavalry were coolly repulsed
by the Prussian infantry, which now retreated in
good order upon the heights, whence the Prussian
army continued its retrograde movement upon
Tilly. The villages of Bry and Sombref were kept
occupied during the night, and the corps under
General Thielman began slowly, at day-break, to
retreat towards Gembloux, where the 4th corps,
under General Count Bülow, had now arrived.
The 1st and 2d corps proceeded, in the morning,
behind the defile of Mount St. Guibert. Marshal
Prince Blücher held it advisable to take up a
position, on the evening of the 17th, near Wavre,
that he might be nearer his reinforcements, and be
able to form a complete junction with the army
of the Allies, under the Duke of Wellington.

The loss of the Prussians at the battle of Ligny, on the 16th, was great; but no prisoners were taken by the enemy, except a part of the wounded. The troops fought with a bravery which equalled every expectation; their fortitude remained unshaken, because every one retained his confidence in his own strength. On this memorable day, however, Field-marshal Blücher had encountered the greatest dangers. A charge of cavalry led on by himself, had failed; while that of the enemy was vigorously pursuing, a musket-shot struck the Field-marshal's horse; the animal, far from being stopped in his career by this wound, began to gallop more furiously, till it dropped down dead. The Field-marshal, stunned by the violent fall, lay entangled under the horse. The enemy's cuirassiers, following up their advantage, advanced; the last Prussian horseman had already passed by the Field-marshal; an adjutant alone remained with him, and had just alighted to share his fate. The danger was great, but Heaven watched over him. The enemy, pursuing their charge, passed rapidly by the Field-marshal without seeing him; the next moment, a second charge of cavalry having repelled them, they again passed by him, with the same precipitation, not perceiving him any more than they had done the first time. Then, but not without difficulty, the Field-marshal was disengaged from under the dead animal, and he immediately mounted a dragoon horse.

The Prussian army had concentrated itself on advantageous ground, in the environs of Wavre. The Duke of Wellington issued the necessary orders to form a junction with Marshal Blücher; the English army, in consequence, made a corresponding movement with that of Blücher's, and fell back upon Genappe, and then on Waterloo, on the morning of the 17th, at ten o'clock. The enemy did not attack Blücher or the English army in their march, but only followed with his cavalry.

The battle of Ligny was marked by the peculiar fury and hatred with which the Prussians fought the French. Their mutual animosity was beyond conception. The slaughter made by the Prussians was immense; they refused to take quarter, as much as the French refused to give it; and it may be easily supposed that there never was such havoc made as here, for, where men fight with equal desperation, the loss on both sides is always terrible. It was evident, from the tardiness of the pursuit, that the French felt but little confidence of success from any further efforts.

The loss of the Prussians may be estimated at about 10,000 men, killed and wounded.

The Duke of Wellington, after the action of Les Quatre Bras, had taken up a position with

the army of the Allies, on the road to Brussels
(see *Plan of the Battles of Waterloo and Ligny*),
having his right wing leaning upon Braine la Leu,
the centre near Mont St. Jean, and the left wing
against Ter la Haye. The Duke wrote to the
Field-marshal, that he was resolved to accept
battle in this position, if the Field-marshal would
support him with two corps of his army. Our veteran Hero promised to come with his whole army.
He even proposed, in case Napoleon should not
attack, that the Allies themselves, with their
whole united force, should attack him the next
day. This may serve to show how little the battle
of the 16th had disorganized the Prussian army,
or weakened its moral strength. Thus ended the
day of the 17th.

On the 18th, Napoleon had detached his right
wing, under Marshal Grouchy, in pursuit of the
Prussians towards Wavre ; he himself fixed his
head-quarters at Planchenoit, and, with his left
wing and centre under Marshal Ney and Jerome
Buonaparte, took up a position, with his right on
the heights in front of Planchenoit, his centre at
La Belle Alliance, and his left leaning on the road
to Brussels, and nearly opposite the village of
Mont St. Jean. The cuirassiers and the guards
were posted in reserve on the heights behind. —
(*See Plan of the Battles of Waterloo and Ligny.*)

The movement of Prince Blücher to Wavre, on
the 17th, had, as already mentioned, induced the

Duke of Wellington to remove his head-quarters to Waterloo.

The position of Waterloo is in advance of that place, where the high road from Brussels to Namur crosses that which leads to Braine la Leu. Though this ground is open and without any remarkable feature, it rises almost suddenly upon this point, to the distance of half a league. There is at the right extremity of the front of this elevation, a farm, consisting of a stone house, a wall round the premises, and a wood, intersected by natural hedges and ditches.

It was upon this ground that the Duke of Wellington resolved to wait for the enemy. He placed his batteries, occupied the farm and the garden, and ranged his army along the eminence, protected by its heights from the enemy's fire. The army being composed of troops of different nations, he took the precaution to support each of them by English infantry, all dispersed in such a manner as to be able to succour the point that was threatened.

On the 18th, at noon, the French army, commanded by Buonaparte, commenced the attack; his first efforts were against the farm of which we have spoken. After several attempts he succeeded, about half past one o'clock, P. M. in dislodging some part of the troops. The Duke hastened to the spot, and ordered two battalions to retake it, and to defend themselves there to the last extremity. His orders were punctually obeyed.

The enemy then directed two strong columns against the centre. The Duke in person led some battalions of infantry against these columns, and Lord Uxbridge the cavalry. They charged with the bayonet; the French were overpowered, and their cavalry broken. In this charge were taken an eagle, a standard, and 1200 prisoners. The victorious troops instantly returned to their place, and again formed.

The attack on the farm continued; the enemy penetrated to it, but could never establish a footing there.

Buonaparte, seeing that he could not obtain any advantage, manœuvred, with all his cavalry, and a part of his infantry, against the right of the Allies, attempted to outflank it with 17,000 cavalry, and began a most vigorous attack. The Duke made his arrangements accordingly: the cavalry of the two armies charged; the squares of infantry remained immovable, and repulsed every attack. This attempt of the enemy was baffled. At last, about six o'clock, he made another attack upon the centre, and reached the eminence. The Duke attacked him, overthrew and pursued him, and the rout soon became general.

The army of the Duke of Wellington did not exceed 50,000 men, actually engaged. The enemy was very superior, particularly in cavalry.

The head-quarters of the Duke of Wellington were removed to Nivelles after the battle.

Meanwhile the army under the command of Marshal Prince Blücher began again to move from the environs of Wavre at break of day on the 18th. The 4th and 2d corps marched by St. Lambert, where they were to occupy a position, covered by the forest, near Frichemont, to take the enemy in the rear when the moment should appear fa-; vourable. The 1st corps was to operate by Ohain, on the right flank of the enemy; the 3d corps was to follow slowly, in order to afford succour in case of need. The conflict began about ten, A. M. In a short time the battle became general along the whole line. It seems that Napoleon had the design to throw the left wing upon the centre, and thus to effect the separation of the English army from the Prussian, which he believed to be retreating upon Maestricht. For this purpose he had placed the greater part of his reserve in the centre, against his right wing; and upon this point he attacked with fury. The English army fought with a valour which could not be surpassed. The repeated charges of the old guard were baffled by the intrepidity of the Scotch regiments; and at every charge the French cavalry was overthrown by the English cavalry. But the superiority in numbers of the enemy was too great; Napoleon continually brought forward considerable masses, and with whatever firmness the English troops maintained themselves in their position, it was not possible but that such

heroic exertions must have a limit.   It was half
past four o'clock.   The excessive difficulties of
the passage by the defile of St. Lambert, had
greatly retarded the march of the Prussian columns, so that only two brigades of the 4th
corps had arrived at the covered position which
was assigned them.   The decisive moment was
come ; there was not a moment to be lost.   The
Generals did not suffer it to escape.   They resolved immediately to begin the attack with the troops
which they had at hand.   General Count Bülow,
therefore, with two brigades and a corps of cavalry, advanced rapidly along the rear of the enemy's right wing.   The enemy did not lose his
presence of mind ; he instantly returned his reserve
against the Prussians, and a murderous conflict began on that side.   The combat remained long uncertain, while the battle with the English army still
continued with the same violence.   Towards six,
P. M. news was received that General Thielman, with the 3d corps, was attacked near Wavre
by a very considerable corps of the enemy, and
that they were already disputing the possession of
the town. The Field-marshal, however, did not suffer
himself to be disturbed by this intelligence ; it
was on the spot where he was, and no where else,
that the affair was to be decided.   A conflict, continually supported with the same obstinacy, and
kept up by fresh troops, could alone ensure the victory ; and if it was obtained here, any reverse

sustained near Wavre was of little consequence.
The columns, therefore, continued their movements. It was half past seven—and the issue of
the battle was still uncertain. The whole of the 4th
corps, and a part of the 2d under General Pirch, had
successively come up. The French fought with a
desperate fury; however, some uncertainty was
perceived in their movements, and it was observed
that some pieces of cannon were retreating. At
this moment the first column of General von Ziethen
arrived on the points of attack, near the village
of Smouhen, on the enemy's right flank, and instantly charged. This movement decided the defeat of the enemy. His right wing was broken in
three places; he abandoned his positions. The troops
rushed forwards at the *pas de charge*, and attacked
him on all sides, while, at the same time, the
whole English line advanced. Circumstances were
entirely favourable to the attack formed by the Prussian army : the ground rose in an amphitheatre,
so that their artillery could freely open its fire
from the summit of several heights, which rose
gradually above each other, and in the intervals
of which the troops descended into the plain,
formed into brigades, in the most perfect order,
while fresh corps continually unfolded themselves,
issuing from the forest on the height behind. The
enemy, however, still preserved means to retreat,
till the village of Planchenoit, which he had on
his rear, and which was defended by the old guard,

was, after several bloody attacks, carried by storm *.

From this time the retreat became a rout, that quickly spread throughout the whole French army, which, in its dreadful confusion, hurrying away every thing that attempted to stop it, soon assumed the appearance of the flight of an army of barbarians. It was half past nine: the Field-marshal assembled all the superior officers, and gave orders to send the last horse and the last man in pursuit of the enemy. The van of the Prussian army accelerated its march. The French army, pursued without intermission, was absolutely disorganized. The causeway presented the appearance of an immense shipwreck; it was covered with an innumerable quantity of cannon, caissons, carriages, baggage, arms, and wrecks of every kind. Those of the enemy who had attempted to repose for a time, and had not expected to be so quickly pursued, were driven from more than nine bivouacks. In some villages they attempted to maintain themselves; but as soon as they heard the beating of the Prussian drums, or the sound of the trumpet,

---

* Napoleon's corps of old guards was posted at Planchenoit as reserve. It was the 15th regiment of Prussian infantry, led on by Major von Keller, and supported by some battalions of Prussian landwehr, that stormed their position, and completely put them to the rout. The greater part of them were bayoneted—no prisoners were made, and no quarter was given.

they either fled or threw themselves into the
houses, where they were cut down or made prisoners. It was moonlight, which greatly favoured
the pursuit; for the whole march was but a continued chase, either in corn-fields or the houses.

At Genappe the enemy had intrenched himself
with cannon and overturned carriages, at the approach of the Prussians. Suddenly they heard in
the town a great noise and a motion of carriages;
at the entrance they were exposed to a brisk fire
of musketry, which was replied to by some cannon-
shot, followed by a *hurrah*; and an instant after
the town was theirs *. Thus the affair continued
till break of day. About 40,000 men in the most
complete disorder, the remains of the whole army,
saved themselves by retreating through Charleroi,
partly without arms, and carrying with them only
twenty-seven pieces of their numerous artillery.

Few victories have been so complete, and there

---

* It was Major von Keller, at the head of the advance, that
charged into Genappe at the time that Napoleon was driving
through the place in his carriage, attended by his suite in several other vehicles : the Major's movement was so sudden, that
Napoleon had only time to mount a horse to escape falling into
his hands. His hat and sword were found in the carriage. His
treasures, his jewels, his imperial mantle, and the whole of his
baggage, fell into the hands of the Prussians, besides maps,
charts, and military plans, without number; and, above all,
his personal portefeuille, containing the whole of his private and
secret correspondence.

is certainly no example that an army, two days
after losing a battle, engaged in such an action,
and so gloriously maintained it. Honour be to the
troops capable of so much firmness and valour! In
the middle of the position occupied by the French
army, and exactly upon the height, is a farm called La Belle Alliance. The march of all the Prussian columns was directed towards this farm,
which was visible from every side. It was there
that Napoleon was during the battle—it was there
that he gave his orders, that he flattered himself
with the hopes of victory—and it was there that
his ruin was decided. There, too, it was, that, by
a happy chance, Field-marshal Blücher and the
Duke of Wellington met in the dark, and mutually
saluted each other as victors.

The allied army under the Duke pursued the
flying French, till, overcome with fatigue, the
troops could follow them no further. But Buonaparte was not suffered to rest; the Prussians, under General Count Gneisenau, started afresh in
the pursuit, where the British army and the
Allies stopped, and hung on the rear of the
fugitives for the whole night, avenging, amply,
the fate of 10,000 of their brave countrymen, who
had so nobly spilt their blood in the battles of the
15th and 16th.

Marshal Prince Blücher's head-quarters were at
Genappe on the morning of the 19th, from whence

he dated the following autograph letter to the Governor of Berlin, General von Kalkreuth:

" I have to inform your Excellency, that, in conjunction with the British army under the Duke of Wellington, I yesterday gained the most complete victory over Napoleon Buonaparte, that ever was obtained. The battle took place in the neighbourhood of a few houses, situated on the road from hence to Brussels, called La Belle Alliance; and a better name cannot well be given to this important day. The whole French army is in a state of perfect dissolution, and an extraordinary number of guns have been taken. Time will not permit me to state more particulars to your Excellency. The details shall follow; and I only beg you to impart this news immediately to the loyal citizens of Berlin.

" *Head-quarters, Genappe, June* 19,   BLÜCHER.
  Half past Five o'Clock, A. M.*"

---

* At the conclusion of the battle the Marshal also wrote the following letter to his lady:

" MY DEAR WIFE,

" You well know what I promised you, and I have kept my word. Superiority of numbers forced me to give way on the 17th; but, on the 18th, in conjunction with my friend Wellington, I put an end at once to Buonaparte's dancing. His army is completely routed, and the whole of his artillery, baggage, tumbrils, and equipages are in my hands. The insignia

The battle of Waterloo was fought by Buonaparte with every power called into action; he knew that he must infallibly lose all if victory did not overawe his foes and encourage his well-wishers. He made one desperate, bloody struggle, and—he failed.

The immediate fruits of this victory were between 20 and 30,000 prisoners, with more than 250 pieces of cannon, and the almost complete destruction of the only French force which could properly be called an army.

The following proclamation was addressed by Field-marshal Prince Blücher to the army of the Lower Rhine, to be read at the head of every battalion, after the victory of Waterloo, on the 18th of June 1815.

" Brave Officers and Soldiers of the
    Army of the Lower Rhine !

    " You have done great things, brave companions in arms—you have fought two battles in

---

of all the orders he had worn are just brought me, having been found in his carriage in a casket. I had two horses killed under me yesterday. Buonaparte's affair will now soon be terminated.

                                        " BLÜCHER."

" P. S. (Written by his son on the road to Genappe.) Father Blücher embraced Wellington in so hearty a manner, that every one present said it was the most touching scene that could be imagined."

three days. The first was unfortunate, and yet your courage was not broken. You have had to struggle with privations, but you have borne them with fortitude. Immovable in adverse fortune, after the loss of a bloody battle, you marched with firmness to fight another, relying on the God of Battles, and full of confidence in your commanders, as well as of perseverance in your efforts against presumptuous and perjured enemies, intoxicated with their victory. It was with these sentiments you marched to support the brave English, who were maintaining the most arduous contest with unparalleled resolution. But the hour which was to decide this great struggle has struck, and has shown who was to give the law—whether an adventurer, or governments who are the friends of order. Destiny was still undecided, when you appeared, issuing from the forest which had concealed you from the enemy, to attack his rear with that coolness, that intrepidity, that confidence, which characterizes experienced soldiers, resolved to avenge the reverses they had experienced two days before. There, rapid as lightning, you penetrated his already shaken columns. Nothing could stop you in the career of victory. The enemy, in his despair, turned his artillery upon you; but you poured death into his ranks, and your progress caused in them disorder, dispersion, and at last a complete rout. He found himself obliged to abandon to you several hundreds of cannon—and his army is dissolved! A few days will suffice to annihilate those perjured legions who were coming to consummate the slavery and the spoliation of the universe. All great commanders have regarded it as impossible immediately to renew the combat with a beaten army : you have proved that this opinion is ill-founded; you have proved that resolute warriors may be vanquished, but that their valour is not shaken. Receive, then, my thanks, incomparable soldiers, objects of my esteem! You have acquired a great reputation. The annals of Europe will eternize your triumphs. It is on you, immovable columns of the Prussian monarchy! that the destinies of the King and his august house will for ever repose. Never will Prussia cease to exist, while your sons and your grandsons resemble you.

" BLÜCHER."

Marshal Prince Blücher continued in march on the left of the Sambre, and crossed that river on the 19th, in pursuit of the enemy; and his army entered the French territory on the 21st, by Beaumont *. The wrecks of Buonaparte's

---

* The allied forces which were on their march into France at this period, have been estimated as follow :

	Men.
The Russian army - - - - - - - - - - -	225,000
The Austrian army - - - - - - - - - - -	250,000
Carried forward	475,000

army retired upon Laon in the most wretched state; and, in addition to its losses in battle, vast numbers deserted continually. On the

	Men.
Brought forward	475,000
The Prussian army - - - - - - - - - -	150,000
The British, Dutch, and Hanoverian army - - -	100,000
The Saxons - - - - - - - - - - - -	15,000
The Bavarian army - - - - - - - - - - -	40,000
The Würtemberg army - ˌ - - ˎ - - - - -	12,000
The contingents of the German Princes - - - -	20,000
The troops of Baden - - - - - - - - - ·· -	10,000
Total	822,000

Our gallant Veteran issued, at this time, the following proclamation :

" Marshal Prince Blücher to the brave Belgians.

" My army being on the point of entering the French territory, we cannot leave you, brave Belgians! without bidding you farewell, and without expressing our lively gratitude for the hospitality you have shown to our soldiers. We have had an opportunity of appreciating your virtues—you are a brave, a loyal, and a noble people. At the moment when danger seemed to threaten you, we were called to give you aid : we hastened to come, and it was much against our will that we found ourselves compelled, by circumstances, to await so long the commencement of the contest, which we should have been glad to see begin sooner. The presence of our troops has been burdensome to your country, but we have paid with our blood the debt of gratitude which we owe you; and a benevolent government will find means to indemnify such of you as have suffered the most by the quartering of the troops.

" Adieu,

24th Marshal Blücher took possession of St. Quintin, after it had been abandoned by the enemy; and, by the little resistance that was every where made, it was found that it had been impossible for the enemy to collect an army to make head against the Allies, and obstruct their direct march on Paris. The spirit of the French soldiers was broken, the infallibility and invincibility of their General was no more, and the chase of glory was given up at once as an idle dream.

The Prussians, flushed with victory, pursued their rapid march on Paris; their van-guard was attacked at Villars Coterets on the 28th; but Marshal Prince Blücher coming up with the main body, the enemy were repulsed with the loss of 6 pieces of cannon and about 1000 prisoners. This small body of the enemy, on being forced from off the high road from Soissons to Paris, got upon that of Meaux. General Count Bülow fell in with them on this road—he briskly attacked them, took 500 prisoners, and drove the rest across the

---

" Adieu, brave Belgians! The remembrance of the hospitable reception which you have afforded us, as well as the recollection of your virtues, will be eternally engraven on our hearts. May the God of peace protect your fine country— may he remove from it, for a long period, the troubles of war —may you be as happy as you deserve to be!

" *Head-quarters, Merbeu-le-Chateau,*   Farewell.
          June 21, 1815.   BLÜCHER."

Marne. Their shattered remains afterwards got
into Paris. On the 30th, Marshal Blücher passed
the village of Vertus, and, moving to his right,
crossed the Seine at St. Germain ; continuing
his march, he posted his right, on the 2d of July,
near Plessis Pique, his left at St. Cloud, and his
reserves at Versailles. The enemy had strongly
fortified the heights of Montmartre and the town
of St. Denys; and, by means of the little rivers
Rouillon and La Vielle Mar, they inundated the
ground on the north side of that town. The
heights of Belleville were likewise well fortified. Our veteran Hero was powerfully opposed by
the enemy in taking the position on the left of the
Seine, particularly on the heights of St. Cloud
and Meudon ; but the gallantry of the Prussian
troops under General Ziethen, surmounted every
obstacle, and they succeeded, finally, in establishing themselves on the heights of Meudon, and
in the village of Issy. The French attacked them
again in Issy, at three o'clock in the morning of
the 3d, but were repulsed with considerable loss;
and, finding that Paris was then open on its vulnerable side, the enemy sent to desire that all
firing might cease on both banks of the Seine,
with a view to the negotiation, at the palace of
St. Cloud, of a military convention between the
armies, under which the French army should evacuate Paris.

Officers accordingly met at St. Cloud, and a military convention was agreed to and ratified on the night of the 3d of July 1815, by the Duke of Wellington and Marshal Prince Blücher, and, on the part of the French army, by the Minister at War. This convention decided, that the wrecks of the French army were to evacuate Paris, to retire to the banks of the Loire, and the consequent surrender of Paris a second time to the Allies. Louis XVIII. entered the capital of his kingdom on the 8th of July, the same day with the British and Prussian forces.

Their Majesties the Emperor of Russia and the King of Prussia arrived on the 10th of July at Paris.

The three corps of Marshal Blücher's army, under the command of Generals Count Bülow and Kleist, and General von Ziethen, now took up their quarters in the city.

The most extraordinary feature in this occurrence, of the entry of the august Allies into Paris for the second time as victors, was, that the national guards, formed of the mass of citizens, showed so very little enthusiasm and loyal feeling.

If the restoration of the Bourbons is to produce peace between France and Europe, what other pledge can be desired than the unanimity and good faith of the French themselves? and what better proof could they produce of their sincerity, repentance, and return to civic order and domestic virtue, than their standing up, one and all, and hailing their King as their deliverer? But they received their Sovereign and legitimate Prince as tranquilly as if it were a spectacle or a procession they were daily accustomed to.

The occupation of Paris by the Allies must strengthen the general and sanguine opinion, that war and bloodshed are to cease, and that the restoration of the Bourbons is the prelude to a durable state of tranquillity amongst the nations of Europe.

Field-marshal Prince Blücher traversed the capital of France, at the head of his victorious troops once more as conqueror. His military glory had now reached its acme.

Our Hero's life, as it can be viewed by a distant observer, appears to have been an uninterrupted series of uncommon events. Distinguished in the army at a late period in life, called afterwards to the command of that army, advancing in promotion and reputation, until he was made a General Field-marshal, and selected for a post, with the due execution of which, the future existence and happiness of his country were intimately connected; subsequently rewarded by the second dignity of the Prussian realm, the father of gallant sons, and, in a vigorous old age, still able to feel all the honour and glory of his situation, what has he not experienced of those things which are supposed to constitute the splendid or the solid satisfactions of life? That he may long continue to enjoy them, to be the first support of the Prussian monarchy,—the terror of its enemies, —the pride of his Sovereign,—and the idol of his brave troops, is most devoutly to be wished and desired.

THE END.

Army, Prussian, its numbers from 1808 to 1811, 54.
————————, its efficient strength in 1813, 61, 62.
————————, its gallantry at the battle on the Katzbach, 165.
————————, its strength and corps, 147.
————————, anecdote of a soldier of the, 262.
————, Russian, under General Miloradowitsch, 66.
————, Silesian, occupies Saxony, 73.
————————, continues offensive operations, 154.
————————, crosses the Katzbach victorious, 168.
————————, its intrepidity and glorious efforts, 170.
————————, marches into France, 306.
————————, trophies of the, during the campaign of 1813, 381.
————, Swedish, the head-quarters of the, at Liege, 363.
————, the confederate, its numbers on the 14th October 1813, 219.
————, the confederate, its advance upon Leipsic, 221.
————, united, of Russians and Prussians, under General Barclay de Tolly, passes the Bohemian frontiers, and forms a junction with the Austrians, 152.
Arrighi, Marshal, anecdote of, 138.
Augereau, Marshal, is attacked by Prince Lichtenstein, 220.
Austria, Emperor of, declares war against Napoleon, 154.

B.

Balaschoff, General, anecdote of, 59.
Barclay de Tolly, General, repulses General Lauriston, 108.
————————————, attacked by Marshal Ney and General Lauriston, at the battle of Bautzen, 118.
————————————, his corps forms the rear-guard, 126.
———————————— Count, commands the united armies of Russians and Prussians, 152.
———————————————— at the battle of Leipsic, 234.
Bautzen, battle of, 113, 118.
————————, loss of the Russians and Prussians, 126.
————————, loss of the French, 126.
Bavaria, the King of, declares himself as the ally of Austria, 274.
Becker, Mr. anecdote of, 290.
Bennigsen, General, enters Breslaw, 171.
————————, forms a junction with his corps with the grand army, in Bohemia, 207.
————————, forms a junction with his corps at Naundorf, 246.
Bertrand, General, repulsed by General Tauenzien, 192.
————————, repulsed at Lindenau, by General Giulay, 241.
Blücher, Field-marshal Prince, traits of his character, 1, 13, 163, 167, 328.
————————, ancestry of, 3.

Blücher, Field-marshal Prince, born, 3.
———————————————, sent to the island of Rügen, 3.
———————————————, enters the Swedish service, 4.
———————————————, taken prisoner by the Prussians, 5.
———————————————, enters the Prussian service, 7.
———————————————, appointed Captain in the Black Hussars, 8.
———————————————, is permitted to resign, 10.
———————————————, retires into the country, 10.
———————————————, is again restored to the Prussian army, 11.
———————————————, commences his glorious career, 13.
———————————————, is appointed Colonel of the Black Hussars, 14.
———————————————, promoted to the rank of Major-general, 15.
——————————————— Lieutenant-general in 1801, 33.
———————————————, explanation of his title, 17.
———————————————, his partisan exploits in 1793, 19.
——————————————— in 1794, 21. 27. 29.
———————————————, his campaign of 1806, 34.
———————————————, commands the right wing at the battle of Jena, 35.
———————————————, marches to the Lower Elbe, 38.
———————————————, defeats the enemy near Fürstenburg, 40.
———————————————, refuses offers of capitulation from the Prince of Ponte-Corvo, 41.
———————————————, fights his way to Lübeck, 44.
———————————————, his defence of Lübeck, 45.
———————————————, capitulates, 47.
———————————————, his letter to the King of Prussia, 48.
———————————————, is appointed military governor of Pomerania, 49.
———————————————, commands the first corps of the Prussian army, 62.
———————————————, marches out of Silesia, in March 1813, 64.
———————————————, takes position at Altenburg, 76.
———————————————, proclamation of, to his army, 76.
———————————————, is attacked in his position near Bautzen, 121.

Blücher, Field-marshal Prince, his manœuvres and dispositions, 120. 123.

———————————————, is supported by General von York, 123.

———————————————, his ambuscade near Haynau, 130.

———————————————, his complete success, 134.

———————————————, advances towards the Katzbach with his army, 151.

———————————————, pursues General Lauriston, 152.

———————————————, his army posted at Jauer, 160.

———————————————, his manœuvres previous to the battle on the Katzbach, 161.

———————————————, defeats Marshal Macdonald on the Katzbach, 162. 164.

———————————————, his address to the troops, 163. 167.

———————————————, his proclamation to his soldiers after the battle of the Katzbach, 171.

———————————————, receives an autograph letter from the Emperor of Russia, 172.

———————————————, his van-guard crosses the Queisse, 174.

———————————————, his rapid march from Elsterwerda to Wartenberg, 210.

———————————————, beats General Bertrand, 211.

———————————————, receives a letter of thanks from his Sovereign, 211.

———————————————, forms a junction with the Crown Prince of Sweden, 212.

———————————————, defeats Marshal Marmont at Möckern, 227.

———————————————, his conference with the Crown Prince of Sweden, 229.

———————————————, detaches General von York to Halle, 257.

———————————————, his reception in Leipsic by the Emperors of Russia and Austria, 264.

———————————————, pursues Napoleon after the battle of Leipsic, 267.

———————————————, his proclamation to the Silesian army at Francfort, 282.

———————————————, reaches the Rhine with his army, 283.

———————————————, passes the Rhine, 285.

———————————————, his proclamation to the French people, 286. 310.

Blücher, Field-marshal Prince, defeats Napoleon at Brienne and La Rothière, 319. 323.

————— —————————, his address to the troops after the battle, 327.

————————————————, anecdote of, 328.

————————————————, his march on Paris, 332.

————————————————, his retreat from Champaubert, 336.

————————————————, his cheering note to the Emperor of Russia, 343.

————————————————, his manly remarks to the King of Prusssia and the Emperor of Russia, 346.

————————————————, marches from Mery to Soissons, 351.

————————————————, forms a junction with the corps of Bülow, Woronzow, and Winzingerode, 351.

————————————————, defeats Napoleon at Laon, 353. 360.

————————————————, arrives with his army at Chalons and Rheims, 366.

————————————————, forms a junction with the army of the Confederates, and marches to Paris, 368.

————————————————, attacks and carries the enemy's lines, 376.

————————————————, enters Paris, 378.

————————————————, visits London, 382.

————————————————, returns to Berlin from his glorious campaign into France, 391.

————————————————, is again appointed Commander-in-chief of the Prussian armies, 398.

————————————————, his proclamation to the army, 399.

————————————————, arrives at Brussels, 400.

————————————————, concentrates his army, near Fleurus and Namur, 404.

————————————————, battle of Ligny, 406.

————————————————, his narrow escape, 409.

————————————————, victory of Waterloo, 411.

————————————————, letter to his lady, 420.

————————————————, his proclamation to the army, 421.

———————— ————————————— to the Belgians, 424.

————————————————, pursues his rapid march on Paris, 425.

————————————————, his second entry into that capital as victor, 428.

Blücher, Count Francis von, anecdotes of, 12.
————————————————-, son of Marshal Prince Blücher, 12.
————-, Count Gebhardt von, son of Marshal Prince Blucher, 13.
Borizoff, Colonel, partisan exploits of, 137.
Borstel, General von, his bold and decisive conduct, 200.
Bubna, Count de, his interview with Napoleon, 107.
———— ———— ————, joins the Silesian army with his corps, 178.
Bülow of Dennewitz, General Count, commands the 3d corps of
the Prussian army, 63.
————————————————————, takes Halle by storm, 99.
————————————————————, defeats Marshal Oudinot
near Luckau, 136.
————————————————————, storms the village of Gross-
Beeren, 192.
————————————————————, his grand movement at the
battle of Dennewitz, 199.
————————————————————, bombards Wittenberg, 204.
————————————————————, is created Count Bülow of
Dennewitz, 391.
————————————————————, is posted with his corps at
Hannut, 401.
————————————————————, arrives at Gembloux, 408.
————————————————————, falls on the rear of Napoleon's right wing, and decides the battle of Waterloo, 415.
Buonaparte, Napoleon, anecdotes of, 59. 64. 107. 197, 198.
206. 215. 221. 241. 243. 260. 277, 278. 377. 384. 386.
————————————————, passes the Saale at Weissenfels, 81.
————————————————, confounded by the vigorous measures of
the Allies, 82.
————————————————, his situation after the battle of Bautzen,
128.
————————————————, his apathy, 130.
————————————————, offers an armistice to the Allies, 135.
————————————————, sends a flag of truce with a letter to the
Emperor of Russia, 135.
————————————————, reaches Löwenburg with his army by
forced marches, 157.
————————————————, is repulsed near Goldberg, by Marshal
Blücher, 158.
————————————————, returns to Dresden, 160.
————————————————, leaves Dresden with his army for Silesia,
176.
————————————————, is obliged to trace his steps back to
Dresden, 177.
————————————————, advances again to Bishopswerda, 180.
————————————————, is repulsed, and returns to Dresden, 181.
————————————————, hastily leaves Dresden, 219.

Buonaparte, Napoleon, retreats into Leipsic, 259.
———————————, quits it in haste, 263.
———————————, his disorderly flight from Leipsic, 281.
———————————, is defeated by Marshal Blücher at Brienne, 319.
———————————, retreats to Troyes, 328.
———————————, endeavours to cut off Marshal Blücher's army, 336.
———————————, attacks the Prince of Würtemberg at Montereau, 345.
———————————, leaves Troyes, and crosses the Marne, 348.
———————————, attacks Prince Schwartzenberg, 364.
———————————, is repulsed at Arcis, 365.
———————————, signs an act of abdication, and retires to the island of Elba, 386.
———————————, his escape from Elba, 395.
———————————, reorganizes his military adherents, 402.
———————————, leaves Paris, 404.
———————————, his bloody conflicts at Ligny and Les Quatre Bras, 406.
———————————, is completely beaten out of the field by the Duke of Wellington and Prince Blücher at Waterloo and La Belle Alliance, 411.

C.

Carra St. Cyr, General, leaves Hamburgh with his troops, 65.
———————————, his ferocious cruelty towards the citizens of Hamburgh, 102.
Colloredo, General Count, storms the heights of Vandamme's left wing at Culm, 188.
Colomb, Captain von, partisan exploits of, 136.
Congreve's rockets, anecdote of, 254.
Congress at Vienna, 392.
Cossacks, anecdotes of, 98. 268, 269.
———, intrepidity of the, 137.
Czerbatow, Prince, defeats General Puthod at Zobten, 170.
Czernischeff, General, partisan exploits of, 65. 137. 195.
Culm, battle of, 186, 187.

D.

D'Avoust, Marshal, strength of his corps on the Lower Elbe, 77.
———————————, his cruel measures towards the citizens of Hamburgh, 139.
———————————, his memoirs, 289.

D'Avoust, Marshal, his insolence towards the Duke of Weimar, 290.

———————, intrenches himself in Hamburgh, 290.

———————, his ferocity towards the Duke of Mecklenburg-Schwerin, 293.

———————, anecdotes of, 293, 294.

———————, his atrocities towards Hamburgh, 139. 297. 299. 304.

———————, orders the village of Hamm to be burnt, 301.

———————, his spoliation of the bank of Hamburgh, 303.

———————, acts of his monstrous cruelty, 304.

Dennewitz, battle of, 199.

Dölfs, Colonel von, is killed, charging at the head of his brigade of cavalry, 134.

Dörnberg, General, defeats the French General Morand, and takes him prisoner, 74.

Dresden, battle of, 134.

Duroc, Marshal, is killed by a cannon-ball, near Napoleon, 129.

——————— anecdotes of, 129.

E.

Emanuel, General, partisan exploits of, 139.

F.

Falkenhausen, Major von, his brilliant operation, 174.

Fouché, Mr. anecdotes of, 378.

France, King of, makes his public entry into Paris, 388.

Frederick the Great, King of Prussia, his laconic note to Captain von Blücher, 8.

G.

Girard, General, defeated by General Hirschfeldt, 195.

Giulay, General Count, his corps posted at Zschocher, 232.

———————, repulses General Bertrand at Lindenau, 241.

Gneisenau, General, Quarter-master-general to the Silesian army, 65. And to the army of the Lower Rhine, 398.

———————, is created Count Gneisenau, 391.

———————, pursues the French, 419.

Gross-Beeren, battle of, 191. 193.

———————, trophies of the, 194.

Gross-Görschen, village of, near which the battle of Lützen was fought, 84.

Guards, Napoleon's, bayonetted by the Prussians, 417.

H.

Halle, town of, taken by storm by General Bülow, 99.
Hamburgh, city of, her spirit of independence, 65.
——————————, her sufferings under General Carra St. Cyr, 101.
——————————— and spoliations under the ferocious d'Avoust, 139. 297. 299, 300. 304.
Hanau, battle of, 277.
———, the town of, audience of the magistrates of, with Napoleon, 278.
Hanseatic legion, its formation and glorious efforts, 66.
Haynau, the ambuscade of, 131.
Hellwig, Major, his partisan exploits, 74.
Hirschfeldt, General, defeats General Girard, 195.
Hospitals, French and Russian, anecdotes of the, 324.

I.

Italy, Viceroy of, is stationed with his army near Magdeburgh, 67.
——————, is defeated by General Count Wittgenstein near Möckern, 74.
——————, arrives on the field of battle at Lützen, 92.

K.

Katzbach, the battle on the, anecdotes of, 162. 164, 165. 167. 170.
Keller, Major von, is very near taking Napoleon prisoner, 418.
Kleist, General, Count of Nollendorf, in Leipsic, 84.
——————, repulses the enemy near Bautzen, 115.
——————, his corps forms the rear-guard after the battle of Bautzen, 126.
——————, falls upon Vandamme's rear, 189.
——————, is created Count Kleist of Nollendorf, 391.
Klüx, Colonel von, his brigade opens the battle of Lützen, 85.
Kolditz, town of, a severe action takes place between the Prussians and the French, 99.

L.

Langeron, General, defeats General Puthod, and takes him prisoner near Löwenburg, 170.
Lauriston, General, marches to Hoyerswerda, 108.
——————, is defeated by General Barclay de Tolly, 108.
——————, his attack on General Barclay de Tolly, 118.
Leipsic, humane inhabitants of, 94.

Leipsic, the battle of, 223. 232. 234. 236. 239. 245. 250. 257.
———————————— anecdotes of, 258, 259. 262, 263. 269.
————, the city of, assaulted on all sides by the confederate army, 261.
Les Quatre Bras, a farm, the battle of, 405.
Lichtenstein, Prince, attacks Marshal Augereau, 220.
Ligny, village of, the battle of Ligny, 405.
Lippe-Schaumburg, Prince of, anecdote concerning his uncle's horse, 47.
Lübeck plundered by the French, 47.
Luckau, town of, the French unable to drive the Prussians out of it, 136.
Lünenburg taken by General Dörnberg, 74.
Lützen, battle of, 83.
Lützow, corps of Major von, its fate, 149.

M.

Macdonald, Marshal, takes the command of the army in Silesia, 160.
————————————, is completely defeated by Marshal Blücher, on the Katzbach, 166.
——————————————, his routed corps retreat to Bautzen, 175.
——————————————, retreats behind Bishopswerda, 178.
Madatoff, General Prince, his brilliant affair, 177.
Marmont, Marshal, commands Napoleon's rear-guard, 83.
————————————, forced to retreat, by the corps of General von Sacken, across the Bober, 156.
——————————, anecdote of, 225.
——————————, is defeated by Marshal Blücher at Möckern, 227.
————————, his corps surprised by General von York, 359.
Mecklenburg-Schwerin, the dutchy of, its patriotism, 100.
————————————, Prince Gustavus of, his gallantry, 101.
Mecklenburg-Strelitz, Prince Charles of, repulses Marshal Ney, 155.
———————————————————— General Lauriston, 158.
——————————, his conspicuous gallantry, 159.
Meerfeldt, General Count, his corps posted on the Pleisse, 233.
———————————, anecdote of, 240.
Miloradowitsch, General, his corps near Zeitz, 81.
——————————, commands the rear-guard of the Russian army, 99.
————————, the affair at Bishopswerda, 100.
————————, repulses the enemy near Bautzen, 115.
Möckern, village of, battle of, near Leipsic, 226.

Morand, General, defeated and taken prisoner by General Dörnberg, 74.

Müffling, General von, appointed Quarter-master-general to the Prussian corps under General Count Kleist in the Netherlands, 392.

Murat, Marshal, is repulsed by Count Pahlen, 220.

———————, anecdotes of, 48. 222.

Mutius, Colonel von, commands the rear-guard near Haynau, 131.

N.

Ney, Marshal, is repulsed by General Count York of Wartenberg, 108.

——————, his attack on General Barclay de Tolly, 118.

——————, marches his army to Löwenburg, 155.

——————, retreats through Bunzlau, 157.

——————, takes the command of Marshal Oudinot's army, 197.

——————, is defeated, with great loss, near Dennewitz, 203.

——————, crosses the Elbe with the wrecks of his army, 203.

Nostitz, General, charges at the head of the Austrian cuirassiers at the battle of Leipsic, 237.

O.

Oesterman, General, is posted at Königstein, 185.

————————, repulses Vandamme, 186.

Olsufieff, General, his gallantry in defending Brienne, 318.

Orange, Prince William of, repulses Marshal Ney at Les Quatre Bras, 405.

Oudinot, Marshal, is defeated by General Count Bülow at Luckau, 136.

——————, menaces the Mark, 153.

——————, marches with his army on Berlin, 190.

——————, loses the battle of Gross-Beeren, 194.

P.

Pahlen, General Count, repulses Marshal Murat, 200.

Pecheux, General, is defeated by General Wallmoden at Görde, 295.

Poniatowsky, General, his corps marches from Zittau, 175.

————————, is repulsed near Löbau, 177.

————————, and crosses the Elbe to Penig, 182.

Prussia, armaments of, the landwehr, 148.

Prussia King of, his letters to Marshal Blücher, 16, 17. 211.

——————, anecdote of the, 124.

——————, enters Paris, 383.

——————, his proclamation to his subjects, 389, 397.

Prussia, Prince William of, and Marshal Blücher, 229.

Prussian battalions, loss of some, at the battle of Gross-Beeren, 193.

Puthod, General, is defeated by General Langeron and taken prisoner, at Plagwitz, 170.

R.

Reichenbach, village of, the rear-guard affair of the, 129.

Rheims, the city of, carried by General St. Priest, 362.

—————————, occupied by Napoleon, 362.

Russians, the, anecdotes of, 324.

Rudczewitz, General, takes the whole of Marshal Macdonald's field equipage, and the military-chest of his army, 154.

S.

Sacken, General von, forces Marshal Marmont to retreat over the Bober, 156.

Saxons, a corps of, come over to the Allies, 254.

Saxony, the King of, receives a note from Napoleon, 242.

—————————, offers terms of capitulation to the Emperor of Russia, 242.

—————————, pays a visit to the Crown Prince of Sweden, 242.

Schwartzenberg, Prince of, takes the command of the grand allied army, 152.

—————————, defeats Vandamme at Culm, 187.

—————————, his head-quarters at Pegau, 223.

—————————, his proclamation to the confederate army, 232.

—————————, marches to Paris, 371.

—————————, attacks and carries the enemy's lines, 374.

—————————, enters Paris, 378.

St. Priest, General, crosses the Neisse with his corps, 177.

—————————, attacks Poniatowsky at Löbau, 177.

—————————, forces the passage of the Spree, 178.

—————————, charges the rear-guard of Macdonald's corps, 179.

—————————, attacks Rheims, 362.

—————————, is severely wounded, 362.

Sweden, the Crown Prince of, posts his army in the Mark, 153.

—————————, takes up a position between Mecklenburg and the Elbe, 184.

—————————, takes up a position with his army between Spandau and Berlin, 190.

Sweden, the Crown Prince of, gains the battle of Gross-Beeren, 194.

——————————, fixes his head-quarters at Rabenstein, 196.

——————————, is attacked by Marshal Ney, 197.

——————————, defeats him at Dennewitz, 202.

——————————, throws a bridge over the Elbe at Rosslau, 203.

——————————, forms a junction with Marshal Blücher at Breitenfeld, 229.

——————————, anecdotes of, 103. 229.

——————————, his memoirs, 287.

——————————, pursues d'Avoust under the walls of Hamburgh, 296.

T.

Talleyrand, Prince of Benevento, anecdote of, 378.

Tauenzien, General, commands a Prussian corps near Münchenburg, 153.

——————————, forms a junction with Marshal Blücher, 182.

——————————, concentrates his corps near Blankenfelde, 191.

——————————, commands the 4th corps of the Prussian army, 63.

——————————, anecdote of, 198.

——————————, is created Count Tauenzien of Wittenberg, 391.

Tettenborn, General, enters Hamburgh at the head of a corps of Russians, 65.

——————————, his reception there, 66.

——————————, is obliged to evacuate it, 142.

Thielman, General, anecdotes of, 78.

Töplitz, town of, the head-quarters of the three allied Monarchs, 189.

V.

Victor, Marshal, takes position at Freiburg, 182.

Vandamme, General, anecdotes of, 141.

——————————, bombards Hamburgh, 141.

——————————, crosses the Elbe, and marches to Pirna, 185.

——————————, pursues General Oestermann, 186.

——————————, is totally defeated at Culm, and taken prisoner, 187.

W.

Wahlstatt, cloister and village of, near Liegnitz, 17.

Wallmoden, General, defeats General Pecheux, at Görde, 295.

Waterloo, a village, battle of Waterloo, 412.

Wellington, Duke of, arrives at Brussels, 400.

—————————, his victory at Waterloo, 412.

Winzingerode, General Count, commands the van-guard of Marshal Blücher's army, 64.

——————————————, anecdote of, 64.

Wittgenstein, General Count, blockades Magdeburgh with his corps, 65.

——————————, crosses the Elbe, 68.

——————————, gains the battle of Möckern, 74.

——————————, marches towards Leipsic, 76.

——————————, appointed commander-in-chief of the allied army, 82.

——————————, assembles his army at Zweckau, and marches to Gross-Görschen, 83.

——————————, repulses Napoleon at the battle of Lützen, 88.

——————————, retreats to Bautzen, and takes up a position there, 104.

——————————, his dispositions at the battle of Bautzen, 118.

——————————, retreats to Schweidnitz, 126.

Woronzow, General, partisan exploits of, 138.

——————————, his corps storms La Villette, 375.

Wrede, General Prince, signs a convention with Prince Reuss, 207.

——————————, marches at the head of the Bavarian army to Hanau, 270.

——————————, his memoirs, 272.

——————————, defeats Napoleon at Hanau, 277.

——————————, advances with his corps to Brienne, 325.

——————————, drives the French into Troyes, 363.

Würtemberg, Prince Eugene of, falls with his corps on the left flank of Napoleon's army, 91.

Y.

York of Wartenberg, General Count, takes up neutral quarters with his corps, 51.

——————————, commands the second corps of the Prussian army, 63.

——————————, repulses Marshal Ney, 108.

York of Wartenberg, General Count, his gallantry in repulsing Marshal Macdonald at Chalons, 331.

—————————————————, surprises Marshal Marmont's corps, 359.

—————————————————, is created Count York of Wartenberg, 391.

—————————————————, is appointed governor of Liege, 391.

THE END.